Multinationals
and
the Peaceable Kingdom

MULTINATIONALS
AND
THE PEACEABLE KINGDOM

Harry Antonides

Clarke, Irwin & Company Limited
Toronto/Vancouver

Canadian Cataloguing in Publication Data

Antonides, Harry, 1931-
Multinationals and the peaceable kingdom

Bibliography: p.
Includes index.
ISBN 0-7720-1196-6

1. International business enterprises. 2. Canada — Economic conditions. 3. Christianity and economics. I. Title.

HD2755.5A57 338.8'8 C78-001468-5

ISBN 0-7720-1196-6

1 2 3 4 5 HR 82 81 80 79 78

Printed in Canada

For Ann, Dean and Dale

Foreword

The mounting troubles that we face in Canada today are only too well known to bear recounting once again. But they take their toll, not only on our pocketbooks (as inflation and unemployment do), or on the health of our political system, but also on our morale and on our inner sense of well-being. Troubled waters may run even deeper than still ones, and there are growing signs of demoralization and of atrophy in our courage and imagination. These fall into the category of things everybody feels today in Canada, yet few care to talk about.

Our disorientation in a "runaway" world is growing. A biological analogy may make the point: just as our new and superior drugs now tend to produce a breed of even more powerful viruses that defeat them, so in the social sphere our cherished rules of thumb for modern society are being defeated by unanticipated and intractable phenomena. In regard to the joint problems of inflation and unemployment, our Keynesian text-books on economic policy are being put away on the upper shelves of our bookcases. Our massive expenditures on social welfare programs in Canada seem to have made hardly a dent in our uneven pattern of income distribution. The poor are as great a proportion of our population as they ever were. Even the pristine Canadian love affair with the landscape is going awry. Who would have imagined that we could bring the marine life of several of the largest fresh water lakes in the world so close to a lingering death?

For want of better guidelines, the old virtues of laissez faire have become a renewed mandate for doing even less than we have tried to do, and for reaffirming a strained and tattered faith that the social world and its perplexities had best be left to themselves. Tinkering, it is argued, has only made things worse.

Sooner or later, however, we must come to realize that the blind momentum of modern life rides onward in the institutional vehicles of our own design. And nothing symbolizes so truly as the multinational corporation the inexorable global grip on our lives by anonymous institutions and technological processes.

Harry Antonides offers a thoroughly researched study of the background and growth of the multinationals. His analysis is as comprehensive as can be found in any single volume published in Canada. He charts for us the social terrain of the last two decades.

Among the leading industrialized countries of the world, Canada harbours more multinational corporations in its midst than any other. Canadians are now beginning to tally up the costs, both political and economic, after the first rush when they were bedazzled only by the benefits. Slowly we have begun to recognize the economic distortions and difficulties, from the ongoing drain on our balance of payments to the overdeveloped place of the resource sector and the accompanying erosion of our manufacturing base.

Meanwhile other sides of our social existence are likewise affected. In the cultural sphere—books, magazines, films and television—our modes of self-awareness and self-expression have been blurred if not dimmed altogether. A pervasive sense of political dependency, of the growing restrictions on our freedom of action and self-determination haunts the body politic. For Canadians, as Northrop Frye once remarked, "the head office is always elsewhere."

Some would reply, rather fatalistically, that we in Canada are in the "vanguard" or front line of global industrialization. With this must come inevitably the standardization and homogenization of life and culture.

Antonides, however, takes a different view. This is a book that comes not from an academic or a politician, but from a trade unionist—one who has worked on the farms and in the factories of this country. He brings us a comprehensive and sustained analysis of our major dilemmas, but not in the usual antiseptic vein of the social sciences. Antonides offers us the very opposite of moral neutrality or the current fatalism. His work is explicitly imbued with certain deep-seated moral premises.

Antonides shows that we are reaping the fruits of a modern lifestyle that results from a sea change in our basic values and outlook. It is this change, at bottom, that has spawned institutions such as the multinational corporation and paved the way for their easy and uncritical acceptance in Canada.

The helter-skelter flight into modernity has unfortunately left behind the past as a piece of excess baggage. We need urgently to be reminded that the pinions of our society rest on those moral premises which bind our social existence into a coherent whole. The question that Antonides puts to us is: What is the vantage point on which we stand when we seek a way out? The economy, for example, cannot be reorganized without an industrial strategy—a more comprehensive perspective on our immediate goals. But how can these goals be defined without specifying the values to which our society is committed? "The real issue," Antonides reminds us, "reaches down to fundamental questions about the Canadian nation, the nature of industrialization and the very meaning of our lives."

Antonides' critique is radical insofar as it seeks to trace these phenomena to their roots: the uncritical faith in technological "salvation," the compulsion to human self-realization through the domination and abject conquest of nature, and the Enlightenment faith that all these blind forces will converge to some benign culmination of secular "perfection."

The way out for Antonides is nothing less than the invocation of that original spiritual endowment through which Western society was once created. The primacy of ethics over mechanics, of purpose over inertia, of social renewal over a resignation to moral neutrality or indeed moral oblivion.

His own answer is not entirely a fashionable one today. He suggests that the moral fibre we will need to see us through these difficulties involves a return to basic Western values rooted in biblical religion. This is not a fundamentalist tenet designed to narrow our perspective, but rather to widen it. Antonides tells us that as men are inevitably driven to the root questions of their existence they are all religious. And it is these root questions that we now must face up to.

Far too few wish to be reminded today of first principles—that the matrix of our society grows out of the moral parameters of biblical religion—however differently they have been coloured, repackaged and attenuated in secular doctrine. Freedom, equality and community are the values with which we have been indelibly imprinted in the definition of what it is to be a Western society. Antonides is right to take us back to the moral origins of our community.

For anyone who has ever taken part in the battle to preserve something of a meaningful social structure in Canada, who has tried to live up to the promise of our history, there is no lack of awareness of how great the odds are against winning such a battle. There is no more timely moment to listen closely than now.

ABRAHAM ROTSTEIN
Department of Political Economy
University of Toronto.
29 June 1978

A Personal Preface

Canadians ask themselves whether they have become free of Britain's colonial influence only to fall under the spell of the United States economic imperialism. [1]

—*Walter L. Gordon*

But this cultural effect is not peculiarly American. This is imagined only because so many of the multinational corporations have their origins in the United States.... Those who react to the American multinational corporation are reacting, in fact, to the cultural power of the planning system whatever its national identity. [2]

—*John Kenneth Galbraith*

...those who are in the forefront of protest must combine with their action the deepest and most careful thought. The central Christian platitude still holds good. 'The truth shall make you free.' For in the long pull freedom without the knowledge of reality is empty and vacuous. [3]

—*George Grant*

In terms of material resources and living space Canada is one of the most privileged nations in the world. This has been underscored by the mounting concern over critical world shortages in essential resources, especially energy resources.

Consider these facts: Canada's population is a mere 23 million, barely 0.6 per cent of the total world population. Yet we have 7.3 per cent of the world's land surface, nearly 300,000 square miles of fresh water supplies and 17,860 miles of coastline. Canada is a major producer and exporter of asbestos, silver, nickel, zinc, forest and agriculture products, and has an abundance of other minerals, including iron, copper, uranium, cobalt, potash, lead and gold. Furthermore, this country has considerable oil and gas resources in Alberta and the Canadian Arctic Islands. Canada is also richly endowed with swiftly moving rivers whose power can be harnessed to generate vast amounts of electricity.

Canada is indeed privileged,[4] but that is precisely one of the major reasons why the problem of foreign, and especially U.S., ownership of Canadian industry has developed. Another obvious reason for the inordinate extent of U.S. ownership and control of major segments of the Canadian economy is the close proximity of the two countries. We share some four thousand miles of undefended borderline; moreover, Canada's population is concentrated in a narrow belt of scarcely a few hundred miles along that border. The historical forces favouring a north-south flow of people, capital and commodities are numerous and powerful.

What has given the controversy surrounding foreign ownership a sharpened edge of late is the shrinking supply of the U.S. domestic resources needed for the insatiable American industrial machine. Canadians are wary of merely serving as the suppliers of raw materials for the U.S. Americans are enviously looking towards that rich storehouse north of the forty-ninth parallel. According to one economist, writing in 1961, this is how Americans have regarded Canada:

> Canada's new northern frontier is Canadian only in a geographic and political sense; economically, it is a frontier of United States resource investment. The emerging pattern of resource depletion in the United States is fundamental to an understanding of the forces working to integrate the two nations into a continental economic system. [5]

The arguments of the "continentalists" are rather straightforward. They support their position by pointing out that Canada needs outside investment, know-how and markets to realize its potential. Without that outside help Canada would not have reached its present stage of economic development characterized by a high standard of living. In other words, if Canadians want the benefits of industrialization, they have to be prepared to sacrifice a measure of their national independence. Economic growth is a universally accepted goal. Therefore the argument is closed.

At the other end of the spectrum, the nationalists see nothing but evil emanating from U.S. investment in Canada. They want to end all foreign investment by means of outright nationalization. The moderate nationalists can be found somewhere in between these two extreme positions, advocating measures that over time would increase Canadian ownership and control of the economy.

Of particular importance was the emergence in 1969 of a vigorous group of socialists to the left of the New Democratic Party, called the Waffle Group, who produced a number of publications denouncing foreign ownership and the American way of life. They were obviously much influenced by the Marxist concept of class. James Laxer, one of their leading spokesmen, wrote that the issue of nationalism versus continentalism has divided Canadians along class lines. "The majority of Canadians who work for a salary or wage want national independence; the minority, the nation's businessmen, are locked into support for continental economic integration." [6]

The controversy surrounding the issue of foreign ownership in Canada has led to an upsurge of nationalism. This issue is undoubtedly of paramount importance to the Canadian nation. While many on both sides of the debate want to reduce the argument to a matter of dollars and cents, the real issue reaches down to fundamental questions about the Canadian nation, the nature of industrialization and the very meaning of our lives.

In assessing the arguments about foreign ownership we need to trace the emergence and growth of foreign direct investment in general, and the extent of this kind of investment in Canada, as well as the main reactions and proposals emanating from a number of sources. In doing so, we also have to pay particular attention to the nature of the corporation, especially the multinational, and to the outstanding characteristics of technology.

The issue of foreign ownership in Canada is complex and must be seen in conjunction with the global reach of the large corporations, a phenomenon made possible by sophisticated technology and the concentration of massive amounts of capital. Canada is in a unique position. On the one hand, it resembles the developing countries with respect to the significant segments of its industry that are owned and directed by non-Canadian (mostly United States) firms; on the other hand, it is very much unlike the poor countries in that it enjoys a high standard of living. Furthermore, Canada has some multinational companies of its own, including Brascan, Massey-Ferguson and MacMillan Bloedel.

It would be a mistake to think that Canada's problems related to foreign ownership can be solved in isolation. For that reason, I have attempted to place the discussion in a broad framework leading naturally to a three-fold division. Part One concentrates on a few of the historical highlights; Part Two deals with certain major responses to the multinational corporation; and Part Three is an attempt to probe into a number of fundamental questions surrounding the nature of technology, including the major beliefs that have shaped our society.

A special effort must be made to come to grips with the underlying, often unarticulated, religious—some prefer to speak of ideological—presuppositions of individuals and groups. This is important for two reasons. In the first place, the idea that men and women can be value-free, "neutral" and purely "rational" is a myth. Every person is partial, makes certain choices with respect to the ultimate questions of life, and is therefore not neutral in his commitment and analysis. Much would be gained if this were generally acknowledged; it would facilitate a more open and fruitful exchange among differently-motivated people and it would tend to generate a greater measure of tolerance and generosity of mind.

Ultimately, all men are religious, that is, all men are forced to answer the basic questions of their existence. We are all confronted with the questions about the origin and destiny of life, and each one of us attaches ultimate meaning to something or someone in our attempt to make sense out of the world and our place within it. It is therefore erroneous to believe that some people are religious whereas others are not. The difference lies in the way we answer the questions concerning creation and our own existence.

In the second place, it is helpful to realize that words assume their intention only in terms of the perspective in which they are used. Words such as freedom, justice, equality and democracy are often meaningless because they receive entirely different contents, depending on the author's presuppositions. For example, when the term democracy is used to describe a relatively open as well as a dictatorial society, it obviously loses all significance. We are therefore forced to inquire into a person's perspective, that is, their underlying belief or *Weltanschauung,* before we can adequately evaluate their particular position.

This book is undergirded by the conviction that the Christian faith is normative for the entire spectrum of human life. This conviction flies in the face of popular wisdom. The latter holds that religion is but one area or aspect that at best ought to be restricted to the "private" life of individuals and at worst must be vigorously opposed as a dangerous illusion. But those who take the Word of the Lord (the Bible) seriously cannot accept this premise. The Word of God addresses a person in the fullness of their being and it makes all encompassing claims.[7]

The Scriptures enlighten us about the reality of creation and man's place within it. They explain that evil results from man's rebellion and disobedience, but they also reveal that in Christ man is again restored and renewed. The message of the Scriptures is one of hope and life; it affirms the meaningfulness of creation, but it also clearly indicates that this world is not unlimited and will not last forever. All things are made by God and upheld by his Word, that is, His power.

Man has been given a very special place, a place of honor within creation (see Psalm 8). But man is a finite, limited creature who utterly depends on God's faithfulness in maintaining the structures of creation—as the fish is dependent on the water for its life. Therefore, the Christian faith is not a constricting and confining force—as it often is represented—but a life-giving, liberating power. Christians are called to be positive toward the world and toward their fellowmen. As Peter L. Berger, professor of sociology, has written:

> Let me conclude with what I regard as the root insight of Jeremiah's perspective: The transcendence of God and the worldly mission of humanity are not in contradiction. On the contrary, the worship of the God who is utterly beyond the world is deeply, inextricably linked with the most passionate engagement in the moral struggles of this world. Nor is the refusal to worship the creation instead of the Creater a denial of the good things of life. On the contrary, it is precisely in the celebration of the world as creation, and *not* in its worship as something divine, that we taste its hauntingly vulnerable sweetness.[8]

The Christian position runs radically counter to the major premises of Western culture, especially the belief in human reason as the source of truth. The Scriptures are very clear at this point and confront us with the paradox of man's fulfilment in his dependency, his strength in weakness. Such Biblical themes are anathema to most of our contemporaries. But unless Christians again dare to take their stand on the "foolishness" of the Gospel,[9] they will be unable to speak and act prophetically—that is, with insight and power.

Christians who wish to take their place and task in society seriously must come to grips with the alternative faith of humanism, which can be summarized as the belief that man and his powers are primary enabling him to chart his own course through history (human autonomy). It is evident that this belief clashes at the most fundamental level with the Scriptural revelation regarding man's creatureliness and the God-ordained and upheld order of creation. By and large Christians have not been successful in responding to the faith of secular humanism. They have fled in panic, or else they have chosen to arrive at a synthesis between Christianity and humanism. This attempt at synthesis has assumed many faces, but one outstanding embodiment is the social gospel movement.

It must be acknowledged that the social gospel adherents were motivated by a genuine concern for human need and social inequity. It was in one sense a healthy reaction against a theology and a church which uncritically sanctioned the free market and the capitalist spirit, turning a deaf ear to the cries of those who were the victims of a system that glorified self-interest and a ruthless individualism. But in another and more fundamental sense, the social gospel involved a compromise that struck at the heart of the Christian faith. It must be viewed as an attempt to provide a Christian veneer to the spirit of modernity characterized by the belief in human autonomy.

Those who attempt to work out a synthesis faith via the social gospel contribute to the decline of Biblical Christianity.[10] This thesis requires elaboration, but suffice it here to mention the influence of J.S. Woodsworth (1874-1942) and the branch of socialism he represented. He identified religion with human solidarity and the quest for the infinite, but this is couched in language devoid of Biblical content. In discussing the nature of religion, he stated:

> Religion in this broad sense is simply the utmost reach of man—his highest thinking about the deepest things in life; his response to the wireless messages that come to him out of the infinite; his planting the flag of justice and brotherhood on a new and higher level of human attainment and purpose.[11]

Another leading figure on the Canadian scene was Salem G. Bland (1859-1950) who advocated a new kind of Christianity founded on the ideals of brotherhood and democracy. In his *The New Christianity* published in 1920, this Protestant spokesman approvingly cited a description of what he called "American Christianity," clearly indicating its synthesis and non-Biblical nature, as follows:

> American humanism has received from Christianity all the traditional, sentimental, and poetical elements which distinguish a religion from a philosophy. American positivism is only a Christianity which has evolved... The American religion may be called a Christian positivism or a positive Christianity. It has received from the past the traditional and the evangelical spirit. Traditional, it preserves the names and the forms of the Churches even when it changes their customs; it develops them from the interior. Evangelical, it keeps the figure of Jesus Christ before all, even when it does not recognize his divinity.[12]

This same author also wrote in optimistic terms about the "passion for freedom" which seized Germany in the years 1517 to 1524 and France in 1789. He somehow linked this "passion" with the prospects of "the new Christianity."[13]

This attempt at synthesis between two conflicting startingpoints is in sharp contrast with a revival of Biblical thought which took place in the Netherlands beginning in the nineteenth century. The names of the statesman-historian Guillaume Groen van Prinsterer (1801-1876) and the statesman-theologian Abraham Kuyper (1837-1920) must be singled out. Groen van Prinsterer, who at one time served as secretary to the Dutch Cabinet, developed a profound critique of modern political thought by taking his startingpoint in Biblical revelation. In his *Unbelief and Revolution,*[14] this Christian statesman argued that the French Revolution must be seen—despite the justified grievances of the revolutionaries against despotism—as an attempt to impose an arbitrary political order and to eradicate all recognition of a divinely given norm for human society. He called for a radical reformation of politics in terms of the Gospel imperative. Abraham Kuyper, who served as Dutch Prime Minister from 1901-5, continued and deepened the work of Groen van Prinsterer.[15]

It is within this tradition that the significant scholarly work of the two Dutch philosophers H. Dooyeweerd and D.H.T. Vollenhoven must be placed. Beginning their teaching careers at the Free University of Amsterdam in 1926, they developed a new philosophy taking its startingpoint in Biblical revelation and concentrating on the themes of creation, sin and redemption. This philosophy involves a significant attempt to construct a framework of thought in which all of life is seen as service of the living God and all reality is understood to find its meaning in the Creator. Hence the name: the Philosophy of the Cosmonomic Idea.[16] This philosophy has profound implications for theoretical investigation but also for socioeconomic and political life since it seeks to work out a normative concept of man and all societal relationships. It provides a frame of reference in which other theories about reality can be analyzed and evaluated.

The influence of this revival of Biblical thought has also been felt in North America. Dr. H. Evan Runner is one of the most important and articulate spokesmen of this new philosophical school in the U.S. and Canada. He played a major role in establishing the Association for the Advancement of Christian Scholarship and the Institute for Christian Studies in Toronto. This Institute, staffed by a handful of scholars, provides a linkage with the Christian philosophical movement centred at the Free University of Amsterdam.

The insights used throughout this book have been shaped by my acquaintance with this particular movement. Immigrating to Canada in 1948 from the Netherlands, I continued to be influenced by this Biblically-oriented thought. While not pretending to be an authoritative spokesman for this philosophical school, I wish to indicate my spiritual roots and to acknowledge my debt to what I consider to be a most significant stream of thought within contemporary Biblical Christianity. To be sure, the views expressed in the following pages have also been influenced by my years of experience in farm, factory and trade union work in Canada.

One of the destructive phenomena of our time is the systematic undermining of the human person. People are viewed and treated as objects of manipulation and control despite the lip service paid to human dignity and social justice. Guided by the Biblical notion that man is a spiritual and responsible person, we can effectively counter the antihuman forces loose in the world today. Insofar as Christian philosophy helps us to deepen our insights into the God-ordained norms for human life and their effect on societal structures, it can be an aid to the renewal of personhood within the multiplicity of societal relationships. There is no doubt that this renewal is of decisive significance for the future direction of our culture.

This book is not written with any pretension of providing detailed answers and a finished blueprint. It is intended to help clarify the real problems that beset Western society and hence to assist others in their own orientation.

Acknowledgments

Many people have in one way or another helped with the writing and publication of this book. I acknowledge my debt to them all, and particularly to Dr. Bernard Zylstra of the Institute for Christian Studies who generously gave advice and encouragement. The support of my colleagues and of the National Board of the Christian Labour Association of Canada was invaluable. Special mention must be made of Betty Westrik for her cheerful and capable assistance in researching and overseeing this entire project.

Contents

List of Tables

This mood [depicted in Edward Hicks' painting "The Peaceable Kingdom"] *is closer to the haunting vision of a serenity that is both human and natural which we have been struggling to identify in the Canadian tradition. If we had to characterize a distinctive emphasis in that tradition, we might call it a quest for the peaceable kingdom.* *

Northrop Frye

* Northrop Frye. *The Bush Garden: Essays on the Canadian Imagination*. Toronto: House of Anansi Press Limited, 1971.

PART ONE: THE RISE OF A NEW ECONOMIC ORDER

Chapter 1 The Corporation in a Global Setting

The multinational corporation, precisely because it is a threat to the sovereignty and independence of the nation state, may well be the harbinger of further evolution of human society out of barbarism towards a more humane, equitable and non-discriminatory civilization.[1]

Harry G. Johnson

I have long dreamed of buying an island owned by no nation, and of establishing the world headquarters of the Dow Company on the truly neutral ground of such an island, beholden to no nation or society.[2]

Carl A. Gerstacker

The multinational corporations are now at the centre of an ongoing controversy. On the one hand, they are viewed as the channel of prosperity and peace on a global scale. On the other hand, they are met with hostility and distrust because they are seen as the instruments of exploitation and domination.

In Praise of a New World Order

The late Canadian economist Harry G. Johnson, at a conference on the multinational corporation in 1971, contended with his customary candor that to place the discussion in terms of nationalism versus the multinational enterprise would encourage the adoption of "a static and unhistorical framework for the discussion and analysis of an evolving situation." He acknowledged that the national state which gradually emerged out of the wars of the feudal lords was "on balance a force for economic and social progress in the world economy; but it has been increasingly a barrier to further progress and the improvement of world civilization, precisely because it rests on discrimination between nationals and non-nationals and carries the imminent danger of catastrophic armed conflict."[3] This former spokesman for global economic integration cited two reasons for the beneficial effects of the multinationals. In the first place, the multinational facilitates—in the face of impeding tariff restrictions, immigration laws and balance-of-payments restraints—the international diffusion of advanced technology and managerial methods. In the second place, the multinational is eminently suited to lower the cost of new productive technology for nations that otherwise would be condemned to a permanent position of stagnation and poverty.

Frank Tannenbaum, the late American professor and author, concluded that all efforts to organize the world for peace have failed and will continue to flounder given the present format of international relations. He located the main functions of the nation-state in the protection of its citizens from external attack and in the maintenance of internal order. He asserted that the notion of national sovereignty inevitably leads to conflict and that world peace must therefore have a different basis than the nation-state. Tannenbaum believed that if a new basis could be found to eliminate the incentive for, or the fear of, aggression, the external role of the nation-state would gradually disappear. This alternative basis can be provided by the extranational corporate organization, because it is supranational in existence and purpose. Tannenbaum was convinced that when an international company builds an airport, opens up an oil field or constructs a steel mill in a developing country, it sets in motion a process that is more significant than anything that a national government may do. The international corporate body performs an international function; it will continue when governments change or fall. He therefore viewed the extranational corporation as "the logical basis for the contrivance of non-military supranational order."[4]

Tannenbaum questioned whether the transition from reliance on the nation-state as the locus of international relations to reliance on the new extranational corporation can be made before a catastrophic war erupts. He pinned much of his hope on the industrialization of the U.S.S.R. and China and predicted that this industrialization would pave the way for a new world order. He concluded: "It is a question of time and no one can say whether man will allow himself the mercy of surviving long enough to find a way of transferring international political powers to the corporate bodies that have come into being unwittingly and whose commitments are primarily functional, to render service where it is needed—indifferent and untroubled by the issues of national security and sovereignty." [5]

George Ball, former U.S. Undersecretary of State, also looks hopefully to the growth of international corporations as the new vehicle for world prosperity and peace. Writing about the phenomenal growth of these corporations, and the parallel use of the world's resources "with maximum efficiency," Ball warns that this development is well in advance of the prevailing political ideas. He continues: "While the structure of the multinational corporation is a modern concept, designed to meet the requirements of a modern age, the nation-state is a very old-fashioned idea and badly adapted to serve the needs of our present complex world. Most nation-states are totally inadequate as economic units, too small to provide efficient domestic markets."[6] To avoid a destructive clash between these two centres of power, Ball advocates the modernizing of political structures so that the new, worldwide corporations can get on with their task of efficient production and distribution.

Arnold Toynbee, the late, renowned British historian, added his voice to the chorus in praise of the multinational corporations. In an interview published in *Forbes*, Toynbee described the corporation as the new structure suited to bridge the gap between the archaic political organizations of the world and the new facts of economic life. Toynbee elaborated: "The ideal situation would be to have a world government with a world department of economic development, including oil, and have it done by public means. But as there is immense resistance to anything like a world government, then the international corporations are a necessity." [7]

The Growth of Foreign Direct Investment

When considering investments across national boundaries, one must keep in mind the distinction between equity capital (direct investment) and debt capital. Equity capital involves control of investment through reinvested earnings, and therefore perpetuates and enlarges indefinitely the claim on a country's wealth. It also constitutes a drain on a country's balance of payments because profits and various charges are remitted to the home country. Debt capital on the other hand consists of fixed interest securities that over time can be paid off and thus not lead to an ever-enlarging growth of foreign investment. The payment of interest to the lender of debt capital in another country also constitutes a drain on the national account, but this debt will in many cases be reduced and eventually paid off.

As it is often more advantageous in the long run to purchase a house by means of a mortgage than it is to be a tenant in the same house, so it is more advantageous for a country to be the recipient of debt capital instead of equity capital. At least, it is obvious that if the proportion of equity or direct investment by foreign companies leads to extensive foreign control, then a danger point has been reached because a nation is faced with loss of control in a significant area. This is the main reason why recipient (host) countries often develop a love-hate relationship towards foreign direct investment. Countries welcome foreign investment because it results in accelerated industrial activity, but they resent this kind of capital because it reinforces their dependency.

The first instances of multinational direct investment occurred in the late eighteenth and early nineteenth centuries. International trade was of course well established much earlier. But direct investment formed a different kind of international exchange. Mira Wilkins reports that between 1800 and 1860 the ventures begun by Americans in foreign countries numbered more than five hundred. Among the early businesses established by Americans in Canada, she lists a paper mill in St. Andrew, Quebec (1804); a small bank in Montreal (1820); tanneries, foundries and carriage works in Ontario (1830s and 1840s); and companies making agricultural implements and sewing machines in Ontario during the 1850s.[8] Americans were involved in the construction of a railroad in Panama, Mexico and Nicaragua beginning in the 1840s. The Panama Railroad Company, operating a 48-mile railroad, proved to be an exceptionally profitable investment for American entrepreneurs. From 1852 to 1905 a total of $36,377,068 in cash and $2,146,772 in stock was returned to the stockholders.[9]

The forerunners of the modern multinational corporation began to invest in foreign countries in the 1860s. Among these were the German drug company of Friedrich Bayer and the Swedish explosives plant of Alfred Nobel, the inventor of dynamite. The first American company locating overseas was the U.S. Singer Sewing Machine Company which built a factory in Glasgow in 1867. Other American companies that followed suit were General Electric, National Cash Register, International Harvester and Westinghouse Electric.

American companies were involved from the outset with the construction and operation of telegraph lines. In 1881 the Western Union system was linked up with Europe and Latin America; it also controlled holdings in Canada. The telephone invented by Alexander Graham Bell in 1876 became another important basis for international investment. For example, in 1880 the American Bell Telephone Company started and at first controlled the Bell Telephone Company of Canada. The International Bell Telephone Company built a factory in Antwerp in 1882. United States chemical and drug companies became involved in foreign countries. In 1876 the Windsor and Hamilton Powder Mills were taken over by an American trust. In 1879 John D. Rockefeller's Standard Oil made its first foreign investment. By the 1890s American companies were involved internationally in the sale of insurance and in the production and sale of sewing machines, harvesters, typewriters, elevators, printing presses, boilers, electrical equipment, drugs, explosives, film and petroleum.[10]

The era of the multinational had begun, stimulated by the companies' search for new markets, closer control over distribution and other cost advantages. Protectionist measures of home countries often served to encourage direct foreign investment because imports of goods were discouraged but not the establishment of branch plants behind the tariff walls.

American companies were not alone in establishing subsidiaries abroad, but they were the most aggressive. Especially after the 1890s, American companies pushed ahead with their drive for world markets. J.P. Morgan's purchase of an old British company, the Leyland Shipping Line, in 1901 shook the British self-confidence. In 1901 and 1902 three publications appeared in London with the following titles: *The American Invasion, The American Invaders* and *The American Invasion of the World.*[11]

Raw material sources became an important area of American foreign direct investment alongside the manufacturing industries. Investments in oil production and marketing as well as in copper and aluminum were significant. By 1901 Standard Oil was the largest oil company in the world. When this company was broken up in the antitrust action of 1911, nine of its thirty-four separate companies had extensive overseas operations. By 1908 Standard Oil controlled fifty-five foreign enterprises with a capitalization of about $37 million.[12]

The American automobile industry quickly and aggressively expanded beyond the borders of its home country. Ford began operations in Canada in 1904. In 1908 General Motors Corporation entered Canada by associating with the McLaughlin Motor Car Company Ltd. which manufactured Buicks in Canada. In 1912 Ford built an assembly plant in Britain and in 1914 it obtained a small assembly plant in France. At the same time it began selling automobiles in Argentina. By 1914 Ford produced a quarter of all cars manufactured in Britain.

Compared to the foreign investments of other countries, the U.S. stake was not large in 1914. Total U.S. foreign investments were $3.5 billion compared to $18.3 billion for Great Britain, $8.7 billion for France, $5.6 billion for Germany and $5.5 billion for Belgium, the Netherlands and Switzerland combined.[13] Yet, comparisons are deceiving. The fact is that American business leaders, especially those in the new industries, were keenly aware of the immense possibilities for producing and marketing in other countries. Within a few short years after 1914, the U.S. changed from a debtor to a creditor nation and was on the way to becoming the first mass consumption society.

In the inter-war years, companies expanded their international holdings. In addition to American companies, those from Britain, France, Germany, the Netherlands and Switzerland appeared on the scene or strengthened their international bases. Among these were Shell Oil, (Dutch/British), Unilever (Dutch/British), Philips (Dutch), I.G. Farben (German) and Nestlé (Swiss). But the international climate was not inviting. Some companies withdrew to concentrate on their domestic operations.

Actually, the figures for U.S. direct investment in Europe declined between 1929 and 1946.[14] A number of forces were at work during this period to discourage foreign direct investment, including the fear of another war, the rising tide of nationalism, inflation and above all, the outbreak of the depression in 1929.

The outstanding form of international business during the inter-war years was the cartel, which ranged all the way from a mere exchange of information to agreement on pricing and marketing. Cartels had existed prior to this time. Christopher Tugendhat reports that one of the earliest documented instances of a cartel arrangement occurred in 1896 between the Swiss AIAG and the Aluminum Company of America.[15] But it was especially after World War I that cartels came into vogue. The intent was to avoid over-capacity and ruinous competition. However, numerous agreements broke down under stress, including the first steel cartel in 1926 involving German, Luxembourg, Belgian, Saar and French companies. A second, more successful steel cartel was established in 1933, in which the British, American, Czech, Polish and Austrian companies were also included. This cartel strictly allocated exports and sales. An oil cartel was officially formed in 1928 and operated with some success. Cartel arrangements were established in nearly all other product lines, but often the lure of sales and profits proved stronger than the desire to promote the common interest. Christopher Tugendhat, author of *The Multinationals*, describes the significance of the cartels during the inter-war period:

> For all their deficiencies the cartels were a step in the evolution of today's multinational companies. They gave industrialists a training in international cooperation. They also gave them an understanding of national differences and of the need to modify business practices to take these into account. Instead of thinking primarily in terms of supplying their home markets, and exporting surpluses, they became accustomed to approaching the problems of their industries on a world basis. These lessons were to prove extremely useful in the changed conditions of the post-war world, especially to the Americans.[16]

The American Challenge

After World War II there was a veritable outburst of activity on the part of business leaders in search of new markets. The war had left much of Europe's industrial capacity in ruins, whereas American industry had been tuned up to peak performance. A host of new products and techniques had been introduced and Americans were anxious to switch over to peacetime production. The Marshall Plan poured $17 billion of aid into Europe from 1948 to 1952, speeding up recovery and the transition to mass consumption in Europe. With the birth of the European Economic Community (EEC) in 1959, production within this newly-formed huge market became an added attraction for American industry. Until 1956 European direct investment in the U.S. exceeded that of U.S. investment in Europe, but after that the ratio began to change rapidly. In 1957 the Americans were ahead with direct investment in Europe at a value of $4,151 billion versus European direct investment in the U.S. to the tune of $3,753 billion.[17] The modern means of transportation and communication played a crucial role in the development of the international, or multinational, business enterprise. The convergence of a number of these developments added up to a favourable position for American companies, and they exploited their position to the full.

A 1973 United Nations report, *Multinational Corporations in World Development*, providing 1971 figures, indicates that the total foreign direct investment in the noncommunist countries (the market economies) amounted to $165 billion, with an estimated annual production valued at $330 billion. The U.S. share of this investment was $86 billion or 52 per cent, compared to $59.4 billion in 1966. Over four-fifths of this total was owned by the United States, the United Kingdom, France and the Federal Republic of Germany.[18] (Total U.S. direct investments abroad climbed to $137.2 billion in 1976.)

The *Fortune* list of the fifty largest industrial corporations in the world (1976 figures) shows that twenty-two of them are American, while the list of the twelve largest multinationals includes eight American companies. An outstanding feature is their immense size. The twelve largest multinationals had a sales volume of $320 billion in 1976 (up $79 billion from 1975). Table 1 provides details on the twelve largest industrial corporations in the world. Table 2 presents a list of seventy-five of the largest countries and corporations in the noncommunist world in terms of Gross National Product (GNP) and Sales for 1976.

One of the characteristics of the multinationals is their tendency toward oligopoly, that is, the control of a market or industry by very few companies. The 1973 United Nations report reveals that about 250 to 300 firms account for over 70 per cent of the U.S. total foreign direct investment; for the United Kingdom, about 80 per cent is concentrated in 165 firms; in

TABLE 1 THE LARGEST INDUSTRIAL COMPANIES IN THE WORLD (ranked by sales)

1976 Figures (in thousands of dollars)

Rank	Company	Headquarters	Sales	Assets	Net Income	Employees
1	Exxon	New York	48,630,817	36,331,346	2,640,964	126,000
2	General Motors	Detroit	47,181,000	24,442,400	2,902,800	748,000
3	Royal Dutch/Shell Group	Neth./Britain	36,087,130	29,645,758	2,347,766	153,000
4	Ford Motor	Dearborn, Michigan	28,839,600	15,768,100	983,100	443,917
5	Texaco	New York	26,451,851	18,193,818	869,731	72,766
6	Mobil Oil	New York	26,062,570	18,767,450	942,523	199,500
7	National Iranian Oil	Teheran	19,671,064	6,544,991	17,175,182	57,331
8	Standard Oil of California	San Francisco	19,434,133	13,765,397	880,127	38,397
9	British Petroleum	London	19,103,330	14,925,935	324,615	78,000
10	Gulf Oil	Pittsburgh	16,451,000	13,449,000	816,000	53,300
11	IBM	New York	16,304,333	17,723,326	2,398,093	291,977
12	Unilever	Britain/Neth.	15,762,219	7,793,812	517,614	317,000

Source: *Fortune*, May and August 1977

definition is obviously useful. For example, in 1966 these 187 companies accounted for 39 per cent of sales and 45 per cent of assets of all U.S. manufacturing enterprises.[26] Nonetheless, there are numerous smaller companies, operating in fewer countries and on a much smaller scale, that can still be considered multinationals in terms of a broad definition.

The preponderance of American multinationals is an obvious fact, although the trend is changing. (The 1976 figures indicate that of the 50 largest companies in the world, U.S. companies accounted for 56 per cent of total sales compared to 60 per cent in 1973.) The proportionate share of foreign investment by other countries is increasing, particularly as England, Germany and France are deliberately embarking on a program of consolidating companies in certain industries to present a stronger front to the American "invaders." For example, in 1966 the British established the Industrial Reorganization Corporation to facilitate a more efficient structure of British industry through mergers and reorganization with the aim of making it more competitive internationally.[27] The Japanese share of foreign direct investment has increased substantially in recent years. Also, the Middle East oil companies have altered the picture drastically as a result of price increases and nationalization. The National Iranian Oil Company shot to the number seven position on the list of the largest corporations in the world. Despite the trend towards a growing non-American influence, it is the American multinationals that are by far the largest and most powerful today. A number of crucial factors have contributed to the primacy of American companies on the international scene. Most commentators agree that the combination of advanced technology, aggressive marketing techniques and superior management qualities has given the American companies their leading position.

An outstanding characteristic of the multinational corporation is the integration of management, which provides these companies with a decided advantage in exploiting production and marketing capabilities. There is much evidence to suggest that central management at head office exercises tight control. Raymond Vernon has pointed out that this control need not always be spelled out in every detail or be ensured by direct management interference. Rather, he suggests that such centralized control takes place in more subtle ways:

> Enough conditioning, it is assumed, will breed the necessary conformity while allowing for local initiative and local adaptation. . . . But, as a rule, discipline and coordination are maintained much more by common training and conditioning than by a stream of commands from the centre. This style of control reduces the need for continuous consultation with the centre and thus puts off the day when diseconomies of scale may drag the system down.[28]

The Crucial Role of Advanced Technology

Obviously, the phenomenal rise of business activity across national boundaries would not have been possible without the modern means of transportation and communication. Multinationals are adept at exploiting the latest breakthroughs in the area of communications. Ford has linked its engineering centres in Britain and Germany to Detroit by telephone cables so that the main computer at head office can be utilized by British and German engineers. IBM has over 300 international communication centres handling more than 10,000 teletyped messages daily.[29]

There is evidently a direct relationship between the prominence of American multinationals and their reliance on advanced technology. Chemicals, machinery, electrical products and transport equipment account for nearly 60 per cent of all foreign manufacturing investments of the United States. Research and development play a major role in all these industries, which explains to a large extent the prominent role of U.S. companies. (It should be pointed out that research and development are not isolated factors. Many observers have underscored that the large U.S. home market also played an important role, for it gave U.S. companies an opportunity to discover the marketability of their products and to absorb the initial high cost of innovation.)

Rainer Hellman has estimated that in 1966 the U.S. controlled 33 per cent of the refining capacity of the EEC; 25 to 27 per cent of the European automotive industry; 10 to 12 per cent of the European chemical industry; and 16 per cent of electronic production. Hellman also found that in 1967 27 per cent of new investments in the machinery industry (including electrical) within the EEC was accounted for by U.S. companies.[30]

Evidence of the prominence of U.S. firms in high-technology industries is provided in their receipts of royalties, and of licence, rental, management and service fees. Admittedly, these figures, supplied by the U.S. Department of Commerce's study of 1972, probably understate the position of U.S. firms, but they do provide us with a helpful comparison. This 1972 report indicates that total receipts for the period of 1960-70 involving direct foreign investments amounted to $17,029 billion, whereas total payments made by U.S. firms were only $1,584 billion (see Table 3).

This same report affirms that "national technological advantages depend not upon a particular technology, but on the continued development of new technologies and the rate at which new technologies become available for use in foreign countries."[31]

As the modern, science-based industries developed in this century, the lead in innovation shifted from Europe to the U.S. The emphasis increasingly came to be placed on basic and systematic research. One indication of the growing position of the United States in this area is the increase of students enrolled in science from about 30,000 in 1911-15 to

TABLE 3 U.S. BALANCE OF PAYMENTS, RECEIPTS AND PAYMENTS OF ROYALTIES AND FEES — 1960-1970

Non-Affiliated Firms and Affiliated Firms - millions of dollars

	Receipts	Payments	Differences between Receipts & Payments
1960	837	75	762
1961	906	89	817
1962	1056	101	955
1963	1163	112	1051
1964	1314	127	1187
1965	1534	135	1399
1966	1682	140	1542
1967	1845	167	1678
1968	2007	187	1820
1969	2205	221	1984
1970	2480	230	2250
	17,029	1,584	15,445

Source: *The Multinational Corporation - Studies on U.S. Foreign Investment,* Vol. 1. U.S. Department of Commerce, 1972, section 3, p. 17.

100,000 in 1951-53. In Germany the comparable figures are about 10,000 and 16,000. The U.S. share of the world's "inventions and discoveries" climbed from about 37 per cent during the last two decades of the nineteenth century to 54 per cent during the 1930s and to 88 per cent during the 1940s. The U.S. stepped up its scientific lead after World War II. From 1951 to 1969 the U.S. took twenty-one of the thirty-eight Nobel prizes in physics, nine of the twenty-seven prizes in chemistry and twenty-three of the forty prizes in medicine and physiology. U.S. gross expenditure on research and development during the mid-1960s was about fifteen times that of Germany, ten times that of the U.K., and three times that of all Western Europe combined.[32] Needless to say, there was a corresponding development in technology and industry.

About two-thirds of the cost of research and development in the U.S. was financed by public funds.[33] It is also of interest to note that most of the scientific discoveries giving rise to industrial innovation have come from universities rather than from industry or the government. One study of the origins of five major U.S. innovations during the 1950s indicates that the universities accounted for three-quarters of the scientific projects that led to industrial innovations. According to a 1970 report of the international Organization for Economic Cooperation and Development (OECD), 51.2 per cent of the total research and development undertaken by U.S. business enterprises during 1963-64 was financed by defence, space and nuclear agencies. Comparable figures for other countries were as follows: U.K. 32 per cent (1964-65); Sweden 25.8 per cent (1964); France 24.9 per cent (1964); Federal Republic of Germany 13.5 per cent (1964); Austria 10.7 per cent (1963).[34]

During the nineteenth century, breakthroughs in new technology could be achieved by the lone genius or tinkerer. Increasingly, major innovations today require the amalgamation of expertise in different branches of science. Consequently, large-scale organization and high cost have become associated with research and development and especially with the application of the results of that research and development. The development of the supersonic jet, the Concorde, is reported to have cost $2 billion; the development of an engine for the Tristar airbus cost Rolls-Royce about $400 million; in a four-year period IBM spent $5 billion on the development of the third generation computer, the 360 system. There is a direct relationship between large-size and high-technology industry. In 1964, 28 out of more than 2,000 firms engaged in research and development in the U.S. accounted for 63 per cent of the total research and development expenditures; in France, 16 out of 440 firms accounted for 43 per cent of such total expenditures.[35]

Concentration is particularly evident in the computer industry, one of the most science-based industries. IBM manufactures about 65 per cent of all computers sold in the noncommunist world. Only in two noncommunist countries, Japan and the U.K., does IBM have less than 50 per cent of the market. The largest non-American computer firm, International Computers Ltd., controlled somewhere between 1 and 2 per cent of the world market in 1970.[36]

The Power of Money

One area of controversy surrounding the multinational companies is the exploitation and transfer of capital. A quick look at the enormous assets and sales of the large corporations, in many cases dwarfing the Gross National Product of a nation, makes it obvious that there is good reason for concern. This controversy centres around several main problems:

(a) the multinationals' drain on the local money market through borrowing;

(b) the pressure on the host country's balance of payments as a result of the outflow of capital in the form of interest payments, dividends, royalties, service charges and management fees;

(c) the effect of the multinationals' use of transfers aimed at benefiting from fluctuations in exchange and tax rate differentials; and

(d) the uncontrollability of this flow of funds due to internal transfers that can easily be manipulated.

These problems have given rise to the fear that countries are placed in a position of dependency vis-à-vis the multinational corporation. This phenomenon is most severe in the case of developing countries which are obviously the most vulnerable. (See Chapter Two.)

The complaint that the multinational corporations drain off a large share of domestic loan capital is consistently heard in Canada. This places domestic firms, especially the smaller and capital-short companies, in a more difficult position. Servan-Schreiber has voiced a similar complaint with respect to the situation in Europe.

Profit Maximization Through Speculation

A former official of the European Economic Community estimated in 1970 that the liquid assets in the hands of U.S. companies and banks with international operations ranged from $30 to $35 billion. The movement of even a fraction of such funds can play havoc with a nation's policies related to exchange rates, balance of payments and credit availability. By the same token, devaluation of a country's currency can cost a company dearly—at least in terms of accounting procedures. For example, Firestone Tire and Rubber Company is reported to have lost $6.5 million in 1967 and $4.2 million in 1966 through devaluations.[37] To forestall such losses, companies transfer as much money as possible in various forms (e.g., dividends, royalties and the prepayment of accounts) out of a country where currency is in trouble. This is what took place in 1964, 1965 and 1967 when the pound sterling was in difficulties and its devaluation anticipated. When the French currency was under pressure in 1968 and 1969, a number of multinationals in France resorted to the same tactics.[38] It is self-evident that such moves further undermine the position of an already troubled currency. It is also obvious that these measures, if undertaken on a large scale, make obsolete all conventional wisdom regarding international trade, balance of payments and inflation.

An even more ominous practice is the transfer of funds largely, or only, for the sake of benefiting from currency revaluation (upward valuation). Charles Levinson reported that on May 4, 1971, $1 billion was transferred to West Germany in anticipation of a rise in the German mark in relation to the dollar. Most of that amount belonged to the giant multinational corporations. Large German multinationals, including Volkswagen,

Siemens, Bayer, Hoechst and BASF, sold hundreds of millions of Eurodollars for German marks on the same day.[39] This is how Charles Levinson, Secretary General of the International Federation of Chemical and General Workers' Union, describes this new phenomenon that alters drastically the functioning of international business and consequently cuts deeply into the role of the nation-state.

> Corporate money management has become an important feature of modern finance. Some companies like Ford, GM and the oil giants such as Shell and the Standards, have top executives in charge of placing their 'mise' on the *grand prix* hot money circuit. The function of the corporate money manager is to follow markets and determine the best optimal mix for placing and recalling funds, and borrowing and investing short-term assets. These managers in effect put disposable money to work to earn the best yields until its number is called for the long-term input. An international gulf-stream of hot money, billions of dollars long and wide, is coursing around the national money markets of the world in the direction of low to high interest rates, raising and lowering them continuously *usually in a contrary direction to domestic policy*.[40]

However, some observers of the multinational corporations insist that most multinationals are not adept at manipulating their funds to benefit from changes in exchange and interest rates. Two such experts are Sidney Robbins of the Columbia Business School and Robert B. Stobaugh of the Harvard Business School. Professor Stobaugh spent eighteen years working for three multinational companies, Exxon, Caltex and Monsanto. In their study of 187 multinational companies, accounting for about three-quarters of U.S. direct investment abroad, Robbins and Stobaugh paid special attention to the finances of these firms. With the aid of a model of a hypothetical multinational enterprise, they drew a number of conclusions that run counter to generally held opinions. For example, they concluded that many of the multinationals scrutinized did not exploit the opportunities in currency speculation that were available to them. They ascribe this failure to a lack of expertise and the difficulties associated with large size and cumbersome operating regulations and controls by head office. They admit that some speculation does take place. "We don't want to suggest that the multinationals don't speculate. Indeed, I feel they are compulsory speculators. They have to decide on a daily basis whether to collect a receivable from, say, Germany, or to wait, hoping to profit from a rise in the value of the mark."[41]

Manipulation Through Internal Transfers

Robbins and Stobaugh have also concluded that manipulation of company funds with the aim of escaping high tax rates by means of (intercompany) transfer payments is not taking place as extensively as is often assumed. They point out that, in any case, there are increasing restraints on this kind of action through pricing regulations and other controls. For example, France has instructed all French affiliates of U.S. multinational companies to collect their receivables from other affiliates elsewhere when the franc comes under pressure. Also, the U.S. government imposes a (higher) revised tax on declared income by multinational companies if the Internal Revenue Service judges that taxable income has been channeled outside the U.S. by means of underpricing or overpricing. According to the study by Robbins and Stobaugh, if U.S. multinational companies had been more adept at manipulating their finances, they could have increased their 1972 earnings from an estimated $12 billion to $15 billion—an increase of 25 per cent. They do give high marks to the internationally integrated oil companies for maximizing their profits through a sophisticated system of internal transfers of funds, which they call "masterful techniques for controlling international 'float.' "

Stobaugh tells of his experience with the oil companies that overcharged for the sale of crude oil to their refining and marketing affiliates to achieve a more favourable tax position in the home country. These inflated prices caused some affiliates to show a loss. He writes: "These losses were entirely fictitious, but when I worked in the oil industry some years ago, many executives said with great seriousness that the marketing end of the business is unprofitable. Such is the power of self-delusion."[42]

Complaints about this practice of over- or undercharging for goods and services transferred among affiliates, with the aim of benefiting the parent company, consistently occur in the literature on multinational corporations. Most often the purpose is to escape tax payments, but it can also be used to assist an affiliate in a competitive struggle by underpricing its supplies. Again at other times a company may wish to create the impression with the host government that it needs more concessions. It is a practice that is very difficult to control because the companies are not dealing with each other at "arm's length" but their pricing practices are centralized and can be set arbitrarily, at least within certain limits.

The method used to gain tax advantages is to overprice the goods sent to affiliates in countries with high tax rates, so that the profits of these affiliates are low or nonexistent. Conversely, goods sent to affiliates in low tax areas are priced low so that these affiliates show high profits. Obviously, no country looks with indifference to the drain on its potential revenue. Not only tax revenue stands to be lost, but underpricing of exports and overpricing of imports have an adverse effect on a country's balance of payments. Therefore, the practice of manipulating transfer prices is a real bone of contention between governments and the multinationals. Some countries have concluded agreements on taxing policies eliminating certain loopholes. In some instances parent companies are required to pay the difference between the tax rate in the host country of its affiliate and that of its home country, if the former is lower.

Also, revenue departments are becoming more adept at comparing the performance of different companies, and they will impose an extra tax if they find that pricing policies of certain subsidiaries have unrealistically lowered their taxes. The Germans have done this with the oil companies. Similarly, the revenue department of a multinational's home country can reallocate income among the members of a group and assess a higher tax rate. In 1972 Du Pont sued the U.S. Internal Revenue Service (IRS) for the recovery of taxes on profits that according to the IRS were made in the U.S. and not in Switzerland where the tax rate is considerably lower. The IRS charged Du Pont with reducing its export prices to its affiliates in Switzerland.[43]

Litton Industries was charged with undervaluing imports from Mexico to evade $216,000 in custom duties. This company pleaded guilty to forty counts of violating the statute against fraudulent imports and was fined $3,000 on each count. Four of its officers also pleaded guilty and were fined $2,000 each. Another American company with subsidiaries in Mexico paid $3 million as a settlement to escape prosecution for falsified invoices.[44]

Although there is a growing awareness that countries must coordinate their taxation policies, self-interest plays a dominant role and causes foot-dragging and the continuation of loopholes. As one official of the British Inland Revenue Service put it: "When a company is engaged in a practice which lessens its tax liability here, while increasing it somewhere else, albeit at a lower rate, it is expecting too much to suppose that the foreign revenue authority will draw the matter to our attention. It is a case of one man's meat being another man's poison."[45]

Tax havens further complicate the flow of capital among nations. These havens include, according to Charles Levinson, "not only the deviant specialists, but also authentic protestant-ethic, tax-paying countries, such as Canada [and] Holland, and parts of the United States (state of Delaware)."[46] Among the countries commonly thought of as tax havens are Panama, Puerto Rico, the Bahamas, the British Virgin Islands, the Dutch Antilles, Switzerland, Luxembourg, Liechtenstein, Malta, Monaco, and Liberia. For instance, over four thousand holding companies are domiciled in Switzerland.

Not only do the companies "based" in these countries escape taxes, but more serious are the outright fraudulent and even criminal activities carried on below the cover of secrecy. An outstanding example of such fraudulent behaviour was provided by Bernard Cornfeld and Robert Vesco, connected with the Investors Overseas Services (IOS), a one-time large—more than $1 billion in its mutual funds—and fast-growing investment fund. Its managers placed the company's investments on a worldwide market, taking advantage of all possible tax loopholes. In 1966 it paid $375,000 on profits of $6 million.[47] After Robert Vesco and his

International Controls Corporation took control of the floundering IOS in 1970, he proceeded to bilk the latter's richest funds of millions of dollars. This looting took place via a number of dummy corporations and shell banks in the Bahamas, Costa Rica, Luxembourg and Panama.[48]

Money of dubious origin can be sheltered under the lax or nonexistent regulations in these "havens." Richard J. Barber has pointed out that the ten biggest stockholders of the Pennsylvania Railroad just prior to its merger with the New York Central included two Swiss banks which together owned 550,000 shares. Nobody knows who the owners of these shares are since the Swiss banks act on behalf of "representatives" of numbered accounts.[49] We are left to speculate about their real identity, and that of other behind-the-scene owners, although we are not entirely in the dark about the identity of some of them.

Misuse of foreign aid is another facet of the problem. Louis Turner writes that U.S. authorities are increasingly concerned about this misuse by the recipient countries' officials. He indicates that "businessmen dealing with some developing nations find that they are asked to make large payments to numbered Swiss bank accounts in order to get key contracts; the Cosa Nostra (the Mafia), with a turnover estimated by U.S. Government officials at $30 billion . . ., is alleged to smuggle money out of the U.S. into anonymous accounts in places like Switzerland and the Bahamas, and thence back into legitimate businesses serving as covers for large quantities of 'hot' money."[50] Turner reports that the U.S. Department of Justice has named persons who are alleged to be assisting the Mafia in switching money from the American rackets into Swiss accounts and thence into the Caribbean. From that base, these companies are beginning to buy their way into the U.S. market. In one case, the Justice Department limited the stake of a Bahama-based company in Pan American Airways.

Obviously, there is a difference between the multinationals' shuffling of funds and prices and the criminal activities of the Mafia. Yet these tactics are taking place within the same international world of business and finance under the cloak of secrecy. There is an urgent need to remove that cover and to establish international agreements with respect to the incorporation of businesses, the flow of money and the payment of taxes. But the structured and organized barriers of greed and self-interest provide a stubborn obstacle to genuine reforms.

A New International Currency

Since the 1960s a new capital market has arisen outside the regulatory arm of any government: the Eurodollar and Eurobond market.[51] A *Eurodollar* is an ordinary U.S dollar deposited with a European bank. The growth of these deposits resulted from the U.S. trade deficit with the rest of the world, which led to an increase of dollar holdings by non-Americans. In addition, U.S. restrictions on the outflow of private capital, especially the 1963 Interest Equalization Tax, made it much more difficult for foreign governments and corporations to sell stocks and bonds in the U.S. Consequently, foreign banks were able to offer more attractive terms than those available in the U.S., and U.S. loans to foreign borrowers increased rapidly. It would be more technically correct to speak of Eurocurrency since the U.K., French and other currencies have also achieved Euro status, but because the U.S. dollars account for about 80 per cent of the total deposits, the word Eurodollar has become accepted as a general term.

Begun in the late 1950s after the British Government imposed restrictions on the use of sterling as an international trading currency, the Eurodollar market amounted to about $1 billion in 1959. By the end of 1967 it was estimated at $17 billion; by 1970 it had tripled to about $53 billion, of which $45 billion were Eurodollars in the strict sense of that term. By mid-1978 this market had climbed to $400 billion! Loans are arranged with a minimum of delay—that is, if the borrower has a good credit rating—and these may be large amounts ranging from $500,000 to over $100 million. A loan to the Pan American Airways in 1970 amounted to $168.8 million and was arranged by a consortium of twenty-six banks led by the British Bank of London and South America.

Alongside the Eurodollar market has arisen the Eurobond market for long-term financing. Advantages are unrestricted flow of funds among different countries and the absence of withholding taxes. One expert has defined a *Eurobond* as "an international bond issue, which is underwritten by an international syndicate and sold to purchasers who are able to pay in funds not subject to exchange controls with the result that the proceeds can be freely remitted by the issuer."[52] After the 1965 program of voluntary restraints on the outflow of capital from the United States, American companies also began to tap this source of funds. Mobil Oil was the first U.S. company to raise a Eurobond (in 1965).

The enormous Eurocurrency market has greatly facilitated international trade and investment, but it has also raised concern on the part of governments and bankers because of the lack of control and recording procedures. This money market is also used to profit from currency revaluations. It is reported that half of the $4 billion which flowed into Germany during a ten-day period in the 1969 German mark crisis originated in the Eurodollar market. For these reasons this huge capital market further aggravates the worldwide inflationary pressures. A book on this subject by Jane Sneddon Little, an economist with the Federal Reserve Bank of Boston, begins with this statement:

> A latter-day specter is haunting Europe—haunting the entire world, in fact. That specter is the vision of $100 billion on the loose in the Euro-dollar

> market, free to rush with next to no restraint from one nation to another, scattering well-ordered government policies and exchange-rate systems in its path. Not even the wealthiest nations in the world have been able to protect their economies from the meddling of the phantom. The crises that tore the dollar, the pound, the mark—indeed all the major currencies—loose from their official moorings were fed with Euro-dollar funds.[53]

The Power of the Bankers

The worldwide money market is characterized by a high degree of integration between the largest banks and corporations. The 1968 report of U.S. Representative Wright Patman's subcommittee on domestic finance concluded that the 49 largest U.S. banks held 5 per cent or more common stock (often sufficient to ensure control) in 147 of the 500 largest corporations in the U.S. A 1967 *Fortune* article claimed that the core of free world capitalism is comprised of about 60 firms, partnerships and corporations, owned and controlled by some 1000 men. These men are in charge of investment-banking houses in New York City, merchant-banks in London, Banques d'Affaires in Paris and similar organizations in Belgium, the Netherlands, Italy, Germany, Sweden and Australia. A 1971 article in *Der Spiegel* claimed that private banks control and administer 70 per cent of all the voting shares of German industry. There are closely interlocking relationships among the major Italian banks and large companies, including Fiat, Montedison, SNIA, ENI and TRI. The large Japanese enterprises, such as Mitsui, Mitsubishi, Sumitomo, Kawasaki and others, operate their own banking chains. These large companies are guaranteed a supply of funds because of their close relationship with the financial institutions. The latter are involved in many joint ventures with each other giving rise to what Charles Levinson calls "one vast, closely interrelated power block." He describes the effect of such concentration of power as follows: "Instead of raising more funds and contributing to greater liquidity, these institutions, by soaking up funds for the growing appetite of their capital hungry clients, induce scarcities elsewhere and make it more difficult for the smaller firms to acquire long-term capital except at exceptionally high interest rates."[54]

A look at the Canadian scene shows that similar integrating and concentrating forces are at work here. In 1976 the five large Canadian banks (Royal Bank of Canada, Canadian Imperial Bank of Commerce, Bank of Montreal, Bank of Nova Scotia and Toronto Dominion Bank) had assets of $110 billion. The combined assets of the five largest industrial companies (Canadian Pacific Ltd., Bell Canada, Inco Limited, Imperial Oil Limited, Alcan Aluminum Ltd.) reached nearly $23 billion in the same year.[55]

R.G.D. Lafferty, a Montreal investment counsellor, charges that "the banking system is a highly concentrated, monolithic structure with interlocking interests that employs restrictive practices to prevent new initiative and enterprise from challenging its dominant position."[56] The figures certainly bear out his comment about concentration. For example, the Bank of Montreal, according to a 1972 article by Peter Newman, had 53 boardmembers who together held 455 corporate directorships, representing total holdings of $124.9 billion. He wrote that the 261 directors of Canada's eight chartered banks held a total of 3,152 company directorships. One director of the Bank of Nova Scotia sat on 49 corporate boards, which placed him at the top. On a list of 100 bank directors, 44 sat on the board of directors of the Commerce, 36 on the board of the Royal and 16 on the board of the Bank of Montreal. Sixty-seven bank directors sat on the boards of the 17 largest Canadian insurance companies.

Newman wrote that Canada is one of the most successful capitalist societies run by a "cluster of interlocking elites." This elite core of 261 directors is drawn from "a self-perpetuating and enormously powerful social enclave" who "put their mark not only on banking policies but on just about every significant business decision in the country."[57]

The position of the banks is undoubtedly affected by the phenomenal jump in the price of oil from around $3 per barrel to $12. The oil-producing countries associated in the Organization of Petroleum Exporting Countries (OPEC) have put immense economic pressure on the industrialized countries—the result for the developing countries is even worse. There is now a general feeling of alarm and even near-panic about the ramifications of the drain of capital from the oil consuming to the oil-producing countries.

The amount of new money available to the OPEC countries is enormous. A spokesman for the European Economic Community reported in January 1975 that the oil-exporting countries had invested between $43 billion and $47 billion abroad in the first ten months of 1974. One quarter of this money was placed in the U.S. while one third went into the Eurodollar market. The overnight amassing of immense fortunes by the OPEC countries has thrown the international bankers, as well as governments and the entire business community, into a state of confusion, if not shock. Previously arranged channels of international trade and cooperation are now under severe strain.

The Balance-of-Payments Controversy

One of the increasingly controversial effects of foreign direct investment concerns the relationship of the inflow to the outflow of capital. The initial foreign direct investment constitutes a transfer of capital from the home country to the host country. However, over time this initial investment results in an outflow of capital from the host country to the home country in the form of dividends, royalties, management and service payments. This return flow in many cases exceeds the amount of new investments flowing into the host country from the home country. The profits generated by foreign direct investments and not repatriated but reinvested add to the foreign investment and do not become a drain on the home country's balance of payments in the short run. But in the long run, these reinvested (retained) earnings will increase the claim of the home country on the host country, and in effect will cause the outflow of capital to the home country to increase. New foreign direct investment is generally financed largely from retained earnings and other domestic sources of capital, with only a small percentage derived from direct capital transfer from the home country—15 per cent in the case of U.S. multinationals during recent years. This is what causes Canadian critics of foreign direct investment to say that we are financing our own takeover. J.J. Servan-Schreiber made a similar point in connection with the European situation.[58]

It is obvious that the inflow and outflow of capital generated by foreign direct investment has a significant bearing on a country's economic well-being. The cost is high when such investment results in a serious drain on a country's balance of payments. However, it is impossible to look at the inflow and outflow of capital by itself and decide whether foreign direct investment is advantageous for a host country. The situation is more complex because the benefits of such investments often include the import of new technology, more employment, spin-offs for local enterprises, the opening of new markets, regional development and especially import-substituting, domestic production and exports.[59] To evaluate the true advantages or disadvantages, one must know what would have happened if this investment were not made, which is an impossibility.

Furthermore, the ratio between domestic and foreign investment, between debt and equity capital must be taken into account as well as the branch of the economy in which foreign direct investment is located. Moreover, it makes an important difference whether profits are reasonable and fair or exorbitant. There are a host of additional and intangible results that have to be evaluated. Nonetheless, it is helpful to look at the inflow and outflow of capital as a result of foreign direct investment. The figures do tell us something as long as we remember that they do not tell the whole story.

The discussion about foreign direct investment is further complicated by the differing viewpoints brought to the subject by those in home countries and host countries. Within each country one finds pro and con positions. This is quite evident in Canada. The U.S., which is largely a home country, is also divided about the benefits of its role. Especially during recent years, there has been an increasing demand for restraining the U.S.

multinationals and curbing imports, culminating in the Burke-Hartke bill (first introduced in 1971), which was vigorously promoted by the U.S. labour movement.

Evaluating the balance-of-payments impact of foreign direct investment on the host country, Raymond Vernon asserts that its most important effect concerns the trade accounts of the host country, that is, imports and exports. He concludes that if the production resulting from the foreign direct investment (of U.S. firms) would have taken place anyway, the balance-of-payments effect is trivial; if the goods produced would otherwise be imported from the U.S., the effect on the balance-of-payments position of the host country is positive. He summarizes: "There is nothing to indicate that the advanced countries receiving U.S.-controlled subsidiaries in their economies have much to risk in balance-of-payments terms, at least as regards long-run effects."[60]

The 1972 U.S. report on multinational corporations agrees that evaluating the impact of multinational corporations on the balance of payments of host countries is complex. However, it points out that if we compare the capital inflow of new direct investment to the host country with the capital outflow in the form of generated earnings, the balance of payments is generally negative for the host country. Between 1965 and 1970, net foreign direct investment inflow into forty-three developing countries was 30 per cent of the investment income outflow.

The income generated by U.S. foreign direct investment for the parent firms amounted to more than $10 billion in 1972. It is estimated that this amount could easily double by 1980.[61] The total amount earned from direct investments and remitted by U.S. affiliates to their parent firms during the 1960-1970 period amounted to $57.2 billion,[62] an amount that substantially aided the U.S. in obtaining a balance-of-payments surplus. By the same token, countries like Canada that have a high level of foreign direct ownership from which this capital outflow takes place must devote large sums to finance this cost. It is self-evident that this drain on developing countries is especially serious.

The level of profits generated by the multinational corporations is an important consideration in evaluating the balance-of-payments issue. Where profits are high, resentment against multinational companies is bound to arise in the host countries. Oil companies have made very high returns on their investments. What is of particular interest is the fact that the profits of these companies were twice as high in the developing countries as in the developed ones. A 1972 study by the U.S. Department of Commerce reports that the yields on all U.S. foreign direct investments over the 1960s averaged 12.6 per cent. For all industries combined in the developing countries it was 21 per cent, which is a reflection of the high yield of the petroleum affiliates. For example, the 1970 yield in petroleum was 15.6 per cent in all countries and 33.1 per cent in the developing countries. This high rate is blandly explained as a partial result "of the pricing agreements with the governments of producing countries."[63]

The U.S. government's determination to improve its balance of payments by means of restricting the outflow of capital and stimulating the inflow through the multinational corporations is a major source of friction between host countries and U.S. multinational corporations. Beginning in the 1950s, the U.S. experienced an increasing deficit in its balance of payments. To stem the tide, the U.S. government imposed a set of restrictions in 1963. The Interest Equalization Tax, aimed at reducing the foreign use of U.S. capital markets, in effect increased the cost of borrowing long-term capital by foreign borrowers. This in turn stimulated the emergence of a new capital market outside of the U.S. or any other jurisdiction: the Eurodollar market (see above).

To counteract the deteriorating U.S. balance-of-payments position in 1965, President Johnson imposed the Voluntary Capital Restraint Program which was aimed at increasing the flow of capital from the host countries to the U.S. by 15 to 20 per cent over the previous year. A variety of means could be used to accomplish this: increased exports, greater returns on earnings, reduction of capital outflow, return of liquid assets abroad, and more borrowing from foreign sources. In 1968 this was followed by mandatory controls setting quotas for individual companies. Quotas for new investments were set at different rates in three major categories, with the highest quotas for developing countries (110 per cent of the 1965-66 level of investment) and the lowest for Western Europe (35 per cent). The U.S. measures have greatly increased the reliance of U.S. multinationals on the capital markets of host countries, placing added strain on those markets to the detriment of domestic firms. Critics insist that the U.S. is exploiting its power to export its balance-of-payments deficits.

Another important phase in U.S. policy affecting its multinational corporations was the incorporation into the Revenue Act of the Domestic International Sales Corporation (DISC) in 1971. Under this legislation, a U.S. firm can establish a DISC which will allow it to defer taxes on its export profits and to set its intercompany prices more advantageously. Proponents agreed that these incentives would result in better export performance of U.S. companies and thus improve the U.S. balance of payments. The U.S. Treasury Department forecast an increase in export sales of between $1.5 and $2 billion per year and 80,000 new jobs when this scheme would be in full operation. Special care was taken that the new legislation would not lead to the expansion of U.S. production abroad. The American labour movement nevertheless objected to DISC on the grounds that it would lead to "tax avoidance through bookkeeping gimmickery between the DISC and its parent corporation."[64]

These defensive measures of the U.S. had a direct effect on those countries in which American affiliates were established. This held especially for Canada because of its heavy reliance on American direct investment. In effect, parent companies of Canadian (and other) affiliates were encouraged to shift production away from these affiliates to the U.S.-based operations. These and other measures aimed at shoring up the U.S. balance-of-payments position served to underscore the dependency of the host countries on U.S. government policy, and such measures have done much to reinforce antagonism toward that dependency in those countries.

Describing the effects of the U.S. balance-of-payments controls on host countries, Jack Behrman observed in 1970:

> . . . it is evident that the existence of the multinational enterprise alters significantly the impact of international capital controls. It does so in ways that impinge directly on the authority and responsibilities of host governments. Given the U.S. multinational enterprise, the imposition of capital controls by the U.S. government challenges the sovereignty of the host country by dampening the economic growth of the capital-importing country, which otherwise would have had an inflow of capital, or by preventing or reducing reinvestment of earnings by U.S. affiliates, thereby altering the investment projections in the host country. Monetary policies of the more advanced countries are tied more tightly together than would be the case without the multinational enterprise. The imposition of capital controls by one country affects locally generated funds in the capital-importing country. The U.S. multinational enterprise has become clearly and unequivocally an instrument of foreign economic policy. Its existence provides the means whereby unilateral action by the United States is transferred into host countries, through the affiliates.[65]

Chapter 2
Crossing Ideological Boundaries

Throughout the cold war, the Third World has been a battleground for ideological confrontation between East and West, to its own detriment and that of the two contending blocs. . . . As the intense ideological rivalry between communism and capitalism recedes into the background, the Third World has mixed emotions: hope for strengthened peace, and apprehension of being neglected. . . . There is, however, a brighter side to the picture. Following years of universal disenchantment with trade and aid relations between the poorer and the richer nations, the concept of coexistence and commerce between East and West offers the Third World a chance to become the theater of meaningful economic cooperation and development.[1]

Samuel Pisar

Most of the investment of multinational corporations is located in the developed countries of the West. But substantial investments are also made in the Third World, and the multinational corporations are increasingly active in the Soviet Union and its satellites. Each of these blocs of countries involves a very different set of conditions than that prevailing in the Western democracies and the multinationals have shown a remarkable ability to adapt to quite different environments.

Multinationals and the Communist Bloc[2]

An increasing flow of equipment, products and technology between the noncommunist and communist worlds is breaching the Iron Curtain. The extent of this exchange is rapidly building up in recent years and even includes some joint-venture projects in Hungary, Romania and Yugoslavia, as well as barter-like arrangements between American, German, Japanese and other companies to unlock the vast Siberian reserves of oil, gas, coal and timber. In 1975 the industrial countries of Western Europe, Japan, Canada and the U.S. sold more than $22.8 billion worth of goods to the U.S.S.R. and its six East European partners in the Council for Mutual Economic Assistance (Comecon).[3] Western companies, including U.S. corporations, are eyeing the large potential consumer market in Eastern Europe and they are working hard to obtain their share of that market. They are quite willing to adjust their methods to the demands of the centrally-controlled regimes. In 1972 there were some twelve hundred cooperative arrangements between Western companies and socialist states.

Yugoslavia is seen as an important bridgehead between the East and the West because of its relatively open-door policy to both sides.[4] U.S. companies, as well as others, have shown a keen interest in the potential of this bridgehead. They can use a variety of arrangements from coproduction, subcontracting and licensing to fifty-fifty joint-venture operations. American companies operating in Yugoslavia include Printing Developments Inc., National Distillers and Chemical Corporation, Bechtel Corporation, Coca-Cola, General Electric, Control Data, Remington Rand, RCA, Ford Motor, International Business Machines, General Motors, Dow Chemical and Chrysler.

Poland, Romania, Hungary, Bulgaria and Czechoslovakia are also becoming increasingly important partners with Western companies in the production and marketing of goods and services. For example, Hilton International, and U.S. Intercontinental Hotels are operating under various arrangements in Eastern Europe. But at the top of the list are automobiles, petroleum, chemicals, machinery and other such basic industries that are essential for a modern, industrialized nation. The East is anxious to obtain all the technical skills and capital needed for its own development and for strengthening its balance of payments.

West Germany's Lurgi group has built a large petrochemical complex in Romania and one in Czechoslovakia. The British Pilkington Glass Company has built factories under license in the U.S.S.R., Romania and Poland. The French Société Nationale des Pétroles d'Aquitaine and two Polish firms concluded a coproduction agreement for building production and distribution facilities for synthetic rubber. A Swedish firm supplied machinery and the designs for furniture production in Poland. The Swedish machine-tool industry is assisting in the reorganization of the Soviet pulp and paper industry, with equipment and technical expertise. Israel and Romania reached an agreement on the construction of two chemical plants and a petrochemical complex in Romania. Simmons Machine Tool Corporation of the U.S. buys equipment from Skoda of Czechoslovakia on a made-to-order basis. Japan's Toyo Engineering was awarded a contract to construct four big petrochemical plants in the Soviet Union, incorporating U.S. technology. Italy's Pirelli Company has built rubber factories in the U.S.S.R. and one in Romania and has coproduction contracts with other East European countries. This list could go on and on.

In addition to the various forms of coproduction and joint ventures, some Western European companies are producing clothing, furniture and appliances in communist countries and finishing them in the home country before final shipment. Thus Swedish furniture or Dutch clothing may be largely produced in Poland, Hungary or Romania where wages are much lower than in the home country. Shipped to the U.S., these goods enjoy much-favoured-nation status and are therefore subject to lower import duties.

The U.S.S.R. is the most formidable receiver of Western technology and equipment, but this importing takes place without foreign direct investment. In many cases, the U.S.S.R. contracts with Western firms for the building of entire factories. An outstanding example of this policy is Fiat's contract for the construction of a 600,000 unit automobile plant in Togliatti. Fiat supplied the design and equipment, supervised construction and trained Soviet engineers and technicians at a cost of $900 million. The total project, including the construction of a brand new city, cost $1.5 billion. After completion, the plant was turned over to the U.S.S.R. (a "turnkey project") and is now producing the Fiat-124 (the Zhiguli) for the East European market.

The most spectacular current project, heavily dependent on foreign equipment and know-how, is the $5-billion truck plant and city now under construction on the Kama River, six hundred miles east of Moscow. It is the largest industrial project in the world and is designed to produce 150,000 three-axle, heavy-duty trucks and 250,000 diesel engines a year. When completed, this plant will cover forty square miles of land and incorporate equipment from twelve different countries, the latter at a cost of more than $1 billion. The Soviet government has signed contracts with some forty U.S. companies to the tune of more than $500 million worth of equipment for the Kama truck plant alone.

In addition, there is a great deal of capital and equipment involved in other joint projects, which are small in comparison to the Kama truck plant but very large-scale by normal standards. These projects, involving the exploitation of the vast oil, gas and timber reserves of the U.S.S.R., as well as the construction of large industrial complexes (steel and chemicals), are cooperative arrangements between the U.S.S.R. and West European, Japanese and American firms. In 1972, the U.S.S.R. spent $2 billion on Western technology alone. Moscow relies heavily on long-term credit or on barter deals, using oil, gas, lumber, ammonia and other raw materials to pay for new installations. Despite this, the Soviets now use more than 20 per cent of their foreign exchange earnings per year on loan repayments.[5] By 1978 the total Soviet debt to the West had increased to $19 billion: this immense debt, the sluggishness of the Soviet economy and the shortcomings of Soviet industry have considerably lowered the expectations of Western businessmen who had hoped to capture a new lucrative market in the Soviet bloc countries.[6]

The traffic is not all from West to East. East European countries are venturing into Western Europe and other noncommunist countries. Soviet banks operate in London, Paris, Zurich, Beirut and Teheran. Scoldia Volga, 95 per cent owned by the U.S.S.R., assembles Russian cars in Antwerp. The Anglo-Soviet Shipping Company of London operates a Soviet merchant fleet around the world. Nafta oil companies, wholly or partly owned by the U.S.S.R., operate in Britain, Belgium and Liechtenstein. A Soviet trucking company has established routes to six West European countries. The Nafta oil group has entered into an agreement with British Petroleum for the supply of oil products. Romanian contractors are building apartment projects in West Germany.

The old antagonism between Marxism and capitalism has not even prevented joint ventures in banking. The London-based International Investment Corporation for Yugoslavia was founded in 1970 to promote joint ventures between foreign companies and Yugoslav enterprises. Its charter shareholders are fifteen Yugoslav and forty Western European, U.S. and Japanese banks. Another East-West banking consortium is the multinational "Centropa" venture formed by banks from seven countries in 1971. Included are banks from Italy, Spain, Japan, France, England, Austria and Poland. Its aim is "to promote technical cooperation, investment and trade between Eastern and Western countries."[7] Eurodollars are finding their way into Eastern Europe. A banking syndicate, including the Moscow Narodny Bank and the Manufacturers Hanover Trust Company (U.S.), has granted a $7.8 million Eurodollar loan to the Romanian Foreign Trade Bank for financing aluminum-manufacturing technology from the U.S. Led by the U.S.S.R., the Eastern countries have established the Comecon Investment Bank for the express purpose of making profits in the Western capital market. Its primary aim is to raise money for promoting Eastern development.

Samuel Pisar, an authority on East-West trade, has pointed out that the détente between East and West will greatly benefit the Third World. He views the joint ventures between the two sides, which he has dubbed "transideological corporations," as an ideal channel for helping the Third World on the way to development. Instead of getting caught between the two contending world forces, Pisar believes that the Third World will benefit from the new partnership on which the transideological corporation is based. The Third World is aware of the industrial potential of the communist countries; conversely, the latter increasingly need the primary products of the developing countries.

Among the cooperative ventures, Pisar mentions Hungarian and Czechoslovakian enterprises which have recently joined with Austrian firms to build thermal power stations in Lebanon, India and Egypt. French and Czechoslovakian companies have jointly built textile plants in

Iraq. West-German equipment has been used in Morocco with Hungarian know-how.

Pisar writes that East-West cooperation in building an industrial infrastructure (irrigation schemes, energy resources, transportation systems and other basic projects in the Third World) offers a unique combination of safeguards and mutual benefits. He observes: "By its inherent nature, a transideological corporation assures recipient countries against the risk of domination or subversion from abroad. While pursuing its own commercial interest, it assumes negotiated economic obligations with no ideological or political strings attached, since Eastern and Western partners effectively neutralize each other.[8]

It is a moot question whether Pisar's optimistic evaluation conforms to reality, but certainly shifts on a world-wide scale are occurring that affect East-West relations. A wider exchange of people, ideas and goods between East and West is of course to be welcomed, as a means of facilitating an opening-up process. Part of the explanation for the new trends, however, must be sought in the fact that both capitalism and communism have common origins in the Enlightenment with its emphasis on human reason, science and progress. It is also well to keep in mind that this cross-fertilization is taking place at a time when there is growing disenchantment with the role of the multinational corporations in the West, whereas in the East there are still high expectations that the mass-production system, now increasingly turning toward the production of consumer goods, will usher in a better future.

Furthermore, even Marx himself had high praise for capitalism's ability to change the face of the earth through its technical mastery over nature. None other than Lenin spoke glowingly of the Taylor system (scientific management) and he was anxious to copy this system from the Americans for the sake of raising production in Russia.[9] This system of organizing work, aimed at maximum efficiency, has cut work into meaningless fragments, thus reducing the worker to an extension of the machine in the U.S. and in the other industrialized nations. Before uncritically rejoicing over the lifting of the Iron Curtain, we should take a hard look at the underlying similarity between a preoccupation with production and consumption in the East *and in the West.* At least, before concluding that the Soviet system is undergoing liberalization, we do well to consider Hedrick Smith's observation:

> Indeed, change is taking place in the Soviet economic system, but so far it is change within parameters that preclude any fundamental transformation. Foreign techniques are transplanted without generating any basic alteration of the Soviet economic or political system. The current Communist leadership seems as capable as its czarist predecessors of making adaptations for the sake of world commerce while managing to contain the germ of change. [10]

In a perceptive article by Robert Scheer on the operations of PepsiCo, the cynicism and banality of this company's approach are aptly described. The author details the company's effort to market its products in the Soviet Union and other communist countries. He pictures the board chairman Don Kendall as an ardent advocate of international trade. In his contacts with the communist leaders, Mr. Kendall discovered that they were very decent fellows similarly interested in expanding international trade and buying PepsiCo products. Pepsi's chairman who was a frequent visitor to the Soviet Union managed to reduce the awesome dimension of communism to manageable proportions as follows: " 'General Secretary Brezhnev is a very warm, very outgoing person, he's an extrovert, not an introvert. I've got some pictures taken in June and you can see it [emphatically]. He's a *warm* person. He's very outspoken.' "[11]

Pepsi pays a great deal of attention to its advertising in order to persuade the public that its product induces sociability and "thinking young." The 1974 jingle selected in the company's advertising campaign was "Feelin' Free." At first it was feared that some nondemocratic countries might object to this theme for fear that people would take it literally. Alan Pottash, Pepsi's senior vice-president for creative services, explained:

> "This was quickly washed away when we analyzed for ourselves the double meaning of the word or the sense of feelin' free, because if you substitute the word *carefree* for the word *free* you're getting closer to what we're really saying—feeling carefree, not feeling free in the sense of breaking the chains that bind you, but feeling free in spirit, and feeling free in thinking and independent enjoyment. So feeling carefree was the best way to explain what we meant in foreign languages and that's what we've done." [12]

So much for feeling free the Pepsi way. The contemporary leaders of the U.S.S.R. need not fear that the Pepsi invasion will stimulate their subjects into entertaining dangerous thoughts. Advertising is all about creating a make-believe world where the consumption of goods reinforces the illusion of freedom. Thus the "free-enterprise" West helps to bolster the prison walls of the communist regime. The campaign to restore "truth" in advertising is irrelevant and totally ineffective over against this unmitigated perversity.

Multinationals and the Third World

There is a great deal of disagreement about the role of multinationals in the Third World. Some view the multinational corporation as the most suitable channel for upgrading the economies of the developing nations, including professional economists and company directors. They insist that these nations need technology and capital to develop their potential, and it is the multinational corporations that can supply those needs most efficiently. On the other hand, critics of the multinational charge that these companies have enriched themselves at the expense of the poor nations. They can indeed point to many instances of exploitation, especially during the early days when one company, United Fruit for example, could ruthlessly dominate an industry (bananas) in Central America. The more recent events in Chile and ITT's role in that country's coup against the Marxist regime of Dr. Salvador Allende is eagerly used to bolster the antimultinational argument.

In view of the statistics, the argument that the multinationals are able to help close the gap between the rich and the poor nations is not convincing. That gap is widening steadily, leaving three-quarters of the world population in the developing (or underdeveloped) nations further behind. In 1900 the per capita income in the poor countries was about half of that in the rich countries. According to one estimate, this ratio had declined to one-fortieth by 1970.[13]

Two hundred million people in India are struggling to survive on incomes that average less than forty dollars a year. Nine hundred million in the developing world earn less than a hundred dollars a year. By the same token, the supreme test for multinational corporations is their record in helping to bridge the gap between the rich and the poor. They have performed poorly on that score. The fact that the gap is widening is of course not by itself proof against the multinationals. Other elements enter in as well. The situation *might* have been worse in the absence of the multinational corporations. But this deteriorating relative position of the Third World should make us especially attentive to the transfer of wealth and resources between the poor and the rich nations.

A United Nations' study of multinational corporations provides a statistical overview of foreign direct investment in the developing countries in 1967 figures. Total foreign direct investment in these countries amounted to $33,134.6 million of which 50.4 per cent was of U.S. origin (19.9 per cent from the U.K., 8.1 per cent from France, 5.1 per cent from the Netherlands and 4.4 per cent from Canada).[14]

The share of production and sales by the U.S. corporations is substantial in a number of countries: for example, 17 per cent of the gross value of industrial production in Mexico; 13 per cent in the Philippines; and 11 per cent in Argentina and Brazil. In Central America the output of foreign affiliates is estimated at 30 per cent of the manufacturing sector. The share of these companies in some industries is, however, much higher, as in the case of rubber products in Mexico in 1970 where it reached 100 per cent. The export share of U.S. affiliates accounted for 87 per cent of the exports of manufacturers from Mexico in 1966; U.S. affiliates in Argentina and Brazil from 1965-68 accounted for 14.5 per cent and 42 per cent, respectively, of the total exports.[15]

Proponents of multinationals are eager to point to the unique ability of these companies to provide both capital and technology—the two essential elements for industrial development. A close look at the multinationals' performance on these two counts in the Third World reveals some startling and disconcerting facts.

A fundamental requirement for economic and industrial development is the creation of wealth beyond that needed for subsistence. When surplus capital is created as a result of savings, this capital (finance) can be put to use in building the infrastructure of a modern society, including roads, transportation and communication networks, schools, and banks. For this reason it is crucial for developing nations that newly generated capital be used to step up this process of development by means of additional investments. But a very large part of the capital generated by the multinational corporations in developing countries has not been used for strengthening and expanding the economic base of these countries. Instead, this capital has been remitted to the parent company, depriving the host country of much needed capital and deteriorating its balance of payments.

The earlier caution against regarding the transfer of capital by itself is relevant here. The figures showing the inflow and outflow of capital tell only part of the story. But when the figures are consistently and excessively high on the outflow side, there is reason to be concerned.

In discussing the drain on the national resources of the Third World, the 1972 United Nations report shows the discrepancy between inflow and outflow related to foreign direct investment in a selected group of developing countries for the five years from 1965-1970. The outflow is nearly always, with very few exceptions, higher than the inflow. For the year 1970, the outflow from the selected developing countries in all categories amounted to $5,341.8 million; the inflow was $1,612.7 million. The net outflow in all categories for the year 1970 was therefore $3,729.1 million according to this U.N. report.[16]

Louis Turner, author of *Invisible Empires* and *Multinational Companies and the Third World,* observes: "Multinational investments are an expensive bargain for the Third World if one merely looks at the inward and outward flows of foreign exchange. This is a serious drawback at a time when the majority of these countries are struggling with massive foreign debts, which are probably the main check on development in the Third World." In 1965-67, 87 per cent of all aid to Latin America was required for debt repayments; in the case of Africa the figure was 73 per cent; East Asia 52 per cent; and the Middle East 40 per cent.[17] The total debt burden of the Third World had climbed to a staggering $180 billion by 1977.[18]

As these figures indicate, the multinationals are not a plentiful source of capital for the developing countries. They aggravate the problems of hard-pressed local businessmen by soaking up much of the domestic loan capital. These large-scale and financially secure outside corporations are attractive borrowers to local bankers and other investors. A study by Fernando Fajnzylber, published by the U.N. in 1970, shows that during the years 1957-65 American-based multinational corporations financed 83 per cent of their Latin American investments by means of reinvested earnings. He also showed that between 1960 and 1968 American-based corporations, on the average, sent 79 per cent of their net profits out of Latin America. Another study has indicated that from the years 1960-70 about 78 per cent of the manufacturing operations of American-based corporations were financed with local capital.[19] These figures clearly indicate that instead of being a major source of capital for the developing countries, multinational corporations are a severe drain on a scarce supply.

There are numerous other ways in which multinationals can, and do, exploit their power to their own advantage but to the detriment of the developing countries, including manipulating internal cost and prices, overpricing of goods and equipment, destroying local competition and curtailing exports.

The reported profit figures of multinational corporations in one country do not mean much by themselves. It often "pays" a company to declare a high profit in one country and a low one in another. This can be achieved via transfer pricing, whereby a company in effect sells to and buys from itself (see above). It speaks for itself that this practice is especially detrimental to the developing countries. The reported yields on all U.S. direct investments in the developing countries were twice as high as in the developed countries during the 1960s.[20] But a closer look at the profit figures reveals an even worse picture.

Constantine Vaitsos, a Latin American economist, has examined the pricing policies of a number of multinational corporations in Colombia. In comparing the prices charged by Colombian affiliates of multinational corporations with world prices in the pharmaceutical, rubber and electronics industries, Vaitsos found overpricing of 185 per cent in the pharmaceuticals, 40 per cent in the rubber industry and from 16-60 per cent in electronics. Comparing prices for certain imported popular drugs with world market prices, Vaitsos discovered that the Colombian prices for the tranquilizers Valium and Librium were 82 and 65 times their average world prices. The antibiotic tetracycline was sold for 10 times the world price. Transistors sold in Colombia cost 11 times their U.S. price; a certain television amplifier cost 2½ times more in Colombia than in the U.S. These prices are charged in a country where per capita income is about $300 per year.[21]

In Chile, Vaitsos reported that overpricing ranges from 30 per cent to more than 700 per cent. Pedroleón Díaz, Vaitsos' colleague, has shown that the pricing policies of the multinational corporations result in overpricing in Peru, from 50-300 per cent, and in Ecuador, from 75-200 per cent. Vaitsos estimates that in 1968 alone overpricing in the drug industry cost Colombia $20 million in foreign exchange and $10 million in tax receipts.

Richard Barnet and Ronald Müller in their *Global Reach* explain that in order to get an accurate picture of the profits of a multinational's subsidiary, one must calculate the overpricing of imports and the underpricing of exports as well as reported profits, royalties and other fees, and divide that into the net worth of such a company. Obviously, such an exercise is exceedingly difficult to perform in view of the lack of accurate information. All findings must be accepted in this awareness and it must be recognized that accurate results are difficult to obtain. A person's bias will no doubt influence the conclusions to some extent. Nonetheless, it can be enlightening to look at such findings.

Vaitsos made a study of fifteen wholly owned U.S. and European drug manufacturing subsidiaries for the year 1968. He found that the annual rate of return ranged from 38 per cent to 962 per cent with an average of 162 per cent. But the average declared profit for that year was 6.7 per cent. The actual profit in the rubber industry was an average of 43 per cent; the declared profit was 16 per cent. Other studies have confirmed these findings. Economists at the University of Lund, Sweden, examined sixty-four mining operations of American firms in Peru, and they found that between 1967 and 1969 the companies reported profits to the local governments of $60 million but profits of $102 million to the U.S. government. A commission established by the Peruvian government in 1966 investigated the double-accounting methods of the American-based Southern Peru Copper Corporation. It discovered that this company had reported two entirely different amounts in profits to the Peruvian and the U.S. governments, $69 million and $135 million respectively, for the years 1960 to 1965. These manipulations go a long way to explain the animosity toward multinationals in host countries.

A practice reported by several observers is the overcharging by parent companies for used machinery. Louis Turner reports that a U.S. textile firm, Indian Head Mills, contributed $170,000 in cash, and forty-year-old machinery valued at $1.7 million in return for 70 per cent of a $5.7 million venture. It is true that the risk factor is high in these cases since many of the projects undertaken in newly-independent Third World countries are unsuccessful. But this kind of practice is wide open to abuse.[22]

Barnet and Müller describe one case of a company that sold machinery to its subsidiary at a 30 per cent higher price than it sold the same item to an independent Colombian firm. Another similar case involved the sale to a subsidiary in Colombia of used machinery that was valued at more than $1 million by the parent company. When a government agency solicited bids for the same equipment, it found that the going price for new equipment was half of what the parent company was charging its subsidiary for used equipment.[23]

Multinational corporations have often driven out local competition. The Chilean and Brazilian economies included thriving commercial and manufacturing sections during the nineteenth century, but the impact of foreign capital via direct investment all but destroyed a number of domestic enterprises, such as the merchant fleet, copper mines and flour mills of Chile. The same thing has happened more recently to the Peruvian fish meat industry, which is now dominated by multinational companies able to buy out the local businesses. More credit restrictions in Brazil since 1966 have led to the takeover of many local firms by the multinationals, especially in drug manufacturing, textiles, plastics and electronics. Turner writes that a slowdown in the economy often meant the sale of the local company to a multinational corporation because the latter had no trouble weathering the storms. "The multinationals caught cold, while their Brazilian counterparts died of pneumonia."[24]

Barnet and Muller claim that the counterpart of what was called the American challenge in Europe a few years ago is now a *fait accompli* in Latin America. Local entrepreneurs often welcome the penetration of their countries by the multinationals, for it gives them a chance to sell their businesses for a good price. Others are "persuaded" by ruthless competition that it is better to sell. One report shows that, of the 717 "new" manufacturing subsidiaries in Latin America established by the top 187 U.S. multinational corporations during the years 1958 to 1967, 331 or 41 per cent were the result of takeovers. The Brazilian government's antitrust agency claims that the Swiss-based company Brown Boveri, and other multinationals in Brazil, including G.E. and Toshiba, formed a cartel for the purpose of "the systematic destruction of Brazilian national enterprises" through pricecutting. Documents used at anticartel proceedings against Brown Boveri revealed that the cartel was out "to destroy Cemec [a Brazilian transformer producer] and another fifty firms." Government prosecution claimed that dozens of local firms were eliminated.[25]

The multinational corporation's superiority in technological expertise, financial strength and managerial ability often leads to oligopolistic conditions. In pre-Allende Chile, 51 per cent of the 160 largest companies were in the hands of multinational corporations. In each of seven key industries, one to three foreign companies controlled at least 51 per cent of production. The pattern is the same in developing countries around the world. In Argentina, more than 50 per cent of the total sales of the fifty largest companies is handled by multinational companies.

Multinational corporations in many instances place restrictions on the exports of their subsidiaries. A study by the United Nations has revealed that agreements between parent companies and their subsidiaries, or joint-venture partners, in Bolivia, Colombia, India, Peru and the Philippines, often contain clauses limiting or prohibiting exports. Out of a total of 1024 agreements in these countries, the percentage of agreements containing such restrictive provisions for one year or more during the period of 1968-71 was as follows: Bolivia, 90.4 per cent; Colombia, 70.6 per cent; India, 47.3 per cent; Peru, 96.1 per cent; Philippines, 25.2 per cent.[26]

One study in 1955 revealed that sole-supplier agreements between American and Swiss firms and the Indian firm Atul Products Limited caused the latter firm to pay up to double the market price for its raw material. Constantine Vaitsos has shown that out of thirty-five contracts in the chemical and pharmaceutical industries in Colombia, only two contracts permitted a free choice of suppliers.[27]

It is self-evident that these restrictions are harmful enough for the developed host countries; but they are all the more damaging for the developing countries because of their need for precious foreign exchange and a manufacturing base.

Even greater in importance are the patterns of trade between the rich and the poor nations. The present patterns reflect the earlier ties between the major Western nations and their former colonies.[28] Much of the agriculture of Africa, Asia and Latin America is geared to produce cash crops for the Western nations, including tea, coffee, cocoa, bananas, peanuts, cotton, sisal. Prices of these cash crops, with one or two exceptions, have declined. Many of the high protein foods are exported from countries where people are starving. Even fish, desperately needed in Latin America, is shipped to North America and Europe, where it often ends up as cattle and poultry food.

Food and other raw materials shipped from the developing to the developed countries is mostly exported in unprocessed form. Tariffs and various arrangements between exporting countries and multinational corporations are effective barriers against processing in countries where the raw materials originate. The World Bank estimates that the poor nations would earn an extra $30 billion a year (in 1975 prices) if the rich nations would drop their trade restrictions.[29] In adopting a deliberate policy of locking the developing countries into a perpetual state of underdevelopment, the multinational corporations have been utterly selfish and cruel. This is one area where drastic change is imperative.

The technology exported by multinational corporations to developing countries is often an imitation of the home country technology. However, in many instances this is not the kind required by developing nations. The self-interest of multinationals is obvious. They can realize a quicker profit by transferring the production *and consumption* pattern already accepted in North America and Europe rather than attempting to tailor their product to the needs of the developing countries. Advertising via radio and television plays a powerful role in conditioning the poor to spend on luxury items.

An international advertising specialist claimed that we must change our ideas about a poor man's physical needs. He continued: "The psychological significance of his spending his money on a transistor radio may be more important than the physical benefit generated by spending the same money for basic foodstuffs."[30] This theory may be good for a multinational producing transistor radios, but it spells nothing but harm in those parts of the world where malnutrition, with its dreadful physical and mental retardation, is the major scourge. A 1973 Brookings Institution study of world nutrition estimated that about one billion persons suffer from the effects of malnutrition. Yet it has been found that dietary habits of the poor in the developing countries have changed for the worse. Joaquín Cravioto, a specialist in pediatric nutrition, found that the two products most wanted by Mexican peasants as soon as they encounter the advertising message are white bread and soft drinks instead of their own simple but nutritious staple foods.[31]

The transfer of technology from the mass consumption countries to the developing countries has been accompanied by the transfer of a consumption ideology that has had disastrous effects. There is plenty of evidence to suggest that the multinational corporations have not been successful in overcoming the problems of inequality, hunger and unemployment—the three major plagues in developing countries. On the contrary, they have in many instances aggravated the problem. The consumption ideology spread abroad by the multinational corporations is harmful enough in North America and Europe, but it is devastating in the developing countries.

Manpower, the one resource always in plentiful supply in developing countries, is not utilized for the benefit of the people by the multinational corporations.[32] Importing high-technology industry has not improved but aggravated the unemployment situtation in the Third World. These capital-intensive projects have drained away scarce capital from agriculture and other less expensive but more labour-intensive projects. Consequently, unemployment remains a most serious and worsening problem in the developing countries.

A 1960 United Nations report estimated that 27 per cent of the workers in the Third World were unemployed. By the end of that decade, this figure had risen to 30 per cent. Erik Thorbecke, a professor of economics at Cornell University, has estimated that 43 per cent of the Peruvian workers are not needed for that nation's production. The unemployment rate in Colombia is 36 per cent. The last survey done in 1960 showed unemployment in Latin America ranging from 22 per cent in Argentina, Brazil and Mexico to 42 per cent in Central America and the Caribbean.[33] Even in agriculture, the trend toward large, highly mechanized farms has destroyed jobs. The same decline in employment is seen in construction because of the introduction of labour-saving machinery. This machinery was introduced in the developed countries partly in response to high labour cost. It makes absolutely no sense to transfer the same labour-saving technology to the developing countries where the need for employment opportunities is desperate. But that is the policy followed by profit-maximizing companies. A more equitable policy would be to maximize employment and to provide many more opportunities and incentives for training the unskilled in the developing countries. That would require a different kind of technology than the one developed in capital-intensive and sophisticated industries.

The late E.F. Schumacher, a British economist and specialist on developing countries, held that the straight transfer of Western technology to developing countries does more harm than good.[34] He insisted that two major problems in the developing countries must be overcome: mass unemployment and mass migration to the cities. He described the growing inequality within the developing countries between a small elite that is imitating the high-consumption pattern of the developed countries and a large majority of desperately poor flocking from the countryside to the cities where they cannot find shelter or jobs. This "dual economy" effect is dangerously disruptive and must be attacked as a priority task. In that context Schumacher persuasively argued that primary attention must be given to an agro-industrial base from which development can proceed. Needed are millions of (small) workplaces using simple technology and concentrating on the first needs of the developing countries: building materials, clothing, household goods, agricultural implements, trees, and water and crop storage facilities. More ambitious programs can be developed once a sound basis has been laid.

Schumacher called for an "intermediate technology," that is, a technology that exploits local resources for local uses, is small-scale, simple and non-destructive. He believed that less stress should be put on production for export and more on production aimed at greater self-sufficiency at the local level. He was a strong critic of the maximum consumption ideology so prevalent in the West, and of those economists who have turned economics into an abstract, mostly quantitative science rather than viewing it as a "branch of wisdom." Schumacher called for bridging the three-fold gap in the developing countries—between rich and poor, educated and uneducated, urban and rural—with imagination and compassion.

It is that combination of imagination and compassion that one encounters in Schumacher's views and insights that has been notably absent in the activities of the multinational corporations in the Third World. This is not to suggest that these activities have only been evil. A few companies have taken some steps to adjust their methods to the needs of the Third World. One such company is Philips, the Dutch-based electronics firm, which has a special experimental team at work adapting its production to local resources and needs in the developing world. Philips has a small research team working on simplifying production, management and accounting procedures to fit conditions in the Third World. Production is kept as flexible and simple as possible. Tools and equipment are utilized to serve various purposes. For example, sewing machine motors are used to drive other equipment, and irons are used as hot plates. Trainees from various countries work in this pilot plant and their findings are used by top level management to decide on production methods, materials and end products for different parts of the developing world.[35]

A few other companies are moving in this direction, but by and large the multinational corporations cannot lay claim to outstanding performance in this respect. On the contrary, their oligopolistic position has driven out local businesses, their sophisticated technology has aggravated unemployment, their mass-consumption ideology has led to harmful eating and working patterns and their drain on scarce resources has added to the debt burden of developing countries. They have locked these nations into a trading pattern that stymies proper economic and industrial development. Repeatedly, the interests of profit-maximizing corporations and poor host countries have been seen as incompatible. The three major plagues of the Third World, unemployment, inequality and hunger, are spreading. The gap between the rich and poor nations is widening. In the face of this, it is obvious that drastic structural changes are required if the developing countries are to achieve a level of economic health that will enable them to overcome their present distressing plight.

Chapter 3
The Growth of Multinationals in Canada

In building the Canadian nation, Canadians have always been keenly conscious of their gigantic and growing southern neighbour. . . . The tug of war between the desire to be like the United States and the desire to be separate from it has confused Canada's sense of national purpose and thwarted the emergence of distinctly Canadian qualities in the nation's economic and cultural life. [1]

William C. Hood

All the data confirm that foreign control now constitutes a very high proportion of Canadian corporate activity and that it is particularly concentrated in resource exploitation and manufacturing. Within manufacturing, foreign control is concentrated in particular industries, including most of the science-based industries, such as transport equipment, chemicals, machinery and electrical products. In 1968, according to CALURA, close to 35 per cent of the assets of non-financial firms were non-resident controlled. [2]

Gray Report

The most bitter harvest of increasing dependence and diminishing control may yet be reaped in the form of the internal political balkanization of Canada and its piecemeal absorption into the American imperial system. The final outcome of a branch-plant society is a merging of value systems and a meshing of corporate and technocratic elites which must ultimately call into question English Canada's willingness to pay the price of continued independence. [3]

Kari Levitt

The Staple Theory

The staple theory, usually associated with the Canadian economist Harold A. Innis (1894-1952), holds that Canada's economic development has been determined by the production of staple goods such as codfish, furs, lumber and wheat. Some economists persist in viewing Canada as a perpetual producer of staples, despite the fact that modern-day staples have changed from food staples to those needed for a modern industrial economy, such as iron ore, nickel, lead and oil. Melville H. Watkins, a political economist at the University of Toronto, wrote in 1963: "The basic determinants of Canadian growth are the volume and character of her staple exports and the ability to borrow, adapt, and marginally supplement foreign technology."[4]

Economists, including Watkins, have criticized this theory as a conspiracy to perpetuate the role of Canadians as hewers of wood and drawers of water. David W. Carr, author of *Recovering Canada's Nationhood,* points out that the so-called staple theory, applied to the early and somewhat static phase of economic development, is not uniquely Canadian but is applicable to the early stages of economic development in all countries. He writes:

> In the critical 1930s, the staple theory made it easy for its disciples to suggest that a national policy would be of little benefit to Canada because her future was clearly determined by these few staple natural resources, by the limitations imposed by geography and by her dependence on export markets. Interpreted as it was in this way, the staple theory tended to be backward-looking, deterministic and negative. It was thus appropriate perhaps for a country without national objectives: appropriate to encourage support for United States enterprise to exploit these unfavourable conditions in Canada. But it was remarkably inappropriate as a view of Canada's economic prospects and as a rational interpretation of her economic growth potential which by that time was becoming clearly evident. [5]

A more scathing attack against the staple theory has come from the side of those who employ a class analysis of Canadian history. Watkins now belongs to that group. He criticizes his former—though still admired—teacher Innis for failing to recognize Canadian liberalism for what it was, although he admits that Innis did discern the "imperialistic" character of American liberalism.[6]

R.T. Naylor, also an adherent of the socialist view of Canadian history, is convinced that "Canadian history since then [1503] reveals little more than a struggle between various imperial powers to determine whose dominion it shall be."[7] Thus, the emphasis on the staple theory in Canadian economics has nothing to do with geography or the stage of technological development but is solely attributable to the nature of what Naylor calls the "metropole," its stage of development and its structure of capital. The metropoles (France, Britain and now the United States) have determined the economic development of the "hinterland" (Canada). It was in the interest of the metropoles to use Canada as a cheap source of staple commodities, assisted by an accommodating core of Canadian merchant capitalists. Another spokesman for the socialist interpretation of Canadian history expressed it thus:

> Canada's dependency is a function not of geography and technology but of the nature of Canada's capitalist class. The Canadian business class has been dominated historically by financial capitalists who have made their profits on the exchange of Canadian staple products in return for manufactured goods imported from metropolitan countries. [8]

In summary, whether looked at from the side of continentalists or nationalists, there is a certain unanimity about the importance of the "staple theory" in Canadian history despite the diversity of opinion on the meaning of this theory.

The National Policy

The National Policy was a series of measures undertaken to safeguard Canada's existence especially over against its colossal neighbour to the south. This is how the American economist Hugh G.J. Aitken summarized Canada's attitude toward the United States: "If we wish to understand present-day Canadian sentiment, therefore, it is vital to bear in mind the fact that resistance to absorption or domination by the United States is the very essence of Canadian history. If there is any such thing as a Canadian nationality, it can be defined only in terms of the ways in which Canadians regard themselves as being different from Americans."[9] The National Policy is most commonly associated with the nation-building efforts begun with Confederation in 1867 and spearheaded by Canada's first Prime Minister, Sir John A. Macdonald, who served in that capacity from 1867-73 and again from 1878-91. This policy, inaugurated in 1879, contained three main ingredients: (1) a program of railroad building; (2) industrialization protected by the tariffs; and (3) settlement of the West.

The National Policy was adopted after two other options—namely, integration with the British empire or absorption into the American one—were rejected. "The collapse in quick succession of hopes for closer imperial co-operation and for a satisfactory measure of continental interdependence made increasingly urgent the need for a national economy as the one adequate instrument of economic survival."[10]

Writing on the National Policy, Craig Brown, a Canadian historian, raises the question why Canadian nationalism was expressed in such predominantly economic terms. He argues that other nationalist themes such as a common language, a common cultural tradition or a common religion were simply unavailable to the young nation in view of the existence of the two cultural groups. What were regarded as deeds of heroism and victory by one were interpreted as humiliation and defeat by the other. It is this predicament plus the lack of Canadian politicians who were political theorists or philosophers, writes Brown, that gave Canadian nationalism an overriding economic content. Brown also asserts that this was an age in which Darwinism and industrialism coincided with the great age of nationalism. Industrialization was seen as the key to obtain power: ". . . power to withstand the pressures from the south and power to expand and consolidate the Canadian nation. And a political programme that emphasized expansion and industrialism had the added advantage of ignoring the potentially divisive issues that would disrupt a 'political nationality.' In sum, then, the National Policy, a policy for a 'Canadian economy' and a 'Big Canada,' a materialistic policy for a materialistic age, was the obvious policy to give expression to Canadian national sentiment." [11]

Canadian socialists are much more critical of the National Policy. They describe this policy as a sellout to Americans by the Canadian "merchant class." James Laxer, prominent Canadian author and political science professor at York University, writes: "The primary purpose of the tariff then was not to protect Canadian industrialists but to guarantee the monopoly of the trading system of the Canadian merchants and to force American industrialists who wanted part of the Canadian market to establish factories in Canada." [12]

R.T. Naylor makes a similar point. The National Policy, he writes, was not really intended to protect a burgeoning manufacturing industry. On the contrary, it was a scheme designed by merchant capitalists who were more interested in finance, transportation and utilities than in industrial development. They favoured short-term risk investments and were therefore preoccupied with the extraction of staple products. Capital was thus drained away from industrial undertakings. Moreover, the tariff attracted foreign branch plants, presenting another obstacle to the establishment of Canadian-owned industries. [13]

American branch plants established in Canada enjoyed the benefit of operating behind the Canadian tariff wall and within the preferential system of the British empire. This dual advantage is generally acknowledged to be the main stimulus for the beginnings of American ownership of Canadian industry. The socialists see no surprise here, since, according to them, it was all planned that way by the capitalist class in the metropole. Those who are unwilling to accept such neat logic are faced with a real paradox: namely, a tariff system designed to protect Canadian industry that nevertheless paved the way for foreign—mostly U.S.—ownership in Canada. "The funny thing about tariff walls," writes Michael Bliss, "was that we always wanted the enemy to jump over them. Some walls!" [14]

The Extent of Foreign Ownership in Canada

Canada has always had to import capital from outside, at first chiefly from Britain. These funds were needed to finance early waterways and railroads (the infrastructure) as well as the early industrial enterprises. After World War I Britain became less important as the provider of capital for Canada. Its place was taken by the U.S. But what is important to keep in mind is that whereas British capital was largely in the form of loan or debt capital, the flow from the U.S. was increasingly in the form of equity capital (direct investment), thus providing Americans with *control* and a *perpetual* claim on the fruits of their investments in Canada.[15] This control over major segments of the Canadian economy, particularly the resource and manufacturing industries, has become a source of deep concern and spirited debate in Canada.

This is a brief overview of the statistics.[16] In 1867 there was a total of $200 million foreign investment in Canada, of which $105 million was in the form of British debt capital. By 1900 this amount had increased to $815 million in British bonds and $160 million in U.S. direct investments. In 1913 there was a total of $3,850 million foreign capital in Canada. Of this amount, $3,080 million was in the form of fixed interest securities, nearly all of it British. The American share of the remaining investment was mostly in direct U.S. investment ($520 million). Total foreign investment in Canada climbed to $6,003 million in 1926, of which 53 per cent was American and 30 per cent was in the form of direct investment. From 1926 to 1939 the rate of foreign investment in Canada slowed down and total investments increased by only $910 million. Canada imported little capital during the war years and the trend of declining British investment and increasing American investment in Canada continued.

The greatest expansion of foreign investment in Canada occurred after World War II, especially after 1950. United States investment in Canada rose from $4,990 million (1945) to $10,275 million (1955). By 1965 it had more than doubled to $23,305 million.[17] In 1976 U.S. direct investment in Canada amounted to $33,927 million according to the U.S. Department of Commerce.[18]

From 1948 to 1963 the proportion of Canadian industrial assets controlled by foreign investors rose from 20 to 34 per cent. In many sectors, U.S. ownership was well over 50 per cent. In 1966 most of the $32,092 million in foreign investment in Canada was in the form of direct investment ($22,853); the remainder was in government securities, public utilities and miscellaneous investments.[19]

The federal government issued an extensive report on foreign direct investment in Canada, the Gray Report, in 1972. This study provided up-to-date statistical information on foreign investment and considered a number of measures to cope with this issue. In 1968 nonresident-owned firms controlled *34.2 per cent of all Canadian corporate assets.* The Gray Report ventured that $30 billion was a reasonable estimate of the book value of all foreign-controlled firms. Foreign control of Canadian industry is concentrated in manufacturing and natural resources, estimated at *57 per cent in manufacturing* with $11.8 billion of the $20.5 billion total capital employed controlled by nonresidents. Of that segment, $9.4 billion or 80 per cent was in the hands of American residents in 1967.

Of the $9.7 billion capital employed in the petroleum and natural gas industry at the end of 1967, $7.2 billion or 74 per cent was controlled by nonresidents. U.S. residents controlled 81 per cent or $5.8 billion of that proportion.

In mining and smelting, 65 per cent ($3.4 billion) of the total capital employed ($5.2 billion) was controlled by nonresidents. U.S. residents controlled $2.9 billion or 85 per cent of the capital controlled by nonresidents.

The Gray Report pointed out that, within manufacturing, foreign control is concentrated in most of the science-based industries, such as transport equipment, chemicals, machinery and electrical products. In geographic terms, Ontario has received a proportionately larger share of foreign-controlled investment than any other province.[20]

More recent statistics on foreign investment in Canada are supplied by the *Corporations and Labour Unions Returns Act* (*CALURA*), *Report for 1974,* issued by Statistics Canada under the auspices of the Minister of Industry, Trade and Commerce. This report provides a wealth of detailed statistical information on the activities of foreign-owned corporations in Canada. It should be kept in mind that the Act applies only to corporations with gross revenues in excess of $500,000 or assets in excess of $250,000. Crown corporations, and a number of other corporations operating under different Acts, such as the *Radio Act,* are also excluded. Some 6,103 foreign-controlled nonfinancial corporations are covered in the 1974 Report. It is estimated that the additional foreign-controlled firms which do not report under the CALURA number about 2,500. Some of the highlights of *CALURA, Report for 1974* follow.

Assets of foreign-controlled nonfinancial corporations rose by 17.4 per cent to $74.8 billion in 1974 representing 34 per cent of the total assets of all nonfinancial corporations in Canada compared to 34.4 per cent in 1973. There were 474 foreign-controlled corporations with more than $25 million in assets holding a total of $55 billion in assets or 74 per cent of the assets of all nonfinancial foreign-controlled corporations. In all nonfinancial industries except storage, primary metals and public utilities, the average asset size of foreign-controlled corporations was much larger than that of Canadian owned corporations. The average asset size of all foreign-controlled nonfinancial corporations was $12.2 million whereas the average asset size of Canadian-controlled nonfinancial corporations in this category stood at $2.4 million.

Table 4 provides certain percentages on the extent of foreign control in a number of industry groups.

A Threat to Independence

Those concerned about Canada's independence are quick to emphasize the disadvantages associated with foreign control over large sectors of Canada's economy. Because the United States is by far the major source of outside capital in Canada, foreign ownership is often equated with American ownership. The mounting clamour for loosening the hold of foreign corporations in Canada is accompanied and invigorated by a renewed interest in Canadian nationalism. There are those who picture Canada's choices as extremely critical. Either Canadians soon assert themselves and become masters in their own economic house or they will not survive as a nation. Walter Gordon, one of the leading Canadian nationalists, warned his fellow Canadians in 1972 that there was only "one last chance" and very little time left to tackle the two major problems confronting Canada—Quebec and economic independence. He wrote: "If we do not resolve these problems during the life of the next parliament, it may very well be too late to do so. This means, at least in my opinion, that the outcome of the election will more or less determine whether Canada is to survive as a separate independent state."[21]

Criticism of foreign-owned corporations in Canada arises because many people are convinced that the real interests of these corporations and of Canada do not coincide. Corporate policy is concerned with self-interest, growth and profit of the corporations—not with the interest of the host country. Policies designed and controlled by an American head office do not give sufficient weight to Canadian interests. What is more, because of the size and power of large-scale corporations, their decisions regarding research, production, marketing, capital flow and a host of related matters directly affect our environment and our very lifestyle. The extensive control exercised outside Canada has deprived Canadians of an opportunity to experience a measure of economic and national independence without which Canada cannot thrive as a nation.

Professor Hugh Aitken has described the Canadian dilemma, represented by the two-way pull of national autonomy and economic growth, as follows:

> The basis of Canadian anxieties is the conflict between two national aspirations: the desire for rapid economic development and the desire for cultural and political autonomy. There is nothing novel about either of these

TABLE 4 DEGREE OF FOREIGN OWNERSHIP OF CORPORATIONS IN SELECTED INDUSTRY GROUPS IN CANADA

	Per cent Assets		Per cent Sales	
	1973	1974	1973	1974
Major Industry Group				
1. Agriculture, Forestry and Fishing	10	10	8	7
2. Metal Mining	45	45	43	44
3. Mineral Fuels	75	75	87	88
4. Other Mining	55	57	60	59
5. Total Mining	58	59	61	64
Manufacturing				
6. Food	48	49	38	39
9. Rubber Products	93	94	91	91
11. Textile Mills	60	60	57	56
14. Wood Industries	29	28	23	24
16. Paper and Allied Industries	45	44	45	45
18. Primary Metals	16	15	20	19
19. Metal Fabricating	44	52	45	41
20. Machinery	70	68	71	70
21. Transport Equipment	81	80	90	89
22. Electrical Products	65	65	68	65
23. Nonmetallic Mineral Products	66	66	54	56
24. Petroleum and Coal Products	99	100	99	99
25. Chemical and Chemical Products	79	78	84	83
26. Miscellaneous Manufacturing	50	48	52	49
27. Total Manufacturing	56	57	57	57
28. Construction	15	14	12	12
Utilities				
33. Total Utilities	10	9	11	11
34. Wholesale Trade	32	30	29	29
35. Retail Trade	19	18	17	16
36. Finance	12	11	11	11
37. Services	26	25	24	23
39. Total nonfinancial Industries	34	34	37	36

Source: *CALURA, Report for 1974,* pp. 106, 111, 130, 136.

> desires; each of them is characteristic of all cultures that have stemmed from the Western European root. . . . What is relatively novel about the contemporary situation is that Canada now finds itself so placed that the two aspirations are in conflict. [22]

The controversy surrounding foreign investment crystallizes around a number of key issues.

Resources Versus Manufacturing

The concentration of foreign investment in the nonrenewable resource sector has led to an "unbalanced" development and a neglect of secondary industry. It tends to reduce Canada to a "hinterland" and to retard its economic growth. A number of effects stand out.

Firstly, resource development is capital-intensive but creates few jobs in comparison to secondary industry.

Secondly, resource development results in depletion of nonrenewable but essential materials for a modern economy. Rapid development of natural resources, most of which are exported, squanders the life blood of future generations. This argument has grown in importance since the "energy crisis."

Thirdly, resource development involves integration with the U.S. economy, thus making Canada vulnerable to changes in U.S. policy and trade patterns.

Fourthly, an overemphasis on resource development, mostly for export by U.S. corporations, retards a vigorous growth of secondary industry. This is extremely important since secondary industry is essential to economic well-being and a healthy measure of independence. Without a viable manufacturing industry, Canada must import a relatively large amount of finished products, straining its balance of payments and reducing domestic job opportunities. A study undertaken for the Science Council of Canada concludes that Canada is in an unenviable position with respect to the import of sophisticated finished products. The Report asserts:

> For example: we are the world's largest producer of nickel, but we are net importers of stainless steel and manufactured nickel products, including "cold climate" nickel-cadmium batteries; we are the world's second largest producer of aluminum, but we import it in its more sophisticated forms, such as etched and formed foil for use in capacitors and precision aluminum parts for use in aircraft; we are the world's largest exporter of pulp and paper, but we import much of our fine paper and virtually all of the highly sophisticated paper, such as backing for photographic film and dielectric papers for use in electronic components; we are one of the world's principal sources of platinum, but it is all exported for refining and processing and reimported in finished forms; we are large exporters of natural gas and petroleum, but we are net importers of petrochemicals; and, although we are the world's

foremost exporter of raw asbestos fibres, we are net importers of manufactured asbestos. The above is not a selected list of products in which our performance is particularly bad. With the exception of platinum, each of them can be found among the ten products in which our export performance, in net terms, is the best. [23]

The heavy reliance on the exploitation and export of resources has helped to shield us from the effects of our poor performance in the manufacturing sector. Though Canada's overall balance of trade has been mostly in our favour, the trade deficit in manufactured goods reached $10 billion in 1976. Canada is the world's leading importer of manufactured goods. Its per capita import of such products amounted to $463.75 in 1969; the figures for the EEC countries were $239.17; the U.K. $149.46; the U.S. $116.23; Japan $38.31.[24]

This heavy emphasis on raw materials export has had a devastating effect on job opportunities in Canada and is to a large extent responsible for the high level of unemployment in Canada. Furthermore, the service sector in Canada is proportionately too high—about two thirds of all workers—which also serves to underline Canada's vulnerable position. Thus, a three-fold weakness of the Canadian economy with reinforcing tendencies is obvious: dependence on nonrenewable resources to close the trade gap in manufactured goods; a weak manufacturing base resulting in a lessening of employment opportunities; and too high a proportion of our workforce in the service industries, including government services.

The socialists have been scathing in their criticism of this phenomenon, which they have labelled the de-industrialization of Canada. They argue that capitalist development is by definition unbalanced. Watkins asserts: "The role of the hinterland, to export staples and import manufactured goods which embody their own staples, is pre-determined. The metropolis, then, develops—or over-develops—while the hinterland is locked into a pattern of underdevelopment."[25] (It is this conviction which has given added impetus to the socialists' opposition to the massive resource development projects, such as the construction of the Mackenzie Valley pipeline—now abandoned.)

Another consistent complaint against foreign ownership of Canadian plants concerns the lack of efficiency of those manufacturing plants and their failure to pursue export possibilities with enthusiasm. Branch plants fail to do that because their operation fits within the scheme of a multinational firm that may find it more profitable, for example, to produce in different countries.[26] Inefficiency results from the so-called "miniature replica" format of Canadian branch plants, i.e., too many producers in too small a market leading to high unit costs. An example of such inefficiency is the production of refrigerators. Fewer producers would lead to greater productivity and lower costs.[27]

It would be wrong to attribute all these distortions of the Canadian economy to the high level of foreign ownership. What is first of all needed is a reappraisal of our lifestyles and priorities, for these have to be given shape in long range policies governing our economic and industrial development. At the same time, it is quite clear that foreign ownership in important ways has contributed to the problem of a vulnerable economy marked by the structural distortions discussed here.

The Favourite Treatment of the Resource Industries

Among those who have vigorously opposed foreign domination of Canadian industry is Eric Kierans, professor of economics, McGill University, former president of the Montreal Stock Exchange, and former member of the Quebec Cabinet (1963-66) and of the Trudeau Cabinet (July 1968-April 1971). In particular Kierans has emphasized that the corporations involved in resource development, mining, gas, oil and refineries are not pulling their weight in the payment of taxes. Instead, they are receiving unwarranted favourite treatment through government policy. A series of tax concessions to the resource-based industries (including depletion, accelerated depreciation, investment allowances, capital cost, exempt mine income, exploration and development costs allowances, plus other adjustments and allowances) result in a remarkably low rate of taxes. In 1969 the corporations engaged in metal mining reported pretax profits of $611 million, but paid taxes on only $111 million because of a host of exemptions, reducing their actual tax rate to only 11 per cent. However, corporations in the manufacturing sector are taxed the full amount.[28] (In 1973 Kierans prepared a report on the mining industry in Manitoba in which he recommended public ownership of that industry.)

The editors of *Getting It Back* point out that if the taxes were equalized over resource and manufacturing industries, the tax rate could be lowered substantially. They continue:

> The elimination of these special tax concessions would also help to correct the distortion of investment flows which has held back capital expenditure for new plant and equipment in the manufacturing industries in favour of exploration and development in the petroleum, natural gas and metal mining industries. This lower pace of growth in the resources industries would conserve more of our natural wealth for future generations of Canadians; at the same time, it would assure a higher rate of return on the sale of the more carefully rationed supply of resources. [29]

During the past few years, the federal government and various provincial governments have substantially increased royalties and taxes imposed on certain corporations active in resource development.

Entrepreneurship and Technology

Direct foreign investment in Canada represents a *package* of technology, management skills and markets. It is often asserted that this package is needed because Canadians lack the entrepreneurial skills to develop their industries on their own.

There appears to be general agreement that the level of Canadian entrepreneurship is inferior to that of Americans. The Gray Report concurred with that conclusion, attributing the inferiority of Canadian management skills to the fact that Canadian managers of American branch plants merely *execute* the major policy decisions made at head office.[30]

The critics of foreign investment insist that such Canadian inferiority is not inherent but is just another one of the heavy costs associated with foreign investment. Kari Levitt in this connection distinguishes between *managerial* decisions by executives of Canadian branch plants and *entrepreneurial* decisions made by the parent company executives. The latter set the framework in which the former must operate. She sums up: "An economy composed of branch-plant industry must of necessity lack the self-generating force which characterizes successful entrepreneurship. To the degree that Canadian business has opted to exchange its entrepreneurial role for a managerial and rentier status, Canada has regressed to a rich hinterland with an emasculated, if comfortable, business elite."[31]

It is self-evident that there is an intricate relationship between entrepreneurship and the level of technology. In that area, too, the American firms enjoy advantages accruing from large size, an early start, and heavy investment in research and development. Again and again, Canadian-owned companies have found the advantages provided by American firms irresistible when takeover offers were made by Americans. This is how one manager of an American-owned firm sizes up the advantages of a direct link to American technology:

> "We couldn't exist as an all-Canadian company at our present size," Wilkes, who's a Canadian, told me. "It just wouldn't be economic. We couldn't afford the engineering, and that's really the base. We take advantage of our parent company's engineering. We sell a lot of automatic control valves for automated systems. It's a constantly changing field, and, if you're not spending tremendous sums on engineering to continually come out with better designs, you're just not in the business."[32]

Research and development is the key to new and more sophisticated technology without which industry faces stagnation. The branch-plant operations of American-owned firms are reported to have an adverse effect on the development of new technology. Often research and development conducted in Canadian foreign-owned plants is of a secondary nature, fitting within multinational operations of the corporations. A study undertaken by the Science Council of Canada centred on the type of research operations of a company (or industry) "where global or continental manufacturing rationalization has been established. The conclusion was that research would be either present or absent: if present, it would be very sophisticated and tied in with the global research program of the entire corporation; in the case of the Canadian auto industry, research is conspicuous by its absence."[33] This report notes that the little design and research capability that did exist in Canada was transferred back to the U.S. after the Auto Pact was concluded in 1965, resulting in the loss of "advanced automobile expertise" to Canada. Thus Canada finds itself in a position of being a major auto-producing nation, yet it does not have one design team that could design and produce a complete automobile.[34]

The Science Council report explains that increasing rationalization (and centralization) of research and development by the multinationals diminishes opportunities for innovation by Canadian subsidiaries. The Auto Pact is a good (or bad) example of the results of centralization by a parent company. Professor Harold Crookell has remarked that if other rationalized industries behave like the auto makers and rationalize operations from a production standpoint only, then Canadian branch plants will lose their managerial and professional staff and with them any hope of innovating in the future. He summed up the problem this way: *"To lose the power to innovate in a changing environment is to yield control of the future to those who retain that power."*[35]

Another report by the Science Council of Canada concludes that the Canadian record at innovation in key sectors of manufacturing is a "cause for national concern." This report points out that American branch plants are not the best training ground for managers and it also asserts that technological capability of secondary manufacturing in Canada does not present a bright picture. "The achievement of this country in basic research in medicine, in nuclear energy and in many other areas indicates that there is no fundamental lack of creativity. We have rather failed to utilize this creativity for the achievement of economic objectives."[36]

Canada's vulnerability is also evident in the data processing industry. It has been said that in the latter twentieth century Canada's continued independence from the U.S. depends as much on the East-West flow of information as it depended in the nineteenth century on the East-West flow of people and goods. That is why the Canadian Pacific Railway was essential in the 1880s; similarly, Canada's need to obtain control over the computer data field is critical for its independence today. According to some commentators, the picture here is highly disturbing.[37]

The Science Council of Canada observed in 1968 that "the electronic computer may well be the basis in the 1970s of the world's third largest industry, after petroleum and automobiles. . . ."[38] But Canada's prospects in this area do not look well. Again we encounter the adverse effects of a branch-plant economy. Canada's computerized data processing systems are exceedingly vulnerable. Canadian firms operating in the data processing sector experience rough going and some have gone out of business. Why? American-owned firms send their data south of the border for inclusion in their home-based continental system. This has an accumulative damaging effect on supportive industries and their personnel in Canada. They will simply not be needed.

There is a further and even more damaging prospect, writes Richard Liskeard.[39] The trend in the computer data industry is toward interlinking of massive data banks with a corresponding access network to those banks. If Canada does not develop its own banks and its own network, it will have to link up with American ones, and that is exactly what is happening. The large American computer data-centre networks are invading the Canadian market and offering their sophisticated services in Canada at prices against which the less integrated Canadian concerns cannot compete. The Science Council report warns against far-reaching and adverse effects of the alienation of a crucial industry and asserts:

> There is the further possibility that the creation of source material for services, such as information banks and computer-assisted learning, would migrate to the points of supply of these services. Thus much of the information and many of the ideas and values which underpin our society would eventually become largely alien. The Science Council, as a group of concerned and informed Canadians, considers these trends to be unacceptable.[40]

The One-Way Flow of Canadian Capital [41]

Though it carries certain costs, foreign investment in Canada is often thought to be justified on the basis that Canada has insufficient capital of its own and is therefore dependent on outside sources. However, recent analyses and reports suggest that present Canadian savings would be adequate for investment purposes if they were rightly diverted. (This of course was not always so.) Moreover, by far the greatest share of capital now invested in Canada does not come from parent companies but is generated right here in the form of retained earnings or depreciation allowances, or is supplied by Canadian financial institutions.

Cy Gonick, university professor and editor of the Winnipeg-based, Marxist-oriented *Canadian Dimension*, distinguishes three phases in the capital flow resulting from foreign investment in Canada. Until the mid-1950s Canada received more investment from outside than was paid back. After that the capital from abroad (mostly U.S.) was about equal to what we paid out. In the third and current phase, the flow of funds to parent companies has been greater than the amounts received from them. Between 1960 and 1967 Canadian subsidiaries and affiliates sent $1 billion more to their parent companies in the form of profits than they received from them in new investments.[42] The *CALURA, Report for 1971* shows that the total amount paid by foreign-owned *reporting* corporations to nonresidents in the form of dividends, interest and service charges was $2,239 million, which was equivalent to about one-tenth of Canada's total receipts from the exports of goods and services in 1971.[43]

Kari Levitt reports that, from 1957 to 1965, 85 per cent of the funds used to expand U.S.-controlled industry in Canada were provided by Canadian sources. For example, in 1964, of a total investment of $2,557 million by U.S.-owned corporations, $1,244 million was financed from retained earnings, $764 million from depreciation allowances, $423 million from Canadian and third-country sources and only $126 million directly from the U.S. The Dominion Bureau of Statistics estimated that during the years 1946-64 retained earnings mentioned above added $5.2 billion, or 40 per cent, to the increase in Canadian external indebtedness.[44]

The preceding indicates that Canada's own capital supply has much improved over the past decades. The Gray Report concludes that "in an aggregate sense, domestic savings should be sufficient or nearly sufficient to meet capital investment requirements at or near full employment. In practice, since there is a relatively free flow of capital into and out of the country, large amounts of Canadian savings are invested abroad and substantial proportions of foreign savings are invested here."[45]

A substantial amount of Canadian funds is invested outside the country because American corporations refuse to offer equity shares in their Canadian subsidiaries for sale on the Canadian capital market. Their reasons for refusing to do so are obvious, but the result is that Canadians are denied opportunities for investment and for participating in creating new wealth, although that wealth is derived from Canadian resources. Proposals for dealing with foreign ownership invariably include the request that foreign-owned corporations be compelled to offer equity shares to Canadian investors. The lack of sound investment opportunities in Canada is said to be responsible for the substantial amounts of foreign investment by Canadians. This places Canada in a most disadvantageous position, summed up by Kari Levitt: "Not only are Americans buying up Canadian industry with Canadian savings, but they have in effect mobilized Canadian savings to assist in the expansion of the U.S.-based multinational corporations."[46]

Alexander Ross, a former *Financial Post* columnist, has pointed out that, in order to obtain maximum returns, Canadian institutional investors place a large percentage of their capital in the U.S. These funds then go to create new jobs and businesses in that country. "This is how a colonial economy works. This is how our existing structure of our capital market tends to reinforce Canada's role as an economic handmaiden to the American empire."[47]

Concerning the availability of capital for Canadian business enterprises, the obstacles at least partly arise from the large size and greater security provided by American-owned firms in Canada. Canadian businessmen persistently complain about their difficulties in borrowing funds from Canadian lending institutions. This holds true especially for small and struggling businesses since they are considered to be much less secure borrowers than the powerful American-owned corporations. But it is exactly the availability of capital that is needed for the development of Canadian entrepreneurship and Canadian enterprises.

Many small and promising, yet cash-short, Canadian businesses are also selling out to American owners because of a shortage of funds and the inability to obtain them from Canadian sources. An example of such a predicament involved the publishing company McClelland and Stewart. In early 1971 Jack McClelland, owner of the company, announced his intention to sell the company. One of the reasons he gave was shortage of working capital and his inability to obtain such capital. No Canadian company was interested in buying and the prospect of another publishing company being taken over by an American company was imminent. (Two other large Canadian-owned publishing companies, W.J. Gage Ltd., and Ryerson Press, Canada's oldest publishing house, had just recently been bought by American companies.) In the midst of a growing public concern about American takeover of Canadian publishing companies, the Ontario government interceded and provided a $1 million loan to keep this company under Canadian ownership.[48]

Mel Hurtig, Edmonton publisher and leading Canadian nationalist, suggests that the Canadian banking system has placed itself in the service of foreign-owned corporations and he offers this explanation: "It's interesting to note that many of our Canadian bank presidents and vice-presidents are paid directors of foreign corporations operating in Canada. The presidents of our five leading Canadian banks hold among them about seventy corporate directorships, approximately half of which are with foreign-controlled corporations and, of all these corporations, not one has its head office west of the city of Toronto."[49]

The favourite treatment enjoyed by the large foreign-owned corporations extends to the receipt of grants and special advantages aimed at stimulating economic growth. Hurtig refers to the payment of $10 million to Imperial Oil by the Department of Regional Economic Expansion for building a fertilizer plant near Edmonton. Other similar grants have been paid to Canadian subsidiaries of giant American firms such as Westinghouse, IBM, and Proctor and Gamble. A $13 million grant was given to International Telephone and Telegraph (ITT), one of the largest multinationals in the world.[50] D.W. Carr asserts that more than half of all federal and provincial grants and assistance to industries in Canada was given to foreign-owned corporations, although he adds that the Canadian International Development Agency has given priority to Canadian-owned corporations.[51]

Obviously, the policies of governments and of those in control of the capital market in Canada are in need of drastic change, for it makes no sense to throw all kinds of roadblocks in the way of Canadian entrepreneurs and then blame them for poor performance. As Professor A.E. Safarian of the University of Toronto has repeatedly stated, much of the trouble lies within Canada and with Canadian policy makers. They have the opportunity to bring about changes that will encourage the growth of Canadian entrepreneurship. Safarian says: "One of the major gaps in entrepreneurial capital in this country can only be closed by some type of public-private agency. But I would not let that blind me to the fact that we have shamefully hamstrung domestic entrepreneurship in this country, while heaping scorn on it for 'selling out.' "[52]

Federal-Provincial Relations

There is good reason to believe that foreign ownership of large sections of key industries tends to contribute to the tension between Ottawa and the provincial governments. This is not to suggest that all we need is to repatriate our industry in order to solve the federal-provincial problem. Nonetheless, the foreign presence is a disturbing factor, as Mel Watkins asserts.

> It is inherent in the nature of foreign power to divide and rule, and American corporations are not able to escape from this compulsion. Regions within Canada are understandably concerned to get their fair share of foreign-controlled industry and hence to compete among themselves to the extent of their laissez-faire policies. Only a *national* policy is feasible, and to make common cause against foreign encroachment can be a satisfying component of nationalism.[53]

The provinces control the resources within their borders. Their governments are interested in rapid economic development and the natural resources within their boundaries are the basis for such development. That is why there is such a heavy emphasis by the provinces on resource development and the import of foreign capital. There are a large number of critics who complain about the pursuit of short-term interests by the provinces at the expense of a unified, national policy. Foreign investors, wooed by the various provinces, are able to play off the one province against the other.[54] Professor Aitken has summarized this major dilemma as follows:

> If continental economic integration is in any sense a threat, it is a threat to Canada as a nation. It is not a threat to the provinces as such, many of whom, dependent as they are on American capital and the American market, would find it easier to defend their regional economic interests if they had two senators apiece in the United States Congress than they do at present, when all pressure on the United States government must be exerted through Ottawa. [55]

The solution to regional disparity and provincial competition for foreign capital obviously lies in a more commanding and unifying role by the federal government. This solution is, however, made more difficult by the peculiar tensions between English Canada and Quebec, especially since November 15, 1976, when the separatist Parti Québécois led by René Lévesque came to power in that province. At the same time, Quebec's concern for retaining its own identity, and its suspicion of foreign corporate control could work as a unifying element if firm and courageous leadership were provided by the federal government in reclaiming the economy and protecting Canadian industry.

Kari Levitt warns that it is superficial and erroneous to focus on Quebec as the troublemaker in the current discussion on national unity. She writes: "The unique resistance to linguistic and cultural assimilation on the part of Canada's Quebec-based population of French origin could be a decisive factor working for the continued existence of Canada." She also describes the alternative possibility and its destructive consequences: "The alternative to the explicit recognition that Quebec is not a province like any other is the continued fragmentation of the federal structure, as all the other nine provinces claim the fiscal and other powers which Quebec requires." The key to this issue, says Levitt, is to recognize that the major national problem is not Quebec separatism, but "the problem of maintaining political sovereignty at a time when economic sovereignty is so gravely threatened."[56]

Extraterritoriality

The extension of American jurisdiction over American-owned corporations in Canada is referred to as *extraterritoriality*. This extension of jurisdiction is centred on three main areas: (1) balance-of-payments regulations; (2) trade with communist-controlled countries; (3) antitrust legislation. The attempts of American legislators and courts to apply U.S. regulations to Canadian operations has at times erupted into a public controversy. Especially, the restriction of sales to communist countries has occasionally emerged as a rallying point for the anticontinentalists. The Watkins Report describes the problems of corporations faced with conflicting jurisdictions as follows:

> If the content of the law conflicts with the policy of the host country, the situation simply becomes more tense. The corporation itself is confronted with two peaks of sovereignty: it must choose and might be expected to defer to the higher peak. In the nature of the case, the higher peak will typically be the home country.[57]

Balance of Payments

Every nation aims at a favourable balance of payments. Of vital importance is the relationship between exports and imports and between inflow and outflow of capital. Because of the magnitude of foreign ownership in Canada, the balance of payments is greatly affected by the flow of goods and capital between the subsidiaries in Canada and their parent companies outside the country. American policy leans heavily on the multinationals to achieve a favourable balance of payments. But, as is readily perceived and often highlighted at critical periods, America's interest in this respect does not coincide with Canada's. A few incidents in recent years have amply demonstrated that reality and underscored Canada's position of dependency.

The volume of trade between Canada and the U.S. carried on by the multinationals is significant. The report *Foreign-Owned Subsidiaries in Canada, 1964 to 1971*, covering all nonfinancial companies with assets of more than $5 million, of which more than 50 per cent are owned by nonresidents, indicated that the sales figures of these companies reached $28.1 *billion* in 1971. The exports of this group represented 40.7 per cent of all Canadian nonagricultural exports. The American-owned companies sent 85 per cent of their exports to and received 80 per cent of their imports from their parent organizations in the U.S.[58] About two-thirds of Canada's merchandise import and export trade is with the U.S.

It should be kept in mind that a major source of concern with respect to the flow of capital between Canada and the U.S. results from the high level of U.S. *direct* investment in Canada. This kind of investment, *even if no additional capital is imported from the home country*, will increase in volume as a result of retained earnings. Therefore, the cost of servicing direct investment, through dividends, interest and other service payments, has risen sharply and looms large in any consideration of Canada's balance-of-payments position. Thus, Canada is placed in a double predicament. Where earnings of foreign-owned companies in Canada are retained, they add to Canada's indebtedness and to the long-term burden on the balance of payments. Where those earnings are remitted to the parent company, they constitute an immediate drain on our balance of payments. Canada's balance of payments has been placed in serious jeopardy at critical times during the past fifteen years as a result of the U.S. measures to improve its position.

In July 1963 the U.S. balance of payments was critical and the U.S.

government placed restrictions on the outflow of capital by imposing an interest equalization tax, increasing the cost of borrowing capital by about 15 per cent. This move, coming in the wake of a serious balance-of-payments crisis in 1962, was a severe blow to Canada.

Another critical run on Canada's foreign exchange reserves ensued. In response to urgent pleading, Canada was exempted from the interest equalization tax, which provided immediate relief—but at a cost. Canada agreed not to allow its exchange reserves to rise above $2.7 billion. In 1965 and 1968 Canada was again exempted from further U.S. controls on the flow of capital in return for additional restrictions on Canada. These special arrangements with the U.S. provided short-term benefits but the long-term costs were substantial and served to "lock" Canada into a continental monetary system as a junior partner to the U.S.

The carefully-worded Gray Report expresses concern about the high cost attached to the benefits of exemptions from these U.S. regulations. It refers to the limited opportunities for Canadian financial firms resulting from the restrictions on capital exports. Then it states:

> Much more importantly, during the period of the ceiling on exchange reserves and the maintenance of a fixed exchange rate *the choices* available to the monetary authorities *in regulating credit conditions were reduced*. In particular, the level of interest rates had to take account of the need to minimize capital inflows. While the inflows could, up to a point, be offset by Canadian government purchases of non-marketable United States securities when excess exchange reserves were being accumulated, this did not constitute an entirely satisfactory response. Thus, the exchange reserve limitation involved *some restriction on the use of monetary policy as an instrument to fight inflation.*[59] (Emphasis added.)

Kari Levitt expresses the same problem in less restrained language:

> Evidently, Canadian monetary and fiscal policies have both been harnessed to serve the U.S. Treasury in their efforts to close the U.S. balance of payments gap and protect the value of their dollar. This is indeed the classical position of a colonial economy.
>
> The cost of special status has been very high. Deal by deal, beginning in 1963, Canada has moved towards a colonial monetary system whereby surplus foreign exchange earnings are automatically lent to the metropolis.[60]

The latest development began with President Nixon's new economic policy in 1971 aimed at curbing inflation, reducing the growing deficit in the U.S. balance of payments and increasing U.S. industrial production. A surcharge of 10 per cent was applied to imported manufactured goods, and American multinational companies were given tax incentives to buy or produce in the U.S. rather than import from abroad. The Domestic International Sales Corporation (DISC) was established to facilitate this program. About two-thirds of Canada's export trade is with the U.S.; consequently, Canada stood to lose a great deal, especially since the new surcharges would hurt our manufacturing industry. A substantial section of Canada's exports were again exempted from the new regulations, but not the critical manufactured products. A government survey of Canadian firms predicted that Canada would lose $900 million in export trade and 90,000 jobs within one year. It was hinted that the U.S. government would consider deleting the surcharge on Canadian goods in exchange for dropping the Auto Pact safeguards and for a continental energy policy. Subsequently, the U.S. lifted its surcharge in return for an international agreement to devalue the dollar.

Canada's balance-of-payments figures of recent years show a disturbing trend. Despite a favourable overall balance-of-trade picture over the past twenty-seven years—with the exception of the $795 million trade deficit in 1975—Canada's current account deficit has grown alarmingly. Averaging about $1.2 billion in the period between 1965 and 1973, it grew to nearly $5 billion in 1976. (The favourable trade balance must be evaluated in light of the fact that Canada's trade deficit in manufactured goods has increased from $2.5 billion in 1970 to more than $10 billion in 1976.)

A number of factors contribute to current account deficits including the outflow of dividends, interest and other charges, borrowing by corporations and governments in foreign money markets and tourism. Canada's indebtedness represents a staggering figure and places Canada in an extremely difficult dilemma. Some economists are deeply worried and warn that soon Canada may find itself in the same position as the non-oil-exporting, underdeveloped countries, such as Brazil, Mexico and Chile.[61]

For obvious reasons Canada's balance-of-payments predicament is immediately related to our dependence on foreign-controlled capital and technology. Furthermore, this predicament raises fundamental questions about the basis of our high standard of living, and suggests that we would be foolish to imagine that we can continue at our current rate of spending. This is one reason why restraint rather than a mad pursuit of an ever-growing standard of living is now demanded.

Trade with Communist Countries

The U.S. *Trading with the Enemy Act* of 1917 forbids all American companies and their subsidiaries to trade, directly or indirectly, with an enemy country. Specifically, trade with Cuba, China, North Korea and North Vietnam is forbidden. In 1969 and again in 1971 these provisions governing China were relaxed to some extent. Nonetheless, on a number of occasions American-owned subsidiaries in Canada were barred from selling materials to Cuba, Vietnam and China.

In 1965 the Canadian government concluded a wheat sale with Russia, tied in with the shipment of flour to Cuba. The three largest milling companies in Canada—Robin Hood, Quaker Oats and Pillsbury (Canada) Ltd.— are all subsidiaries of American companies. Complying with U.S. law, they could not fill the order. A solution was found by transferring the sale to Canadian-owned companies. Further incidents involved the shipments of medical aid to North Vietnam, trucks to China and locomotives to Cuba.

Because this particular issue is rather straightforward and easy to grasp, it has caused strong public reaction whenever similar restrictions on companies operating in Canada hit the headlines. They usually result in a flurry of editorial comment and public indignation—soon to be forgotten except by those who are aware of the underlying reason for the long arm of the U.S. reaching into Canada. Mel Watkins writes in this connection: "When an incident occurs, it evokes a response that is hot, because U.S. policy is so obviously illiberal. But the response is *ephemeral*, because, after a moment's thought, it is clear that *the problem inheres in the situation*."[62] (Emphasis added.)

Antitrust Legislation

U.S. antitrust legislation applies to subsidiaries of American companies in Canada. Under provisions of the *Sherman Act* and the *Clayton Act*—the two most important U.S. statutes against restraint of trade—the U.S. government has initiated action against parent companies in the U.S. involving their subsidiaries in Canada. U.S. courts have asserted jurisdiction over firms in Canada; they have sought to secure evidence from the files of Canadian companies and they have ordered corrective action to be taken by American-owned companies in Canada.[63]

In addition, U.S. antitrust law has so influenced the behaviour of Canadian companies that inefficiency has resulted. At least, a consistent complaint is that the existence of too many U.S. companies in one branch of the industry in Canada has led to inefficient production and, consequently, to higher costs. It is argued that American-owned firms would be able to produce more efficiently if they were not hampered by U.S. antitrust legislation.

It would appear that the last two problems—namely, the extension of U.S. laws governing trade with enemy countries and those regulating restraint of trade (antitrust)—do not belong to the most serious effects of foreign ownership. Although some instances of the intrusion of U.S. law into Canada have at times provoked considerable public resentment, it should not be too difficult for the Canadian government to counteract U.S. legislation and to ensure that companies doing business in Canada are subject to Canadian law. It is probably correct to describe the problems in this area as the tip of the iceberg.

Cultural "Cocacolonization"

Foreign influence in such culturally sensitive areas of activity as book publishing, newspapers, magazines, entertainment, advertising and higher education presents a most difficult challenge to Canada. Certain restrictions have been placed on foreign ownership in "key sectors," for example, communications and finance (see below), yet the American impact from cultural "spillover" and American ownership is immense in Canada.

The Gray Report devotes a section to the impact of foreign control on Canadian culture and society. The Report takes issue with the notion that Canadians need not worry about U.S. ownership of Canadian businesses, but should get on with developing cultural and political integrity. "There is no way of leaving the 'economic' area to others so that we can get on with the political, social and cultural concerns in our own way. There is no such compartmentalization in the real world."[64] The Report ascribes the lack of Canadian heroes and distinctive symbols, as well as the Canadian diffidence toward nationhood, to Canada's colonial past. It is also of interest to note the Report's assessment of Canada's elite in the process of cultural homogenization. It offers this opinion: "The fact that Canadian society has tended, particularly in the past, to be dominated by an establishment based more on social connections than ability and providing only limited scope for social mobility has contributed to the failure of Canada to develop entrepreneurs at the same rate as the United States. Social rigidity has induced the expectation and mentality of working for others."[65]

The publishing industry is one of those key links in shaping a national consciousness. It is dominated in Canada by American-controlled firms and by American books. The plight of the Canadian publishing industry came dramatically to the fore in 1970 when two Canadian companies, W.J. Gage Ltd. and the Ryerson Press, were sold to American companies. McClelland and Stewart narrowly escaped a similar fate.

A large number of American firms set up branches in Canada during the 1960s. The competition for the smaller and poorly-funded Canadian publishers became tough. Canadian firms sold out and the Canadian publishing industry became an extension of the U.S. industry. In 1969, according to a report published in 1970 by the Department of Industry, Trade and Commerce, 80 per cent of imported books were American; American firms produced 59 per cent of *Canadian* books; and about 60 per cent of all books sold in Canada were American publications. Forty-two per cent of all imported books (that is, $62 million worth) bought in Canada were sold directly from outside Canada. Only 29 per cent of the textbooks sold in Canada in 1969 were of domestic origin.[66]

The distribution of newspapers and magazines reveals much of the same—a preponderance of American influence. Though the newspaper industry is largely Canadian owned, the spillover effect from south of the border tends to further the Americanization of Canada. Think in this connection of the popularity of American columnists such as Ann Landers and Art Buchwald. Canadian news services rely heavily on American services. The Canadian (English) newspaper industry is dominated by three major chains owning a total of about 55 of the 107 dailies in Canada: Southam Press, Sifton-Bell (F.P. Publications Ltd.) and Thomson Newspapers. Because of heavy reliance on advertising, and therefore on large-scale, often American-owned corporations, newspapers tend to reflect the business-oriented outlook that predominates in the U.S.[67]

The facts regarding the (now discontinued) special treatment granted to *Reader's Digest* and *Time* magazines are well known. In the early 1960s Canadian magazines were finding it difficult to survive over against their American counterparts. The *Report of the Royal Commission on Publications* (the O'Leary Commission) in 1960 advocated that advertising in Canadian editions of foreign-owned publications no longer be allowed as a tax-deductible expense. In the first quarter of 1964 *Time* and *Reader's Digest* obtained 52 per cent of all advertising in Canadian consumer magazines, compared with 47 per cent in 1963.[68] When the Pearson government intended to impose the new rule on all foreign publications, intense lobbying resulted with reported pressure from the highest echelon of the American government. The Cabinet, with Walter Gordon reluctantly consenting, gave in and passed legislation in 1965 to exempt *Time* and *Reader's Digest*.

In explaining his role, Gordon refers to the threat that the U.S. would not agree to the Auto Pact if the Canadian government would not exempt *Time* and *Reader's Digest*. He wrote: "I was quite aware of the power and influence of Mr. Luce [publisher of *Time*] and of the difficulties being encountered in getting the U.S. Congress to approve the automobile deal."[69] Thus, another Canadian industry failed to get a measure of protection which it sorely needed over against much stronger foreign competition. This trade-off clearly demonstrates how easily the long-run interests of the nation may be sacrificed for short-run advantages in terms of dollars and cents. (In 1975, the Canadian government passed new legislation which ended the special status of *Time* and *Reader's Digest*, and as a result *Time* discontinued its Canadian edition.)

The influence emanating from American entertainment and radio-TV broadcasting is obviously of great importance in the shaping of Canadian minds. To mention one manifest reason, radio and TV signals do not respect the border along the forty-ninth parallel.

In a 1972 submission it was reported that about 37 per cent of all advertising revenue went to subsidiaries of U.S. companies. Thirty of the top fifty advertisers in Canada were owned or controlled by U.S. parent corporations. The 1970 Senate Report on the mass media warned that in ten years more than half of the Canadian advertising industry would be in the hands of foreign-owned corporations.[70]

A look at the country of origin of Canadian university teachers indicates a high proportion of U.S. citizens in this group. It is inevitable that American professors are influenced by their own background in teaching, course structure and selection of textbooks.[71]

Summary

International trade was not begun by the modern multinational corporations. But what is new in their operations is the existence of subsidiaries in many different countries coordinated by a central management located in the home country.

The U.S. multinational companies occupy a commanding position in the world because of their superior technical, financial and managerial performance. This in turn is directly related to the fact that the U.S. is the most industrially advanced, mass consumption society in modern times.

The rapid growth of the multinational corporation is viewed with optimism by those who believe that this kind of large-scale enterprise will help overcome the limitations of the nation-state. Others regard the multinational corporation as a threat to national wellbeing because its interests, especially its preoccupation with profits and technological advance, are seen to be in conflict with those of the nation-state. Ambivalence results since economic growth and national autonomy are desired simultaneously.

The multinational corporations play an important role in the expanding flow of goods and services between East and West. The U.S.S.R. and other European communist-bloc countries are eager to benefit from Western technology, but they prefer to keep majority control in their own hands by means of joint-venture undertakings or they rely exclusively on the so-called turnkey arrangements. Some are hopeful that the extension of the operations of the multinationals into communist-bloc countries will dampen the ideological hostility in the world. But there is little evidence to suggest that the communist leaders are prepared to relinquish their totalitarian control.

Proponents of the multinational corporation insist that this type of business enterprise is able to provide the capital and technology the Third World countries need to escape their poverty and position of dependency. It would be incorrect to blame all the problems of the Third World on the developed countries and particularly on the multinational corporations based in these countries. Nonetheless, a relationship of dependency and even exploitation exists between the developed countries and the Third World, marked by extreme disparity in standards of living. Multinationals play an important and often ambiguous role in this context. On the one hand, these corporations are able to provide a stimulus towards the needed industrialization. On the other hand, because of their preoccupation with profits and technical sophistication, they are often at odds with the real needs of the Third World, especially the need to overcome the problems of hunger and unemployment.

The ambivalent role of foreign direct investment and multinational corporations is also evident in Canada. This kind of investment, mostly by American companies, is more extensive here than in any other Western country (responsible for 34 per cent of all nonfinancial industries). A complex of factors have contributed to this phenomenon, notably Canada's proximity to the U.S., its rich storehouse of natural resources, and a pattern of political and economic policies inspired by a shared belief in the virtue of an ever-rising standard of living. A number of structural weaknesses and distortions (such as the extensive reliance on the exploitation and export of nonrenewable resources, a weak manufacturing base, a high level of unemployment, a large service sector and a serious balance-of-payments problem) are at least in some ways related to this high level of foreign direct investment in Canada.

In the centre of the controversy surrounding multinational corporations is the question about the nature of the nation-state and the corporation. It is a matter of importance and even urgency that the interrelationship between the two structures be clarified in such a way that both can properly perform the functions required of them.

PART TWO: RESPONSES TO THE NEW ECONOMIC ORDER

Chapter 4
Warning Voices

The multinational is a problem precisely because its decisions are based on economic rationality and divorced from political sovereignty. There is no solution. The multinational is a political problem not because of anything it does or does not do. It is a problem because political sovereignty and economic reality no longer coincide. [1]

Peter F. Drucker

Paradoxically, the precondition for effective international regulation, in our view, is the restoration of certain powers to national governments and local communities to manage their own territory. [2]

Richard J. Barnet, Ronald E. Müller

There are important differences in the way countries have responded to the presence of multinational corporations. That response is invariably marked by the recognition that foreign investment brings benefits but also poses a threat to the host country. Hence there is an uncertainty on the part of many nations in their dealings with the multinational corporations in their midst.

Increasingly, host countries are devising ways to monitor and control the spread of foreign investment. In France and England, for example, a foreign investor must obtain permission for new investment from governmental agencies. Japan has traditionally been reluctant to allow any foreign investment but has relied heavily on the import of foreign technology through licensing agreements. More recently, Japan's tight-fisted policy has been relaxed somewhat in response to the demand of its trading partners. Six Latin American countries—the Andean Pact countries—have imposed extensive restrictions on foreign investment coupled with mandatory joint ownership, technology transfer and even divestment arrangements. The European Economic Community is now struggling to achieve a measure of harmony in its policies with respect to multinational corporations.

J.J. Servan-Schreiber Sounds the Alarm

In 1968 the Frenchman J.J. Servan-Schreiber issued one of the most noteworthy warnings against the inroads of American companies in Europe. His description of this phenomenon struck home and his book, *The American Challenge,* became a bestseller. (It was first published in French in 1967.) Since there are certain parallels between the French and the Canadian situation—apart from the extent of foreign ownership in both countries—it is worthwhile to review Servan-Schreiber's arguments.

He described the growth of American investment in Europe, which at that time amounted to $14 billion in fixed assets, and predicted that fifteen years hence the world's third largest industrial power, after the U.S. and the U.S.S.R., would not be Europe but American industry in Europe. Servan-Schreiber informed his readers that the source of new American investment capital in Europe was mostly European. Only 10 per cent of new investments in 1965 came directly from the U.S.; the remainder consisted of retained earnings, subsidies and loans from the European capital market. In the 1965-66 period, American investment rose by 17 per cent in the U.S. but 21 per cent in the Common Market.[3]

Furthermore, Servan-Schreiber noted the strategic character of the American investment since it was concentrated in the fast-growing high technology industries. For example, a 1963 report showed that American firms in France controlled 40 per cent of the petroleum market, 65 per cent of the production of film and photographic paper, 65 per cent of farm machinery, 45 per cent of synthetic rubber. The author singled out the electronics industry as the most crucial one for future developments. American corporations in Europe controlled 15 per cent of the production of consumer goods in that industry—radio and TV, recording devices, and so on—50 per cent of semi-conductors, 80 per cent of computers and 95 per cent of the market for integrated circuits. He underscored the importance of the last-named figures by stressing that electronics is not an ordinary industry but "is the base upon which the next stage of industrial—*and* cultural—development depends."[4] He stressed that the secret of the American success story is not in money, nor even in technology, but in the American flair for organization and management.

The American lead, Servan-Schreiber claimed, is derived from a better educational system, more confidence in human capabilities than is prevalent in Europe, and closer cooperation between American industry, universities and public agencies. He contrasted the American flexibility and readiness to innovate with the inflexibility of European industrialists and politicians and especially their lack of forging an aggressive and united, or European-wide, industrial policy.

This French author envisioned three options for the French and the other Common Market countries:

1. Continuing the present trend, which would result in further decline and eventual "industrial annexation."
2. Playing a complementary role to the American giants concentrating on those areas where Europe still has an advantage; but this would permanently reduce Europe to a second-rate position, or "satellization."
3. Choosing competition, calling for European businesses, especially those in the science-based industries, to enter the global market. This strategy would require government assistance, "particularly in such areas as electronics, data processing, space research, and atomic energy."[5]

Servan-Schreiber opted for the third choice and proceeded to discuss the manner in which this could be achieved. It would require a shake-up of deeply rooted habits and structures in France, as well as in the rest of Europe, aimed at greater mobility, better and more education, more efficient and larger industrial firms, more cooperation between industry and governments and, above all, more integration of efforts among the Common Market members. He called for a determined effort to concentrate on research and development, which is the key to industrial progress. What is required to give more life to the Common Market members is nothing less, wrote Servan-Schreiber, than the building of a unified scientific and industrial policy. The members of the Common Market have failed because they have been preoccupied with their own narrow interests. Therefore, what is needed is a revitalized Common Market with strong central powers and the financial and administrative means to back up that power. Servan-Schreiber suggested replacing the original confederal organization of the Common Market, which makes decisions by unanimous vote, with a federal organization that would make decisions by majority rule instead. At the same time he stressed the need for such a federal authority to be limited to a specific area, and accompanied by the decentralization of authority and power in all other areas, so that national identity and effort could have full sway.

The aim of growth and progress is justice, Servan-Schreiber insisted, and he appealed to the Left in Europe to make good on its "capital of confidence" rather than on its "capital of discontent." He described the Left's ambiguity and internal divisions, and called on the labour leaders and politicians of the Left to cooperate in the effort of rebuilding

Europe's industrial and scientific capabilities so that Europe could successfully meet the American challenge.

The American Challenge is not an "anti-American" book. It does not even offer a critique of American capitalism. The author cautions against a negative and restrictive response to American investments in Europe. He acknowledges that American investments bring important, and even irreplaceable, benefits. The responsibility for the European lag lies with the Europeans. Servan-Schreiber's book is a warning against European dependency on the U.S. and an urgent appeal to meet the Americans on their own ground. The author maintains that this challenge can be met only by intensive development in science and the science-based industries, accompanied by innovation in organization and management. All of this must be done, he says, within the framework of a genuinely cooperative and unified Europe.

What Can the United Nations Do?

The United Nations has become a forum for the study and discussion of the role and power of the multinational corporations. In July 1972 the Economic and Social Council requested the Secretary-General to appoint "a group of eminent persons . . . to study the role of multinational corporations and their impact on the process of development, *especially that of the developing countries,* and also their implications for international relations, to formulate conclusions which may possibly be used by Governments in making their sovereign decisions regarding national policy in this respect, and to submit recommendations for appropriate international action." (Emphasis added.) Out of this recommendation came the appointment of twenty persons who presented their report in May 1974: *The Impact of Multinational Corporations on Development and on International Relations.* A previous study published by the United Nations Department of Economic and Social Affairs in 1973, *Multinational Corporations in World Development,* served as a basis of discussion and source of information. The twenty-member group of eminent persons (hereinafter referred to as the Group) held two plenary sessions in New York and Geneva where it heard testimony of fifty leading persons from government, business, trade unions, special and public interest groups, and universities. This testimony is published in condensed form in another UN publication.[6]

The Report of the Group contains two major recommendations: (1) to set up a twenty-five-member commission on multinational corporations, and (2) to establish an information and research centre to assist this commission and other bodies in gathering information and formulating policies. It emphasizes the overriding need to obtain sufficient and reliable information about controversial issues, such as restrictive business practices, transfer pricing and taxation. The Report represents the consensus of many divergent viewpoints ranging from those who underline the positive contribution of multinational corporations to those who emphasize the negative effects. As a result the Report lacks consistency and clarity. Nine members, although they endorsed the contents, added an appendix listing a number of reservations and qualifications. The core problem was summarized succinctly by one of the Group in these words:

> There is a clear case to be made today for accelerated economic growth among developing nations, coupled with slower and restrained growth among the developed (high consumption) nations, but co-operation and self-restraint are not the characteristics of our day. Rather we see everywhere reductions in the flow of aid, reluctance to remove trade and monetary impediments, and continuing import restrictions imposed by developed nations upon third world products. A growing need for co-operation is being met with increased competition.
>
> The single most important action which the United Nations might take concerning multinational corporations today, therefore, is that of persuading *developed* nations to reactivate and to fulfill their early commitment to *developing* nations for improving their legitimate access to wealth, food, education, research, and other resources. [7]

The Group asserted that the underlying reasons for distrust and tensions surrounding the multinational corporation are actual and potential divergence between the interests of the corporations and of their host countries, the glaring inequalities within and among countries, and the lack of bargaining power on the part of many developing countries. A number of specific recommendations were put forward to alleviate these inequalities and to set up a framework in which peaceful and beneficial development could take place.

In the first part of the Report the following recommendations are presented: host countries should clearly define the permissible public activities of the affiliates of multinational corporations, excluding all subversive political forms of intervention; nationalization should be accompanied by fair compensation; home countries should not interfere in disputes between multinational corporations and host countries; and the possibilities for international agreement on the issue of extraterritoriality should be explored. The Group sees the long-term objective as "the conclusion of a general agreement on multinational corporations having the force of an international treaty and containing provisions for machinery and sanctions." [8]

The main body of the Report deals with key problem areas and certain recommendations covering such items as ownership, capital flow, technology transfer, employment, marketing, transfer pricing and taxation. The recommendations are aimed at achieving a better balance between the interests of the foreign investor and the host country.

The comments by the late Canadian economist Stephen Hymer, presented at one of the plenary sessions of the Group, are important because he attempted to break up the logjam of words by articulating some specific and hard-hitting counterproposals to the main recommendations of the Group. Since Hymer died shortly after his appearance before the Group, his written and oral remarks were reproduced in full.

Hymer conceded that the emphasis of the 1973 UN Report on the need to strengthen the hands of developing nations vis-à-vis the multinational corporations was valid but "myopic." He faulted the Report for not analyzing the current structure of the world economy and not confronting the problem of dependency. He raised two questions that have been overlooked: (1) Is a world system based on private multinational capitalism compatible with "our hopes for a peaceful and prosperous world"? and (2) "Are there alternative systems of organizing the world economy which rely much less on private multinational capital and are more promising for reaching these goals?"[9] He answered the first question with a No, and the second with a Yes, and argued that the multinational system concentrates control and power in a few metropolitan centres leaving the rest of the world—the hinterland—in a permanent state of underdevelopment and dependency. He advocated a system of independent socialist countries "in which information and technology flows freely between countries, but capital, i.e., power, does not."

Arguing that the chief defect of the 1973 Report was its lack of historical perspective on the multinational corporations, Hymer referred to John Maynard Keynes (1883-1946) who, in a 1933 article on national self-sufficiency, suggested that world peace, prosperity and freedom could best be achieved by emphasizing national self-sufficiency rather than international market capitalism. Keynes wrote:

> I sympathize, therefore, with those who would minimize, rather than with those who would maximize, economic entanglement among nations. Ideas, knowledge, science, hospitality, travel—these are the things which should of their nature be international. But let goods be homespun whenever it is reasonably and conveniently possible, and above all, let finance be primarily national.[10]

Keynes supported his position with these arguments: the world market does not create peace; modern technology makes local production easier; and private competitive capitalism is not a sound basis for human society.

Hymer proceeded to contrast Keynes's views with those who believe that industrial capitalism, spearheaded by American business with its unrivaled technical achievements, will usher in an international New Deal. He referred to a 1942 *Fortune* article which proclaimed: "American imperialism can afford to complete the work the British started; instead of salesmen and planters, its representatives can be brains and bulldozers, technicians and machine tools."[11] But, Hymer pointed out, this same imperialism vigorously pursued by American business has given rise to the "law of uneven development" at work within the hierarchical structures of corporations. Moreover, this law is also reflected in the corresponding uneven development of urban and rural areas—the dichotomy between metropolis and hinterland. The result is not conducive to peace, prosperity or freedom because of the internal strains and contradictions, the uneven division of labour and the loss of capacity for people to plan their own future.

Searching for alternative insights, Hymer proposed two kinds of research projects. In the first place, we should try to project the multinational corporate system into the future, and this, he predicted, would give us an unsatisfactory picture in terms of status, income distribution and employment. Secondly, we should attempt to find an alternative goal for the developing countries, one that does not involve development in the traditional sense—integration into the world economy—"but rather the removal of misery." In this context, Hymer advocated setting fifteen or sixteen targets to remove misery, for example, to make penicillin and other necessary drugs available to everybody in the world, and to have minimum standards of food, clothing, housing and communications that would give everybody a basic standard of living.

Such a plan would not call for a large role by the multinational corporation, he said, because it would only involve the use of the technology required for producing basic goods, "and the multinational corporation's strength does not lie in basic goods for minimum standards of living, but rather lies usually in very highly advanced products for the consumption of the middle class and the upper middle class. . . . "[12] As an example of basic goods production, Hymer mentioned the need for poor people to have shoes. A target of two pairs of shoes per year for everybody would result in large production runs and call for special machinery and techniques that could utilize the unskilled labour so abundant in poor countries.

In the question-and-answer session Hymer reiterated the conviction that we must look for alternatives to the dominant role of multinational corporations and to the international market. In reply to a question about the political influence exercised by multinational corporations, Hymer revealed insight into the deceptive character of the headline-creating sensational events such as the so-called Watergate affair. He stated:

> I do not think that is the most serious or most important thing to concentrate on. . . . The real thing is what goes on every day, in every-day life. And there it is much more important to notice that most of the government officials of the United States associated with foreign policy or other policy do in fact come from a background of corporate executives: their friends and their training. And that gives them a certain perspective of the world, a certain idea of what is

> right and a certain idea of the way to do things. And it gives them one-dimensional thinking.[13]

Hymer's appeal for open alternatives and his specific suggestions to help the poor people of the world with the kind of production that suits their own circumstances deserve careful consideration.

Third World Responses

The exorbitant oil price increases since October 1973 have drastically altered the relationship between some developed and developing countries. Suddenly it seems that the erstwhile helpless and impoverished countries, at least the oil producers, have discovered that they have the power to drive up prices and literally dictate to the industrialized world. The Organization of Petroleum Exporting Countries (OPEC), for the first time in history, organized the major oil producing countries of the developing world into an effective cartel. Almost overnight prices skyrocketed and the oil embargo imposed after the 1973 Arab-Israel war shocked the world into the realization that the tables were turned. Because of their utter dependence on energy resources, the industrialized nations found that the very source of their power—advanced technology—was their Achilles heel.

The vulnerability of the West showed up starkly in another area as well, namely, in the supply and use of capital. The tripling of oil prices has poured immense wealth into the producing nations. But that wealth has been drained from the consuming countries at an alarming rate. The drastic change in the world flow of capital resulting from the price increases imposed by the oil producers has put severe strains on a number of countries, notably England, Italy and Japan. Every consuming nation is hard hit, including the U.S., which saw its annual bill for oil imports jump from \$3.9 billion in 1973 to \$24 billion in 1974. Japan's increase for the same years was from \$3.9 to \$18 billion.

This capital drain on the industrialized world is seriously aggravating the already difficult problem of inflation. However, the effect on the poor countries is considerably worse. The sharply increased cost of oil will make it even more difficult, if not impossible, for these countries to reach that state of economic health that will provide a source of independence and prosperity. The cost of oil for the developing countries rose to a staggering \$15 billion in 1974 from \$3.7 billion in 1972. Fertilizers, crucially needed to improve agricultural yields in the developing countries, have become much more expensive as a result of the rise of oil prices. The cost of other imports is also rising, draining off scarce foreign exchange and tightening the grip of starvation and hunger on the poor nations. The term Fourth World has been coined to describe those developing nations which do not own oil reserves or other significant resources.

Economists and bankers are at a loss how to cope with the recent and abrupt shift in the flow of capital. Meanwhile, the fabulously rich Arab countries are eyeing the industrialized world for investment opportunities and there are many who are fearful of what might be called a takeover in reverse.

The oil exporting countries are not the only ones grouping together for a more effective bargaining position vis-à-vis the industrialized countries. Other nations exporting strategic raw materials are beginning to follow OPEC's example. The four major copper exporters in the world, Zambia, Chile, Peru and Zaire, have organized along similar lines. (Fluctuations in the prices of copper and other minerals indicate that the measures taken by these countries have not been as effective as those of the oil producing countries.) Resource-supply countries are coordinating their activities across product lines. Copper and aluminum producing countries are cooperating in their efforts to oppose substitution. Coffee and tea producers are also closing ranks. In 1973, thirty African countries agreed to coordinate their trading policies. Developing countries are inviting competitive bids from different companies and they are turning to more portfolio instead of direct foreign investment.

The Latin American countries, perhaps because their development is ahead of African and Asian countries, have gone the furthest in coordinating their policies. The Andean Pact is an agreement formulated by Bolivia, Chile, Colombia, Ecuador, Peru and Venezuela to coordinate their policies with respect to tariff barriers, foreign direct investment and industrial development. It assures that the multinationals will not be able to play off one country against the other. (Chile has dropped out of this group.) These countries have established a central data-collecting agency that will aid them in exchanging information quickly. The major provision of their Pact is the requirement that all foreign companies must divest themselves of majority interest within fifteen or twenty years. Several American affiliates have been nationalized in the Andean Pact countries, including mining and oil companies. Foreign investors are banned from key areas of these economies, such as banking, insurance, domestic trade, communication and transportation. These Latin American countries have served notice to the U.S. that they are determined to loosen their dependency on the U.S. Japanese and European investors are helping to dislodge the U.S. companies from their prominent position.

The winds of economic independence are blowing through Latin America, least so in Brazil where continuing cooperation with American policy is desired. Brazil has been described as a country "impelled by its vision of one day joining the ranks of the world's great powers (as futurist Herman Kahn and others think it will). It has elevated economic pragmatism to the status of a state religion, with the planners as priests."[14]

Despite these recent changes in the relationship between the rich and the poor countries, especially affecting the role of the multinational corporations, the developing countries are faced with incredible difficulties. Their historical role of raw material suppliers to the rich countries has led to structural underdevelopment. Unemployment and hunger are difficult to erase and the mounting debt load of the Third World is like a millstone around its neck. The developed nations cannot deny their responsibility for this misery in the Third World. Furthermore, the effect of cooperative moves, such as the Andean Pact, among developing countries has been much less than initially anticipated.[15]

The most important question now is whether the new relationship between developed and developing countries will be cultivated in a climate of revenge and confrontation or in such a way that the earth's resources will be distributed and enjoyed by all rather than by a privileged few. The latter would require either a changed role for the multinational corporations in the developing countries or their elimination. But more than that is needed. A redistribution of the necessities of life, that is food, clothing, shelter and employment, will require a shift of resources from the rich minority to the poor majority. That entails a willingness to accept a lower standard of living in the industrialized countries. An immediate beginning must be made by tackling the injustice of the present pattern of trade and capital flow between the rich and poor countries. That would of course fundamentally undermine the obsession with economic growth as an end in itself in the developed countries. Yet nothing less than that is now required and the time to make such a switch is quickly running out.

One thing is sure. Unless the West is willing to relinquish its present neocolonial ties with the poor countries, it has absolutely no moral basis to accuse the Arabs of price gouging. The Arabs' mentors are the businessmen and diplomats of the industrialized countries!

Reforms in the U.S.

A discussion of the major proposals for reforming the multinational corporation logically includes a look at the reform efforts in the U.S., since this study is especially concerned with the power and role of U.S.-based (multinational) corporations.

The Rise of Anti-Corporate Action in the U.S.

The climate in the U.S. affecting the position of the corporations has undoubtedly been altered by the spectacular events surrounding the so-called Watergate affair. The aftermath of this sordid episode has uncovered instances of collusion between government officials and corporations. At the centre of this collusion there were the political parties hungry for funds, especially at election time, and the corporations, willing and able to supply large amounts of money. U.S. courts have contributed to an exposure of this practice.

A number of large U.S. companies have admitted giving funds to former President Richard Nixon's 1972 reelection campaign, contrary to legislative restrictions. One of the companies is Northrop Corporation, the California aerospace company that made illegal political contributions from a slush fund built up by kickbacks. In an unprecedented decision, federal Judge Warren J. Ferguson ordered the restructuring of Northrop's board of directors and the introduction of new stockholder prerogatives. The judgment also deprived Thomas V. Jones of the presidency while he remained chairman and chief executive officer of the company. The court furthermore ordered that the board of directors be enlarged by four persons, all named in consultation with Judge Ferguson and New York lawyer Jay Springer, the stockholder who initiated the class-action suit.

Sixty per cent of the directors must be genuine outsiders and these independent directors will dominate the company's executive, audit and nominating committees. Springer, who only owns two shares of Northrop stock, will continue to play a watchdog role over the company. In case he detects any departures from the settlement, he can complain to Judge Ferguson, who retains jurisdiction.

Corporate legal scholars cannot recall any similar case in which minority shareholders imposed permanent organizational changes on a company. Some observes consider the Northrop settlement a major breakthrough on the way to making management more responsible to shareholders and society. Sceptics, however, contend that it is questionable whether, for example, even Northrop's new independent board would have discovered the company's slush fund.[16]

The judgment against Northrop is only one among many. By mid-1975 seventeen American companies and fifteen high-ranking business executives had pleaded guilty to the charge of making illegal political contributions. Among them were American Airlines, Goodyear Tire & Rubber, and Gulf Oil. A company that received a great deal of publicity was Minnesota Mining and Manufacturing Company (3M) employing over 80,000 employees, with sales of nearly $3 billion in 1974. Evidence uncovered by federal agents found 3M had a $500,000 slush fund. Funds were laundered in Switzerland, then passed on to political fund raisers in the U.S. Top officials of the company pleaded guilty and consequently resigned. One of them explained that what business was seeking with campaign contributions was a chance to "open some doors to be heard."[17] The system of bribe payments engaged in by the Lockheed Corporation involved millions of dollars and reached into the highest echelons in Italy,

Japan and the Netherlands. It caused the resignation of top government officials who had accepted millions of dollars in return for certain favours.

The prosecution of these companies is indicative of a new sentiment in the United States. In addition, the heightened awareness of corporate abuses has also given new impetus to the antitrust activities of the U.S. Department of Justice. For example, the Justice Department has sued American Telephone and Telegraph, the world's largest private corporation, for its alleged monopoly over telecommunications in the U.S. A.T.&T was ordered to divest itself of Western Electric, its manufacturing arm. Similarly, IBM has been confronted with a demand to divest itself of some of its subsidiaries. The struggle in the courts is expected to be long and costly.[18]

A third area of renewed activity concerns the shareholders' efforts to exert influence on company policies by means of policy statements and proposals submitted to the annual meetings of companies. Various organizations and individuals are active in promoting social responsibility on the part of shareholders. In 1975 the Council on Economic Priorities, a nonprofit organization doing research on corporate practices for the purpose of encouraging social responsibility, estimated that eighty-four shareholder actions would take place that year at fifty-nine corporate annual meetings.

A number of church groups figure prominently in the current renewal of shareholders' interest. Fourteen Protestant church groups and Roman Catholic orders of nuns and friars, representing $9 million worth of IBM stock, submitted a proposal to IBM management in 1975 for ending the sale, lease or service of computers to the South African government because they believed this equipment was being used for military and strategic purposes in support of white supremacy policies. The Interfaith Center on Corporate Responsibility, a movement affiliated with the National Council of Churches, is concentrating its efforts on a number of large corporations. Six orders of nuns asked the Bristol-Myers Company to report on their sales of infant formula products in developing countries. They suspected that such products might be linked to rising rates of malnutrition and infant mortality by undermining breast feeding. A group called Clergy and Laity Concerned has aimed its guns at corporate involvement in military production.

This is how one official of a large accounting firm summed up the present climate in the U.S.: "Shareholders are going to get in depth into what used to be the sacred ground called management decision. There will be questioning of business decisions and management will be put on the spot to come up with a lot of answers."[19]

Neil H. Jacoby, an American economist, argues that the boards of directors of large corporations must become more independent to perform their main function of auditing the performance of management. He points out that many directors do little more than rubber-stamp management's decisions. Outside directors often lack the necessary information for effective supervision, whereas inside directors, although they have the knowledge, are reluctant to challenge their superiors. Jacoby also underscores the need to limit the number of directors coming from financial institutions to avoid conflicts of interest. He asserts: "The key to better corporate government is to increase the power, the independence, the range of competence, and the compensation, of outside directors in public corporations."[20]

Ralph Nader Versus Corporate America

Ralph Nader, the self-appointed watchdog of corporate behaviour, has done much to bring into the open the corporations' abuse of power in American society. He has tirelessly devoted himself to the revelations of corporate fraud, corruption and privilege. Testifying before a Senate subcommittee investigating automobile safety, Nader gave this account of himself:

> As I became more and more aware of the tremendous gap between what was possible and what was actual, I became, in a sense, incensed at the way there can be a tremendous amount of injustice and brutality in an industrialized society without any accountability, without any responsibility. That people sitting in executive suites can make remote decisions which will someday result in tremendous carnage, and because they are remote in time and space from the consequences of that decision, there is no accountability.[21]

The book *Unsafe at Any Speed,* published by Nader in 1965, rocked the automobile industry when it was under heavy fire on account of the rising public concern about U.S. traffic accidents. (In 1964 there had been 48,000 traffic deaths in the U.S.) Nader's bestseller was a scathing attack on the Corvair, a compact car produced by General Motors, which he described as unsafe and dangerous. At this time, irate owners of the Corvair had lodged more than one hundred lawsuits against GM. The company fought back by putting detectives on Nader's trail in order to find damaging information that could be used to discredit him. James M. Roche, chairman of the board of directors of GM, subsequently apologized for this action. Nader sued the company for invasion of privacy and obtained a $425,000 settlement. This money launched his career as an irrepressible critic of the corporations.

To expose numerous areas of corporate abuse, Nader has sent teams of investigators into government agencies and corporations. His name has become synonymous with a consumers' revolt against shoddy products and other forms of exploitation of the consumer and worker. He has been acclaimed a hero, and denounced as a dangerous subversive out to destroy the American free enterprise system.

Nader's investigations have uncovered a host of malpractices by companies and government regulatory agencies alike. He is unsparing in his criticism of government agencies that do not regulate but serve as umbrellas for corporations. His in-depth investigations of various industries have led to more extensive regulations and reforms. The food and drug industries have come under Nader's scrutiny and have been forced to discontinue some harmful practices. For example, after Nader unearthed shocking, unsanitary conditions in the meat-packing industry, the federal government stepped in with new legislation and tighter controls. Nader and his team have turned out a rash of well-researched reports and books that have lifted the corporate veil and resulted in corrective action. His books include one on the Du Pont operations in the State of Delaware (*The Corporate State*) and one on the Food and Drug Administration (*The Chemical Feast*).

In addition to heading the Center for the Study of Responsive Law, Nader is channeling his investigative work through the Auto Safety Center and the Public Interest Research Group. He has been instrumental in establishing research groups and consumers' organizations across the U.S. But consumer protection in the form of exposure, litigation and legislation (Nader works closely with several congressmen) is not the only avenue employed by Nader. He has turned his attention to corporate law and the need to open up the closed circle of the corporate elite. The book *Corporate Power in America* is the product of the Conference on Corporate Accountability held in 1971. This book contains contributions from various authors who address themselves to the problems of corporate power and their remedies. Writes Nader in the preface: "Our large corporations are unparalleled as buffers shielding their executive decision makers from public inquiry and accountability. A supposed democracy should not suffer the exercise of such uncontrolled power."[22]

In his own contribution to this collection, "The Case for Federal Chartering," Nader argues for federal incorporation of companies because the states have failed to establish a unified and fair system of incorporation. As a matter of fact, the existence of many different incorporation powers (vested in the individual states) has given rise to rivalry and competition which in turn have created a host of loopholes and unequal advantages. The State of Delaware has the worst record and has served to attract a disproportionate number of corporations. As long as there is even one state that continues to give a virtually free hand to corporations looking for easy tax laws as well as a great deal of leeway for their boards of directors, no reforms are possible. Hence, Nader argues for exclusive incorporation at the federal government level, at least of all major corporations engaged in interstate business.

He advocates the adoption of a "corporate bill of obligations" providing for a measure of control over management by shareholders, consumers and employees, and removing the veil of corporate secrecy (over such details as earnings by subsidiaries, the identity of the real owners, safety testing procedures and product control standards). In addition, this suggested bill of obligations would contain antitrust restrictions, for example, by limiting to 12 per cent the share that any one corporation may own in an oligopolistic industry. Other provisions would protect consumers against shoddy and dangerous products.

There is always the danger, as Nader points out, that a federal chartering agency may become as unresponsive and inefficient as some of the present regulatory and enforcement agencies. But he is hopeful that the pitfalls can be avoided if we can learn lessons from the past.

The American professor and author Andrew Hacker, another contributor to the same series, takes issue with the federal charter solution because he is convinced that the question is not so much which government charters a corporation but whether such a government is determined to exact accountability from the corporations and to exercise its power when the corporations evade their responsibility. He points out that some of the most notorious corporations, particularly some of the railroads, were incorporated by the federal government.[23]

Generally, the proposals for reform centre on ways to impose restraints from the outside or on ways to democratize the corporation from within. A number of specific proposals were put forth by various participants in the Conference on Corporate Accountability. For example, John J. Flynn advocated that employees of the large corporations be nominated as the "constituency" and given a voice in management, which would provide a meaningful check and balance upon corporate power. He said this would change the position of the worker from "seller of his labour" to owner of the enterprise and would drastically change the function of labour unions.

Robert Townsend, former chairman of Avis Rent-A-Car and author of *Up the Organization,* presents a "modest proposal" in the form of advocating the appointment of a "public director" to all manufacturing companies with over $1 billion in assets. This would cover approximately 110 U.S. companies in the industrial sector. Townsend recommends that each public director have a budget of $1 million a year of the company's money with which he would be able to hire all the staff needed to examine the performance of the corporation. Directors should be appointed from a pool that is created especially for that purpose and assigned to corporations by lot. They furthermore should be rotated every four years. Townsend recommends an *ad hoc* legislative committee of representatives and senators which would serve as the authority overseeing the performance and appointment of the public directors. He is hopeful that his recommendation would avoid coopting and corruption, since he believes that his proposals would lead to maximum independence of a highly competent group of people assigned to oversee the large corporations.

Others are more pessimistic about the possibilities for reform. They do not believe that the government nor the public at large is prepared to make the necessary changes. Andrew Hacker writes that "government does not even deserve to be called the executive committee of the bourgeoisie. Rather, as indicated, it is a subsidiary branch of the corporate community."[24] He describes a number of specific areas where priorities have to change, but he is doubtful that the government is prepared to insist on the changes. For example, there is the need to command General Electric to stop manufacturing refrigerators in sixteen different colours, which he calls a "scandalous waste of resources"; to tell General Foods that it must cease putting crinkle cuts on its french fried frozen potatoes; to instruct Western Electric that it must find better use for its capacities than making Princess telephones. He is doubtful that a government would be prepared to tell companies that they cannot make and market snowmobiles or electric pencil sharpeners until other more pressing needs have been met. He points out that the issuing and enforcement of such directives would require men and women to be

> impervious to the threats and blandishment of the business community. They would have to survive without campaign contributions, not only from corporation executives but also from local businessmen who finance candidates of all major parties. Moreover, they would have to pitch their appeals to voters who are employees of corporations, whose livelihoods depend on producing our cornucopia of superfluous products, ranging from oversized airplanes to under-nourishing cereals; they will certainly be aware that official interference will jeopardize their jobs. To elect such a Congress would require the perceptions of politics quite different from those now held by the majority of American voters. [25]

The route of strengthening the shareholders' position is discussed by some of the contributors and is mostly found wanting. What one author calls the "renaissance of shareholder dissent" is a disappointment. A number of attempts to influence company policy by shareholders at annual meetings are evaluated. These reform efforts often ran aground on the invincibility of management and the apathy of shareholders.

An outstanding example of this type of reform attempt is Campaign GM. Begun in 1970, it was an effort to open up GM's board of directors and its annual meeting to the shareholders in order to impose reforms. Its first proposals included an expansion of the GM board from twenty-three to twenty-six directors and the formation of a special shareholders' committee for corporate responsibility. Other attempted changes concerned amendments to the corporate charter forbidding GM to undertake activities inconsistent with the public interest, imposing certain policies related to air pollution, minority employment, product warranties, public transit and employee health and safety. Only two items were ordered to be placed on the proxy statements mailed to every shareholder. In 1971 Campaign GM tried to introduce further improvements in terms of corporate disclosure, shareholders' rights and placing workers, dealers and consumers on the board of directors.

Campaign GM achieved a certain amount of success. A public policy committee was set up. A new vice-president in charge of environmental activities was appointed, and Leon Sullivan, a distinguished black activist, was appointed to the board of directors. Yet, it is acknowledged that no concrete results have been attributed to any of these reforms. Where Campaign GM and similar movements have attempted to mobilize the shareholders in opposition to established company policies, they have often met apathy, or even opposition, from the side of shareholders who do not want to be deterred from reaping maximum returns on their investments.

Corporate Power in America focuses on the evils of vast concentrations of power in the large corporations. It pinpoints many facets of the disharmony resulting from such power, including misallocation of resources, unequal distribution of wealth, pollution of the environment, and even fraud and crime. It proceeds to list a host of specific recommendations for reform. Many of these recommendations are undoubtedly important, particularly those that focus on the need for opening up the closed elitist structures of the corporate decision makers, spreading responsibility and income, curtailing the inordinate size of some corporations and removing the veil of secrecy that now often beclouds corporate conduct, all of which are aimed at bringing the public interest and corporate behaviour into harmony. But somehow the suspicion lingers that most of these efforts concentrate on symptoms and largely ignore underlying causes.

Other Voices

There are now numerous critics, inside as well as outside the U.S., who seek new methods, other than those derived from socialism, for channeling the resources of the multinational corporations into more constructive ways. Peter F. Drucker, in discussing the appropriate form and behaviour of the multinational corporation, asserts that we are still in a transition stage, because the nineteenth century multinational is doing the twentieth century task of a transnational. He describes four types of multinational structures that he considers unacceptable.

One of these is what he calls "the Canadian pattern," which is marked by the failure to build the multinationals into the political reality of their host countries. Furthermore, Drucker considers the nineteenth-century pattern of foreign domination and control of infrastructure businesses (electric power, transportation and telephone) unworkable in our time.

He also singles out as untenable the near-monopoly position of a company such as IBM simply because it goes beyond the limits of what any company should be allowed. He suggests that a totally new way of resolving IBM's dilemma may be to convert it into the first truly trans-national public utility that might continue enjoying worldwide leadership but be "anchored in the economic and even political structure of the host countries, through partnership with local government, local part ownership, and local regulation."[26]

Finally, Drucker observes that the wholly-owned subsidiary does not fit the developing countries because it discourages rather than encourages what these countries need most: "native investment and capital formation, and native managers and entrepreneurs."[27] He is convinced that multinational corporations need to have a flexible approach and use different forms of relationships suitable to the needs and interests of the host countries.

It has become quite obvious of late that the wholly-owned subsidiary in the host country is becoming increasingly unsatisfactory.[28] Various recommendations have been made to facilitate the transition from foreign ownership to partial or complete local ownership. The divesture arrangement, whereby a company is ordered to sell all or part of its shares to local investors, is incorporated by the Andean Pact countries. This seems to be a suitable method to bring about the transfer of ownership over a stated period of time. Raymond Vernon has suggested that divesture arrangements, which are optional and renewable periodically, could be made part of the agreement under which foreign investment enters the host country.[29] The parent company could then plan for eventual divesture, but the flexibility built into such arrangements would be conducive to a less strained relationship.

A number of authors concerned about the disadvantages of foreign direct ownership, especially the loss of sovereignty in the host country, have advocated strengthening domestic industry. J.J. Servan-Schreiber's book was an appeal to his fellow Europeans to match the American companies in size and competence through cooperation and mergers. Britain, via its Industrial Reorganisation Commission, attempts to meet the "American challenge" by reinforcing its domestic companies through streamlining and mergers. Members of the EEC seek to move in that direction, but self-interest and nationalism have stood in their way. Professor Behrman's remarks about the European response point to a dilemma faced by those who want to compete with the Americans:

> A stronger competitive position of the nationally or regionally owned enterprises in Europe would reduce the fear of the foreign-owned elements. And success in building European-owned entities in key sectors would reduce the fear of strategic dependence on the foreigner. To build such corporations may require that Europe emulate the American pattern, emphasizing U.S. management techniques, U.S. selling tactics, and U.S. business behavior—a concept of capitalism they have not wanted. [30]

Richard Barnet and Ronald Müller, authors of *Global Reach: The Power of the Multinational Corporations,* do not believe that multinational corporations as presently constituted are suitable vehicles for a balanced development within either the developed, or the developing, world. "Driven by the ideology of infinite growth, a religion rooted in the existential terrors of oligopolistic competition, global corporations act as if they must grow or die and in the process they have made thrift into a liability and waste into a virtue."[31] These authors warn against expecting reforms from self-correction or self-policing on the part of multinational corporations. Nor do they believe that all the focus must be on international regulations although they do not discount the need for international coordination and cooperation. They write that "the precondition for effective international regulation, in our view, is the restoration of certain powers to national governments and local communities to manage their own territory."[32] They emphasize the right to know what multinational corporations own, what they are doing and what they plan to do. Therefore they advocate the opening of the corporations' books. In this context they point to the need for harmonizing disclosure requirements among the major countries in which multinational corporations operate.

Another major step advocated by these two authors is to establish clearly articulated national priorities arrived at through open debate and democratic procedure. A national development plan is needed that sets out a number of basic goals which will contribute toward opening up possibilities for living. They are critical of the drift toward overspecialization and disharmony, calling for variety and a "holistic" approach, that is, a way of life in which the social, ecological and the psychological balances are maintained. That requires participation, experimentation, a more equitable distribution of wealth and income, the strengthening of public institutions and local interests, and more self-reliance in terms of raw materials. Futhermore, they pay special attention to those policies that will assist the developing countries, such as preferential trade agreements with the poor countries, divestment of foreign ownership, stimulating locally-owned industry and paying higher prices for raw materials from the developing countries.

Barnet and Müller are convinced of the urgent need to undertake remedial action especially in view of the gross inequalities between the poor and the rich countries. They assert: "Whether there is enough statesmanship and true international spirit in the rich countries to recognize that changes in bargaining power and resource pricing (including human labor) are long overdue in the interests of global justice and global stability will determine the character of world politics in the coming generation."[33]

John Kenneth Galbraith—Canadian-born, American professor of economics, former ambassador to India, prolific writer and critic of his colleagues—has done much to demythologize economics and challenge conventional wisdom. He accuses his colleagues of engaging in theorizing about a world that no longer exists. He holds that neoclassical economics is still preoccupied with the workings of a free market whereas in reality the market is successfully brought under control by the "planning system," whereby he means the large-scale, technically advanced oligopolistic corporations. Galbraith's *The New Industrial State* (1967) and *Economics and the Public Purpose* (1973) develop this theme and have been widely debated.

In these works Galbraith describes the new "industrial system" and enumerates its six outstanding features. The system exhibits an increasing time span between the initial concept of the product and the completed task, it is highly capital-intensive, it is inflexible as a result of the foregoing, and it requires specialized manpower, complex organization and planning. Hence the modern industrial system aims at removing uncertainty by controlling the entire range of activities from the initial stages of production to the final marketing process. Galbraith calls this the "imperatives of technology" and argues that the shape of economic society is determined by those imperatives and not by the images of ideology.

The "planning system" is not subject to the market because of its control over capital, technology, supply and demand. The core of this system is the "technostructure," that is, the managerial and technical experts on whose knowledge and organizational talents the corporations depend. The primary goal of the corporation, says Galbraith, is not maximum profits but maximum growth aided by innovation and advertising. This has led to socially and ecologically damaging production and consumption. On the other hand, useful services such as housing, medical care and education suffer from chronic underdevelopment. Galbraith argues for restoring the balance between the planning and the market system (i.e., small-scale nonoligopolistic business enterprises) through government controls, monetary and fiscal policies, public ownership of the large oligopolistic and monopolistic corporations and through strengthening the market system, thus balancing the "countervailing powers" more evenly. He advocates price and wage controls in the planning system.

Galbraith's analysis and critique of neoclassical economics and the "technostructure" is refreshing on many counts. He discerns the dangerous and manipulative role of advertising as a means to stimulate demand for an ever-rising GNP which has been elevated to a priority goal. He also perceives that economic growth has been promoted to a new religion. "That social progress is identical with a rising standard of living has the aspect of a faith."[34] Galbraith explains that the imbalance in development on a national scale because of the preponderance of the technostructure is transposed on the international scene by the multinationals. "What has been called the American challenge is not American; it is the challenge of the modern planning system. . . . Those who react to the American multinational corporations are reacting, in fact, to the cultural power of the planning system whatever its national identity."[35]

Yet in the end, Galbraith's proposals, though they may appear to be radical, do not help us very far along. He addresses himself to the symptoms of a distorted economy. Many of his suggestions are undoubtedly valuable, but he does not come to grips with the underlying cause of distortion. He refers to that cause when he describes the obsession with growth and technology as a faith, but he fails to show how that deceptive faith can be confronted with true faith. That explains why Galbraith's proposals for reform are contradictory and half-hearted. In *The New Industrial State* the author belabours the fact that the technostructure draws into its sphere of influence and subordination all sectors of society, including the state and the educational institutions. "Modern higher education is, of course, extremely accommodated to the needs of the industrial system." But he pins his hope for breaking free of this stranglehold on the educated elite. The resulting predicament is evident in the following statement:

> The industrial system, by making trained and educated manpower the decisive factor of production, requires a highly developed educational system. If the educational system serves generally the beliefs of the industrial system, the influence and monolithic character of the latter will be enhanced. By the same token, should it be superior to and independent of the industrial system, it can be the necessary force for skepticism, emancipation and pluralism.[36]

A similar contradiction is found in Galbraith's *Economics and the Public Purpose.* Here the author refines the case presented in *The New Industrial State.* He describes the similarity of the goals of the public and private bureaucracies. This tendency toward a common purpose is referred to as the "bureaucratic symbiosis." Yet Galbraith turns to the state as the source of emancipation. Again the conflict is obvious in the author's prescription for reform:

> The role of the government, when one contemplates reform, is a dual one. The government is a major part of the problem; it is also central to the remedy. It is part of the problem of unequal development, inequality in income distribution, poor distribution of public resources, environmental damage and bogus or emasculatory regulation. And it is upon the government that reliance must be placed for solution.[37]

But how can the patient be the doctor? To put it in Galbraith's own inimitable terms: "No one can appeal with confidence for vital therapy to the local doctor if he serves even more devotedly as the local undertaker."[38] There is little in Galbraith's prescriptions that can help us out of this dilemma because he does not confront the underlying cause for the distortions he describes. Galbraith thinks that if we can only muster sufficient courage and intellectual stamina and restore the relative balance of the various power centres in society, we will be emancipated. That involves an underestimation of the seriousness of the human condition. It cannot be emphasized too strongly that the inequality and distortions which are the subject of Galbraith's books are directly related to the deepseated, spiritual crisis affecting Western culture at its very foundation. By the same token, any critique that does not come to grips with this crisis merely deals with symptoms, no matter how novel and brilliant it may appear to be.

The Position of the AFL-CIO

Looking at the U.S. from the outside, we see an immensely powerful, highly industrialized nation which is the envy of many others. Its far-flung corporations dominate business in the noncommunist world, often bringing about drastic changes in living and working patterns that cause serious dislocations. These adverse effects are also felt within the U.S. itself.

The American Federation of Labor and Congress of Industrial Organizations (AFL-CIO), the joint voice of organized labour in the U.S., has shown increasing antagonism toward the U.S. multinational corporations. In 1973 it issued a report, *U.S. Multinationals: The Dimming of America,* in which it demanded a series of restrictions on U.S. multinational corporations. These demands were incorporated in the controversial Burke-Hartke bill which would curtail imports through mandatory quotas, increase the tax burden on multinational corporations and invest the President with power to prohibit the export of technology and capital. These restrictions were inspired by labour's major grievance against the multinational corporation: it is an exporter of jobs. American labour partly shares the views of the critics of multinationals in host countries, but partly the attitudes of these two groups are exactly opposite. U.S. labour is inclined to support the U.S. multinationals (e.g., with respect to exploiting their technological dominance) exactly on those counts where host countries focus their harshest opposition.

The opening statement of the AFL-CIO report claims: "Proud countries are losing the power to shape their own destinies, to guide their economies, to collect their taxes, to better the lives of their people. They are increasingly at the mercy of stateless, soulless, anonymous multinational corporations."[39]

After this salvo, it points out that U.S. corporations have grown to immense size and power but in this process they have undermined the power and integrity of the U.S. itself. The report warns "This greatest industrial power in the world's history is in danger of becoming nothing more than a nation of hamburger stands . . . a country stripped of industrial capacity and meaningful work . . . a service economy . . . a nation of citizens busily buying and selling cheeseburgers and rootbeer floats."[40]

The Dimming of America describes the process of change from international to multinational, transnational and finally supranational corporations, which in turn has given rise to a new manager whose loyalty to the corporation precedes his loyalty to the nation in which his company happens to operate. The reason for "runaway" plants is said to be the company's desire to locate in countries where wages and taxes are low and regulations lax.

Carborundum Company is a relatively small multinational, but its worldwide operations allow it to shift production to those countries where labour is cheapest. It has production facilities in the U.S., Britain, Germany, Mexico, Brazil and Argentina. If all companies were to follow Carborundum's policies, American industry would become dependent upon non-American manufacturers for this vitally important product used in the production of a wide-ranging scale of goods from roller bearings to contact lenses. Interruption of this supply could bring American industry to a "grinding" halt, the AFL-CIO report warns.

The AFL-CIO report aims its guns at a list of practices of the U.S. multinationals that hurt the U.S. economy. These include resorting to the Eurodollar to escape U.S. controls, undermining the U.S. dollar, tax-dodging, exporting American technology and speculating on the international money market. In the report, the latter practice is tagged as "sinister" since it holds "the potential for creating worldwide financial chaos."[41] The AFL-CIO is especially incensed over the export of jobs to low-wage countries, such as Mexico, Taiwan and Hong Kong. It claims that at least a million Americans are unemployed because their jobs have been shipped overseas. In this context, the report asserts that currency speculation and tax avoidance are only a "reflection" of the basic problems. Those problems are "decreased production and employment, decreased merchandise exports and increased imports."[42]

American labour views the export of technology as a powerful stimulant to overseas production in such items as shoes, textiles, clothing, steel, autos, ceramic tiles, radios, TV's, leather goods. America's share of the world's auto production declined from 76 per cent in 1950 to one third in 1970. America's mills produced 47 per cent of the world's raw steel in 1950; in 1970 this had dropped to 20 per cent. After World War II, the U.S. was the world's foremost shipbuilder; now it produces less than 2 per cent of the world's merchant ships. Traditionally, America was the world's leading machine tool builder; today it is only in fourth place.

In its report, the AFL-CIO describes an impressive list of instances to back up its charge that the U.S. multinationals are creating unemployment and hardship for American workers and introducing new problems for workers in the host countries. For example, 50,000 new jobs were created in Mexico. These new employment opportunities in Mexico were accompanied by increased social tensions reflected in a rise in delinquency and prostitution, family breakdown, overcrowding and overloading of existing facilities. Numerous case histories are cited to demonstrate the culpability of the multinationals.

It is claimed that American-based multinationals earned $17.5 billion in overseas profits in 1970 but paid only $900 million in taxes, an effective 5 per cent tax rate. In 1971 United States Steel had profits of $154.5 million but did not pay anything in federal income tax. A U.S. *Oil Week* study revealed that eighteen major oil companies had a combined income of $10.2 billion but paid only $683 million in federal income taxes, a rate of 6.7 per cent. The case of U.S. Gypsum Company reveals an extraordinarily imaginative method of tax evasion.

> The case involved rock mined in Canada by the Canadian affiliate of the U.S. Gypsum Company. While the rock was on a dockside on a conveyor belt it belonged to Canadian Gypsum. However, for shipment the rock was to be dropped from the conveyor belt into the hold of a waiting ship. During the split second the rock was falling from the conveyor into the ship, it was bought, in mid-air, by U.S. Gypsum Export and instantly resold to the parent, U.S. Gypsum Co., at a profit of 50 cents a ton. Because first the mid-air buyer, U.S. Gypsum Export Co., did not buy the rock until it had left the turf of Nova Scotia, it paid no tax on its profits to Canada. But Gypsum Export Co. was a "Western Hemisphere" trading corporation and entitled to be taxed at 14 per cent below the domestic corporate rate, under a law designed to promote trade. Therefore, U.S. Gypsum Export received a preferential tax rate on its 50 cents a ton profit. This arrangement saved U.S. Gypsum more than $700,000 in U.S. taxes. No figures are available on the amount of Canadian taxes U.S. Gypsum avoided because of the maneuver. [43]

The AFL-CIO dislikes the dilution of American technological dominance and therefore opposes the export of technology by the U.S. multinationals, through joint ventures, licensing or other forms of sharing knowledge with non-American firms. In short, the AFL-CIO wants to end tax breaks and other privileges of the multinationals and to replace these with stringent restrictions and protectionist measures against the import of goods and the export of technology. That is why it was opposed to the DISC legislation but aggressively supported the Burke-Hartke bill. (It speaks for itself that the restrictions on U.S. imports would have serious repercussions for Canada. A U.S. Commerce Department study estimated that if the Burke-Hartke bill had been in effect in 1971, Canada would have lost $3.6 billion in exports to the U.S.)

A Response to the AFL-CIO

U.S. labour's assessment of American multinationals no doubt grates on the nerves of non-Americans who already resent the overwhelming presence of U.S. affiliates in their own country. American labour argues that the power of the U.S. multinationals is waning—at least insofar as their dominant position as world producers is no longer secure—and advocates measures that would make other countries even more dependent on the American ability to innovate and produce.

Although the AFL-CIO position is essentially selfish, reflecting the narrow interests of this organization, it is valid and appropriate in at least two important areas. In the first place, the AFL-CIO's criticism is justified insofar as it condemns the deliberate efforts of the U.S. multinationals to evade the scrutiny of host as well as home countries for the sake of maximizing their own growth and profits. The companies' adroit use of every possible loophole to escape their obligations and to benefit from currency and transfer pricing manipulation deserves to be condemned. The multinationals' aim of transcending national boundaries and thereby placing themselves beyond the reach of any other jurisdiction—particularly that of the nation-state—needs to be challenged. Multinationals should not be entrusted with that kind of prerogative.

In the second place (although this may be difficult to accept by those who resent the U.S. dominant position in world trade), the real hardships encountered by American workers who are unemployed because U.S. production is shifted to other countries should not be underestimated. It is true that, when looked at through macroeconomic glasses, the U.S. position is impressive. But the microeconomic realities, that is, the shutdown of a specific plant in a particular community leading to unemployment of long-term and semiskilled blue collar workers, and to regional underdevelopment, are a real scourge in the U.S.

Imports have cut heavily into U.S. jobs. In 1971, imports from Japan, Korea, Taiwan, Singapore, Mexico and elsewhere supplied 54 per cent of black and white television sets in the U.S., 18 per cent of colour sets, 32 per cent of phonographs, 91 per cent of radios and 96 per cent of tape recorders. Growing imports in other industries also led to more plant closures and unemployment. Steel imports rose from 1.15 million tons in 1957 to 18.3 million tons in 1971. Several unions, including the International Association of Machinists, the United Shoe Workers of America, the International Ladies Garment Workers' Union, and the International Union of Electrical, Radio and Machine Workers, have declined in membership during past years. The laid-off workers are often middle-aged people, women or members of minorities—all groups difficult to retrain and relocate. Irwin Ross points out that it is easy for economists such as Paul Samuelson to advise that American resources should move out of cheap textiles and shoes into more efficient lines of production, but extremely difficult for a fifty-nine-year-old unemployed woman textile worker to find other work.[44] Behind the statistics and graphs in the U.S. as in other countries, there are real, living human beings to be considered, men, women, children, families and communities, experiencing genuine hopes, fears, pain and joy.

Barnet and Müller, writing in *Global Reach* published in 1974, also describe the wrenching changes that are created by these corporations in the U.S. They speak of the "Latin-Americanization" in the U.S. during the previous five years accompanied by a reduction in the standard of living among the American middle class and, even more seriously, among those below that category. These authors characterize the drastic changes as follows: the globalization of oligopoly capitalism; world profit *maximization,* which may be accompanied by profit minimization in some countries; the shifting of principal sites of new production to the poor nations of Asia, Latin America and Africa, traditionally the hewers of wood and the drawers of water for the international economy; and a new concentration of political power in private hands.

These authors also claim that the managers of the multinational corporations are creating a system which will change the U.S. from a producer of industrial goods to a "service economy" and producer of "software," the know-how for others to use. In this process heavy reliance is placed on exporting staple goods such as agricultural products and timber to maintain a positive balance of payments. These authors claim that the change in employment patterns in the U.S. "has led to a redistribution of wealth and income which, once again, is more in the tradition of the underdeveloped world than in that of the Affluent Society."[45] Workers are earning a decreasing share of the national income.

How closely the views of Barnet and Müller reflect reality will be a point of dispute for a long time, but there are some weighty reasons to take their assessment seriously. For the truth is that there is more than one America. There is also "the other America," visible beyond the Affluent Society. This realization will prevent us from wholesale denunciation of the American "system" and the prescription of solutions that overlook the complexity of reality. The dislocating and harmful effects of a ruthless pursuit of growth, profits and technical innovation, engaged in by the multinational corporations on a global scale, is cutting through national boundaries in many ways. What may be in the short-term interest of a U.S. multinational, and of those who reap the "rewards" at the top, is often not in the interest of the American people and particularly of those at the lower-income levels. This complicates the situation, but an awareness that the harmful effects of the globalization of business extend across national boundaries *and also cut through the U.S. itself* could stimulate cooperative and constructive reform measures on an international scale. The alternative is that each nation look out for itself only and resort to a negative and harshly protectionist stance, pitting one nation against the other.[46] The AFL-CIO report centres, unfortunately, on the latter approach. Three major elements of the AFL-CIO position deserve further attention.

The AFL-CIO position is inspired by a static concept of international trade. It is assumed throughout that if the U.S. companies had not moved investment and production abroad, that production would have taken place in the U.S. and the goods would then have been exported, much to the benefit of U.S. employment and the balance of payments. As it is now, production is moved abroad where the goods are produced more cheaply, adding to the profits of the multinationals but increasing imports, unemployment and pressure on the balance of payments in the U.S.

On the other hand, the proponents of U.S. foreign investment insist that it has increased employment in the U.S. and that, in the absence of such investment, the goods that result from it would not have been supplied by American firms but by non-American competitors. They argue that foreign investment by the U.S. corporation is largely for defensive reasons.

In 1971, the Harvard University Graduate School of Business Administration, on behalf of the U.S. Department of Commerce, undertook a study of foreign direct investments by U.S. multinationals, and their effects on U.S. employment and on the U.S. balance of payments. Nine case histories were examined, including a new paper mill in Canada. The assumption underlying the study was that in the absence of this foreign direct investment, the market would have been captured by non-American competitors.

This study concluded that the U.S. foreign direct investments resulted in an additional 600,000 jobs for U.S. workers and the positive effects of investments in foreign manufacturing plants on the U.S. balance of payments amounted to at least $3 billion, including net trade effects, dividends, royalties and management fees.[47] To prove that U.S. export performance has been improving in certain sections (thus countering the AFL-CIO's criticism regarding the loss of U.S. exports), the study lists a number of product lines that show an increase in exports (see Table 5).

TABLE 5 EXAMPLES OF PRODUCT LINES IN WHICH U.S. TRADE PERFORMANCE HAS BEEN IMPROVING

U.S. Exports Minus U.S. Imports

Industry (SIC No.)	Absolute ($ millions) 1963	Absolute ($ millions) 1970	As a Per cent of U.S. Production 1963	As a Per cent of U.S. Production 1970
Plastic materials and resins (2821)	295	550	10.6	11.2
Construction machinery (3531)	826	1,530	31.5	36.9
Mining machinery (3532)	81	210	24.2	32.5
Oil field machinery (3533)	135	225	23.6	25.7
Pumps and compressors (3561)	131	276	11.4	13.5
Electronic computing equipment (3573)	181	1,001	9.0	26.3
Electrical measuring instruments (3611)	59	175	7.8	12.7
Electronic systems and equipment (3662)	362	480	6.0	6.6
Aircraft and parts (372)	1,305	2,985	10.0	16.3
Measuring and controlling instruments (3821)	183	309	18.6	20.6
Photographic equipment and supplies (3861)	66	188	4.0	4.9

Source: *The Multinational Corporation, Studies on U.S. Foreign Investment Abroad,* Vol. 1. U.S. Department of Commerce, March 1972, section 2, p. 33.

The AFL-CIO's opposition to, and the U.S. Department of Commerce's defense of, U.S. foreign direct investment, together with their estimates of either negative or positive effects on employment and the balance of payments, are not convincing. These two conflicting positions and findings are based on the assumption that it is known what would have happened if history had been different. That is a very shaky assumption—and the conflicting findings bear this out. The AFL-CIO's assumption that the products would have been exported from the U.S. if American-based corporations had not built their branch plants overseas is unrealistic. It suggests that non-American firms would not have been able to produce these goods. That is underestimating the capabilities of other nations and the possibilities for knowledge transfer. (The AFL-CIO opposition to transferring technological know-how through joint ventures and licensing is related to this underestimation.)

The U.S. Department of Commerce study contains much food for thought, especially for critics of U.S. direct investment in Canada. It has shown in the case of the Canadian paper mill that U.S. direct investment in Canada results in a heavy drain on Canadian resources.[48] The irony in this is that the arguments and evidence produced to persuade the AFL-CIO that U.S. foreign direct investment is good for U.S. workers reveal the disadvantage of such investment to the host countries. (A note of caution: It would be wrong to conclude that there were only disadvantages for Canada. There are also some benefits, for example, in the form of employment opportunities. But the emphasis should be placed on the heavy cost to Canada and, above all, on the need to rely more—which does not mean exclusively—on Canadian-owned and managed developments.)

It seems to have escaped the AFL-CIO that their position is also contradictory in the sense that they demand of other countries what they themselves reject. If imports from other countries to the U.S. must be warded off and be replaced by exports to those countries, why should those other countries not feel the same way as the AFL-CIO does and oppose imports from the U.S.? In other words, the AFL-CIO says what's bad for us is good for you, and vice versa. But that is a most unconvincing argument. If other countries were to assume the same posture, a trade war would be inevitable with ruinous results for everyone.

This brings us to the second major point of the AFL-CIO report. The AFL-CIO laments the declining position of the U.S. in a number of important industries, such as automobiles, steel, shipbuilding and machine tools. These figures underscore the fact that the U.S. has enjoyed a very favourable position for a long time. *But why should that disparity between nations continue?* There is no logic to that continuation—only self-interest. This matter is especially urgent in view of the stark contrast between the rich and the poor nations. The only way in which that contrast can be leveled off is by a more equal distribution of wealth, but the key to that is a country's productive capacity and its supply of capital. This is why the AFL-CIO's opposition to the transfer of technology from the U.S. to other countries through joint ventures and licensing agreements is grossly unfair to those countries that so desperately need new technology. A comparison, for example, in 1974, of per capita income in the U.S. ($5,486) and in Bangladesh ($70), as well as a look at the phenomenally disproportionate use of resources in the U.S. (with 5.7 per cent of the world population it consumes about 40 per cent of the world's production of natural resources), drives home the reactionary and selfish stand of the AFL-CIO.

Finally, the AFL-CIO position is unconvincing because it does not get at the source of the dislocation and injustice caused by the multinational corporations. That source is the overriding commitment to the goals of maximum economic growth, profits and unlimited technological innovation as ends in themselves. The elevation of such ends has played havoc with justice, social and ecological harmony, and the opportunity for meaningful and enriching work. The AFL-CIO does not come to grips with this at all. It only wants to ensure that it will continue to benefit from the actions of American corporations. It wants to keep them at home so that from that home base they can all the more effectively pursue their goals and perpetuate their dominant role in the world, and thus enrich the American workers.

The AFL-CIO reaffirmed its dedication to the free enterprise system.[49] That system, in its present form as well as in its underlying assumption, is based on the belief that individual man pursuing his self-interest is the motor of "progress." The AFL-CIO acts consistently with that picture of man and for that reason is unable to make a fundamental and lasting contribution to the vitally needed redirection of the multinationals' behaviour and to the more equitable distribution of the world's resources. That is most unfortunate, even tragic; for, given its power and role, the AFL-CIO could have been a real force for renewal had it determined its priorities in a different manner.

Chapter 5
The Canadian Response

When virtually every other nation in the developed and industrialized world follows a policy of conserving and reducing the drain on its natural resources, we encourage their consumption by outrageous tax concessions accorded to no other sector of our economy.[1]

Eric Kierans

I wrote this book because I'm fed up with the nonsense I read about our supposed enthusiasm for our glorious new nationalism. I think this spurious patriotism has hurt the average Canadian in his pocketbook, his opportunities, and most of all in his morale.[2]

Alan Heisey

For however incoherent in its expression, this country has a rage to live.[3]

Abraham Rotstein

In 1958 the *Royal Commission Report on Canada's Economic Prospects* (the Gordon Report) dealt briefly with foreign ownership of Canadian industry. A decade later there was an upsurge of interest in this Canadian problem. Between 1968 and 1972 the three following studies were published under the auspices of the federal government:

1. *Foreign Ownership and the Structure of Canadian Industry: Report of the Task Force on the Structure of Canadian Industry,* 1968 (the Watkins Report)
2. *The Eleventh Report of the Standing Committee on External Affairs and National Defense, Respecting Canada-United States Relations,* 1970 (the Wahn Report)
3. *Foreign Direct Investment in Canada,* 1972 (the Gray Report)

The Gordon Report[4]

In June 1955, during the heyday of C.D. Howe, the crusty czar of the Department of Trade and Commerce, a Commission chaired by Walter Gordon was appointed to study Canada's economic prospects. Gordon had turned down an offer to serve in the St. Laurent Cabinet because of his disagreement with Howe's policies. He was becoming concerned about the "open door" policy of the government and its long-range adverse effects on Canada's political independence. This is how Gordon's biographer describes that time:

> While Canadian politicians paid lip-service to the independence of Canadian interests, this notion was unconventional in 1955 for someone close to the Liberal party. All federal political parties were loyal adherents of the Western alliance with its Cold War assumptions and its presumption of American righteousness. The progress of mankind, and Canada, was almost universally seen to rest with the unimpeded leadership of the American colossus. Within that mental framework, it was difficult to conceive of separate Canadian interests. Canadian resources were needed to fire the furnaces of the American economy; the exploitation of these resources would bring prosperity to Canada; expanding American economic power was needed to hold the frontiers of the Free World; and Canadians, among others, were all citizens in that Free World. A thousand speeches since 1948 had reminded Canadians of their privileged position in that scheme of things. If Canada were to adopt an independent stance in relation to the United States, it would have to be within the very narrow margins allowed by this overriding community of interest recognized by all parties. For the Liberal party, with its continental economic perspective, the margin for manoeuvre seemed even smaller.[5]

The preliminary Report was presented in December 1956 and the final Report was published in April 1958. In the meantime the government had changed hands; the Diefenbaker years had begun. Both governments ignored the moderate proposal for change in Gordon's Report. C.D. Howe called the views expressed in the Report "some of the greatest rot" he had ever heard.[6]

The Report dealt with a wide spectrum of economic matters and ventured a number of forecasts up to the year 1980. They dealt with population increase, economic growth, national energy, tariff and commercial policy, wheat marketing, regional development, manpower and educational policy. The Commission's forecasts were predicated on the assumption that there would be no major wars, recessions or mass unemployment.

Although the policy recommendations regarding foreign investment were modest, they nevertheless stirred up controversy. The Commission stated that foreign investment had brought advantages to Canada and would continue to do so. But it suggested that investment from outside Canada should not continue without some corrective measures. Otherwise, the Commission warned, concern among Canadians "could lead to actions of an extreme kind being taken at some future time." With this in mind, it recommended more foreign investment in the form of debt rather than equity capital; at least 20 or 25 per cent of Canadian equity ownership in foreign-owned companies; more Canadian personnel in senior management positions; use of Canadian engineering services and

Canadian-made goods by foreign-owned corporations; public disclosure of their financial operations; incentives for more Canadian participation in foreign-owned companies via changes in the tax laws; control of Canadian banks and life insurance companies by Canadians; greater flexibility in the investment policies of life insurance companies and other financial institutions.

The Commission did not set a timetable and did not recommend that these measures be made mandatory. Rather, it counseled reliance on goodwill and, at the most, on tax concessions. Altogether, the recommendations did not add up to a drastic change in policy and no action was taken on the Report. Nevertheless, it marked the beginning of a growing awareness among some Canadians that there are costs as well as benefits in foreign ownership.

The Watkins Report

In 1967 Melville H. Watkins, an economist at the University of Toronto, was appointed chairman of the Task Force assigned to study the structure of Canadian industry with special reference to foreign ownership. (Walter Gordon was at this time in the Pearson Cabinet where he enthusiastically favoured this inquiry—but quite a few of his colleagues were opposed.) The Task Force also included Abraham Rotstein, another professor at the U. of T., who occupies an important place in the ranks of Canadian nationalists.

The Task Force presented its Report entitled *Foreign Ownership and the Structure of Canadian Industry* in January 1968.[7] This exhaustive study details the extent of foreign ownership in Canada. It indicates that by 1963 foreign ownership in the Canadian manufacturing industries had increased to 54 per cent, in the mining and smelting industries, to 62 per cent. Total foreign investment in Canada had grown to $33 billion in assets by 1964.

The Report states at the outset that national independence and economic growth are uppermost goals in the minds of Canadians. It reviews and considers a large number of elements of foreign ownership and their effects on Canada. The Task Force cautions that Canadian policy toward foreign investment has been piecemeal and gradual within a policy framework provided by a "favourable attitude on the part of Canadian governments at all levels toward foreigners who wish to invest in Canada." The Report asserts that "the major deficiency in Canadian policy has not been its liberality toward foreign investment *per se* but the absence of an integrated set of policies, partly with respect to both foreign and domestic firms, partly with respect only to foreign firms, to ensure higher benefit and smaller costs for Canadians from the operations of multinational corporations."[8] The Report insists that new policies aimed at greater benefits from foreign investment must take "full account both of the constitutional rights of the provinces and the property rights of foreign owners."[9]

The Task Force recommended the establishment of a special agency to coordinate policies governing multinational companies. Its tasks would include gathering of data on foreign-owned firms, facilitating international cooperation and examining taxation procedures to ensure that Canada would get its just share of taxes. Furthermore, it was recommended that multinational companies be required to file returns with the government and make them available to the public; that the provisions of the anticombine legislation be strengthened while still allowing suboptimal firms to merge; and that the Canada Development Corporation be created as a large holding company "to assume a leadership role in Canada's business and financial community . . . ," with special emphasis on resource development and the rationalization of Canadian industry.

To deal with the so-called issue of extraterritoriality, the Task Force recommended that a government export trade agency be created with power to ensure that export orders are filled. Where an American subsidiary would refuse to fill the order (in compliance with U.S. legislation governing trade with enemy countries) the agency would assist in having the order filled with a Canadian-owned firm. Failing that, the agency would purchase the item for resale to the customer. It would be a criminal offense to refuse to sell to the agency.

Tax incentives were recommended to encourage foreign-owned subsidiaries to offer shares to Canadians. The Task Force also favoured measures to exempt the subsidiaries from antitrust orders and balance-of-payments guidelines originating in foreign countries.

When the Report was tabled in the House of Commons on February 15, 1968, it was presented significantly as "an expression of the views of the members of the Task Force and not those of the government."

The Wahn Report

The Wahn Report, named for Ian Wahn, the chairman of the Committee, was presented in July 1970, and covers much the same ground as the Watkins Report. The major recommendations of this Report centre on: improving the efficiency of Canadian-owned firms; more Canadian equity participation in foreign firms (51 per cent of voting shares in important sectors); counteracting American jurisdiction over U.S. subsidiaries in Canada; establishing a Canadian Development Corporation; forbidding takeovers in "key sectors" of the economy; and establishing a Canadian Ownership and Control Bureau that would provide information on foreign-owned firms and supervise takeovers of Canadian firms. In case foreign-owned firms refuse to sell to certain countries, the Report recommended that they be compelled to comply with the public utility regulations applicable to railroads and telephone companies.

Although this Report did not come with any drastic new proposals, it reflected a mounting concern on the part of Canadian parliamentarians about the effect of foreign ownership in Canada. Abraham Rotstein commented on the Wahn Report in *The Canadian Forum* and issued this warning:

> This is probably the last chance we will have for an all-party endorsation of a foreign investment programme. In a country already sharply divided on the issue, the government can only expect *more* dissension rather than less if it fails to move. More radical solutions than the Wahn Report will undoubtedly receive greater impetus if all we get is more foot-dragging by the government in the fall.[10]

The Gray Report

Foreign Direct Investment in Canada (the Gray Report), published in 1972, further elaborated the disturbing figures on foreign ownership in Canada. It reiterated the sentiment that Canada has benefited from imported capital and technology but that there are also definite disadvantages in the form of increased dependency on the U.S. and a consequent loss of Canadian identity.

This Report, prepared under the direction of the Minister of Revenue, Herb Gray, dwelt at some length on the dangers to the integrity of a Canadian culture resulting from foreign, and especially U.S., ownership. After reminding the readers that a distinctive indigenous Canadian culture will depend on domestic talent and creative capabilities, rather than the creation of barriers to foreign influence, the Report warned:

> But it must also be recognized that the creation and development of such Canadian capacities can be stifled if Canada is inundated with influences from other countries which are much larger or much more developed than Canada. The large volumes of United States direct investment in Canada constitute an important part of the massive American influence on Canadian society, although certainly not the largest portion of it. Prohibiting further United States investment would by no means ensure the emergence of a viable and attractive Canadian culture. Some further capacity to control such investment, however, may contribute to the creation of a strong national identity and a stimulating and distinctive culture.[11]

The main recommendation of the Gray Report was the establishment of a screening agency which would be given extensive power to supervise the operations of foreign-owned firms and to review all foreign direct investment in Canada. The agency would be empowered to block investments that contribute nothing to the Canadian economy. The Report favoured this somewhat flexible approach over the "key sector" or "fixed rules" approach, since it was feared that the latter might well block investments in certain areas that would result in considerable economic benefits.

The Report was leaked to the editors of *The Canadian Forum* who took the unprecedented step of publishing a major portion in the December 1971 issue of that publication. The editorial committee explained: "Our purpose is to induce the Government to release the full text and, we hope, to act on its recommendations." The same committee offered this evaluation of the Gray Report: "The policy proposals are feasible and straightforward. The report is an excellent document of its kind. It should prove a sound guide to those who are concerned with the level of foreign ownership in this country and to those who are seeking further information."[12]

The bill introduced in May 1972 did not meet the expectations of the nationalists. It was an innocuous piece of proposed legislation that applied only to new takeovers and not to internal expansion or new developments of foreign-owned firms. The new measures died on the order paper with the dissolution of parliament in September 1972.

Legislation to govern certain aspects of foreign ownership in Canada was again introduced by the succeeding Trudeau government, and on April 9, 1974, the *Foreign Investment Review Act* became law. This legislation set out a number of criteria by which takeovers of Canadian firms and the establishment of new businesses by nonresidents were to be judged. Such takeovers and new businesses would only be allowed if they were considered "of significant benefit to Canada." A special Foreign Investment Review Agency (FIRA) was established to administer the Act.

Patching the Fence

The rapid growth of foreign ownership in Canada, especially since the 1950s, does not mean that the Canadian government did not take *any* action in protecting certain segments of the Canadian economy against foreign domination. Government policies focused on certain key sectors, such as finance, communication and transportation. Crown corporations were established, including the Canadian Broadcasting Corporation, Air Canada and the Canadian National Railway. The Canadian Transport Commission, the National Energy Board (NEB) and the Canadian Radio-Television Commission (CRTC) are among the major government agencies supervising certain sectors of the Canadian economy. For example, the CRTC has established certain restrictions on imported programs and minimum quotas for Canadian-content broadcasting.[13]

In the mid-1950s, six Canadian life insurance companies were purchased by foreign-controlled firms. Subsequently, amendments in 1957 to the *Canadian and British Insurance Act* provided for the "mutualization" of Canadian insurance companies and stipulated that a majority of directors be Canadian residents. In 1965 the limit of foreign ownership of banks and insurance companies was placed at 25 per cent. In 1967 the maximum ownership by any one shareholder was set at 10 per cent by amendments to the *Bank Act*. Mercantile Bank, the only foreign-controlled bank, was given time to comply.

The *Broadcasting Act* of 1958 set a ceiling on foreign ownership of any broadcasting undertaking at 25 per cent. Applicants for licences were required to be Canadian citizens. Oil and gas leases in the Yukon and the Northwest Territories were to be granted only to Canadian citizens or to corporations of which at least 50 per cent of the shares are owned by Canadian citizens. In 1965 amendments to the *Income Tax Act* and the *Customs Act* effectively prevented the takeover of newspapers and periodicals, as well as the establishment of new newspapers and periodicals, by foreign-controlled firms.

On March 31, 1966, Robert Winters, the Minister of Trade and Commerce, issued a set of guiding principles of good corporate behaviour for Canadian subsidiaries of foreign firms. The guidelines encourage these subsidiaries to pursue sound growth potentials, maximum competitiveness, market opportunities in and outside Canada, and a pricing policy that will provide a fair return for the company and for Canada. They admonish the subsidiaries to procure more Canadian supplies; to engage in more research and development in Canada; to process more Canadian resources; to retain a sufficient share of earnings; to include more Canadian citizens in management; to provide for more equity participation by Canadians; to divulge more information; and to give support to national objectives and Canadian institutions. These guidelines were voluntary and amounted to nothing more than the expression of a pious wish.[14]

Further measures affecting taxation policy, research and development, and the establishment or expansion of Canadian businesses and designed to enhance Canadian ownership and entrepreneurship are scattered throughout a number of federal and provincial pieces of legislation. The Canadian Development Corporation (CDC) was established in 1971 with the aim of helping to develop strong Canadian-controlled firms and to provide greater opportunities for investment by Canadians. Other programs aimed at assisting Canadian-controlled firms are administered by the departments of Industry, Trade and Commerce, and Regional Economic Expansion, and the Bank of Canada. They are: the *Industrial*

Research and Development Incentives Act (IRDIA); the Program for the Advancement of Industrial Technology (PAIT); the Defence Industry Productivity Program (DIP); the Shipbuilding Assistance Program; the General Adjustment Assistance Program (GAAP); loans by the Industrial Development Bank (IDB); and regional incentives grants.

In 1970 the Trudeau government blocked the sale of a substantial share of Denison Mines Ltd., Toronto, to a U.S. firm. Denison Mines Ltd. is a major producer of uranium at Elliot Lake, Ontario. The government based this action on the crucial importance of uranium. Subsequent new regulations restricted foreign ownership of Canada's uranium industry to about 33 per cent; no single foreign investor is allowed to hold more than 10 per cent of the total shares.

Despite these protective measures, Canadian policy with respect to foreign ownership is one of the most liberal in the world. The expansion of foreign control over the resource and manufacturing industries in Canada and the strong cultural pull from the United States continue unabated. This is how A.W. Cockerill, a British observer, describes the effects of Canada's position of dependency:

> . . . Canada has already been cast in the American economic mould and there is simply nothing Canadians can do to extricate themselves from it. Canada's governments, both provincial and federal, appear too preoccupied with the wheeling and dealing domestic issues of federalism, who has dominion over off-shore oil and mineral rights and the like, to pay much attention to the emerging continental resources policy of the U.S. Government.

The same author offers little hope for the future of a viable, independent Canada. He gloomily predicts:

> Hope may spring eternal, but the harsh fact becomes clearer as time passes that Canada, as a sovereign nation, has about twenty years left—thirty at the most—before it will be effectively submerged in the pea soup of the American dream. One is prompted to suggest that one nation's dream is another's nightmare. At that time Canada will no longer be distinguishable as a separate and independent nation except, perhaps, in name only.[15]

Since it would stimulate competition, the Canadian Development Corporation was seen by many as a means to counter the inroads of foreign investors. At the end of 1976 the CDC had assets of over $1.5 billion, had direct or indirect interests in approximately 150 companies and ranked 16th by assets and 36th by sales on *The Financial Post*'s list of the top 200 industrials. Among some of its holdings are Polysar Ltd.(100%)—a company that makes rubbers, latex and plastics in North America and Europe; Connlab Holdings Ltd. (100%)—a pharmaceutical and biological company with branches in Canada and Denmark; and Texasgulf (30.3%)—a natural-resource company operating in Canada, the

U.S., Mexico and Australia in the field of base metals, oil, gas, potash and sulphur. In 1975 CDC Oil and Gas Ltd. was formed following the acquisition of 60 per cent of the Canadian oil and gas holdings of Tenneco Inc. CDC also owns 60 per cent of Petrosar Limited, which in the fall of 1977 completed construction of a $650 million refinery/petrochemical complex near Sarnia.

CDC's shares went on sale to the public in August 1975. To the critics who say that CDC has done nothing to stop foreign takeovers or create new jobs, the CDC's spokesmen point out that these were not among the government's goals.[16]

It is obvious that Canada's prospects for reclaiming a large share of its economy through competition are bleak in light of the extent and characteristics of sectors now under foreign ownership. There is a major difference between the Japanese policy of limiting foreign direct investment from the outset and the Canadian position which has a long history of outside control. Historical trends cannot easily be changed. To be sure, Japan's closed-door policy is now changing. Furthermore, Japan is much more dependent on foreign resources than Canada, making it more difficult to maintain its independence. Yet the results of its deliberate policy compare favourably with the Canadian situation.

A significant area of public concern is the high level of foreign ownership in the resource sector, particularly that of fossil fuels. The renewed concern about energy costs and foreign ownership has resulted in stronger demands for more Canadian control and ownership in this sector. Provincial governments and the federal government have recently moved into this industry. The federal government has a share in Panarctic, a consortium active in the Arctic Islands. Together with the Alberta government, it has invested $600 million in the Syncrude project, a consortium established to develop the Alberta tar sands. The Alberta government is pouring an additional $200 million into the Syncrude development for supportive facilities. The federal government has also established the new crown company Petro-Canada. When Donald Macdonald was still the Minister of Energy, Mines and Resources, he stated that the government did not plan to use Petro-Canada as a vehicle for nationalizing the Canadian petroleum industry but as a supplement to existing exploration and development.

By October 1976, FIRA had resolved 245 applications of which 173 takeovers were allowed, 34 were disallowed and 38 were withdrawn. It has negotiated with applicants for more favourable conditions for Canada in terms of local production, research, employment, exports and other benefits. Some believe that these negotiations have led to important concessions adding to the benefits accruing in Canada. However, others have argued that many companies do not live up to their commitments and that the Agency has failed to enforce such commitments.[17]

Presently the Act applies only to new acquisitions of Canadian firms; it does not apply to new direct investments by foreigners, nor to the expansion of foreign-owned firms. The section of the Act applicable to new investments and expansions was initially scheduled to go into effect shortly after the Act became law. But nothing happened, reportedly because of provincial opposition to restraints on foreign investment. The provinces are reluctant to see their opportunities for attracting capital restricted on account of federal regulations. Furthermore, the federal government is wary of scaring off any of the foreign capital much needed by corporate and governmental borrowers in the face of a massive current account deficit. Obviously, this area too is fraught with pitfalls for federal and provincial politicians, but equally obvious is the fact that Canada must face the issue squarely; and that opens a Pandora's box of problems related to regional disparity and federal-provincial disagreements.

Kari Levitt has correctly pointed out: "In the absence of effective federal initiatives to provide the means of mobilizing and directing Canada's resources towards the elimination of regional disparities, the provinces will reinforce the continentalist trend by joining the competitive scramble for foreign investment." [18] This puts the finger on a sore spot in Canada's political existence, and it is unfortunate that the long-range vision required to assess the needs of Canada as a whole is largely absent. This lack of vision results in continuous jockeying for position and petty squabbling in federal-provincial relations.

The Auto Pact

The Canada-U.S. Auto Pact negotiated in 1965 is interpreted in conflicting ways by the continentalists and the nationalists. One side points to the increase in jobs and incomes, whereas the other side emphasizes the heavy costs in terms of further dependence on foreign-owned corporations.

In 1962 Canada's balance-of-payments deficit with the U.S. amounted to $850 million of which the trade deficit in automotive and truck parts accounted for $580 million. In 1964 Canadians bought 7.5 per cent of cars produced in North America, but only 4 per cent of the total was produced in Canada (in foreign-owned plants). The producers were hampered in their desire to rationalize production because of tariff and other restrictions. To meet both Canadian and American needs, Prime Minister Pearson and President Johnson signed a new agreement providing for a free flow of automobiles and parts across the Canada-U.S. border, which took effect in January 1965 and was to be reviewed in 1968. The safeguards of the Pact are these three provisions: (1) a minimum annual level of Canadian automobile production, based on the value of automobiles and parts produced in Canada in 1964; (2) as sales increased, so would production increase in Canada by at least 50 per cent of sales; (3) the four major automobile producers agreed in a "letter of commitment" that production in Canada would increase during the next three years by $240 million over the minimum levels provided in the Pact.

In June 1967 the Canadian government announced that 16,000 new jobs were created, new plants had been established and existing ones expanded. Production increased dramatically. Canadian hopes for more employment and an improved balance-of-payments position with the U.S. were realized. In 1970 Canada's balance-of-payments position in automotive trade showed a surplus of $200 million, although the net deficit for Canada during the six years the Pact had been in effect was still $2 billion. The 1970 Canadian surplus caused consternation in Washington and started a discussion about dropping some of the safeguards. But the situation soon turned in favour of the Americans again.

Between 1973-76 the total Canadian auto deficit with the U.S. climbed to $4.3 billion. But in other ways too, the results of the Auto Pact were not without costs. Streamlining by the auto makers and the loss of the protective tariff put heavy pressure on independent Canadian-owned parts manufacturers. Many went out of business or were taken over by American firms. By 1971 American firms owned half and controlled 80 per cent of the Canadian automotive parts industry. The Liberal government proudly points to the impressive rates of increase in Canadian car production and employment resulting from the freer flow of cars and parts between Canada and the U.S. However, others emphasize the further loss of Canadian independence in a major branch of manufacturing. Jim Laxer writes:

> Had the Auto Pact not emerged, Canada would have been forced to take protective steps to guarantee the reservation of Canada's market for the sale of cars produced in this country. Considering that Canada's auto industry is almost entirely foreign-owned, there would have been long term pressure in favor of producing a Canadian car, either with government assistance or public ownership. The Auto Pact had the effect of preventing pressure to follow the Swedes and other Europeans, who have produced their own cars. [19]

The various positions on foreign ownership in Canada can roughly be divided into these three categories: continentalists, nationalists and socialists. Needless to say, these distinctions are somewhat arbitrary and not everyone can be categorized in terms of them.

In Defence of North American Integration

The continentalists have had the most influence in the past, which is obvious from the extent of foreign ownership in Canada. Those who hold this position are mainly adherents of a free market economy with its emphasis on efficiency, competition and maximum economic growth. This laissez-faire outlook has greatly accommodated foreign-owned firms in buying their way into the heartland of Canadian industry. The continentalist adheres to the position that national boundaries should not inhibit the free enterprise system.

It is safe to venture that most Canadians identify the good life with economic growth stimulated by a sophisticated technology. The good life and a rising standard of living are generally considered to be synonymous. This drive for economic growth underlies the eagerness to serve as the junior partner to the U.S. Hugh G.J. Aitken has summed it up thus:

> The frontier of development in Canada is no longer a frontier of settlement producing agricultural staples for Europe; it is a frontier of capital-intensive resource industries producing raw materials for the United States. Development, therefore, to the extent that it is based on these staples, must be in the direction of continental integration along north-south lines. This would still be true even if all the capital required for the development of these resource industries came from within Canada. In fact, however, the pull of the American market is reinforced by the corporate linkages that result from heavy dependence on American capital and technology.[20]

The U.S. government has consistently viewed Canada in terms of a continental economy. Testifying before the Wahn Committee, George Ball, U.S. Undersecretary of State, advised that we should "recognize the imperatives of an evolving world and the increasing obsolescence of the nation state as an economic unit."[21] The U.S. government has various ways of bringing pressure to bear on Canadian officials, many of whom appear anxious to please our neighbour to the south. When the Pearson government in 1965 and 1966 introduced legislation to curtail foreign ownership of Canadian banks, a great deal of pressure was put on the Canadian government on behalf of the First National City Bank of New York (the owners of the Mercantile Bank of Canada). The U.S. government sent this note to Ottawa on April 7, 1966:

> The Embassy has been instructed to remind the government of Canada of the concern with which the United States government viewed certain aspects of the banking legislation introduced in Parliament last year but not executed. . . , and express the hope that the banking legislation to be introduced this year will not contain provisions discriminating against American-owned banks.[22]

Another source of pressure in favour of Canadian-U.S. integration consists of a number of agencies aimed at smoothing the flow of capital and goods across the border. The National Industrial Conference Board and the Arctic Institute have provided information and services to facilitate U.S. investment in Canada. The Canadian-American Committee was established in 1957 to study the interrelationship between Canada and the U.S. It did much to encourage the expansion of U.S. investment in Canada.

John Fayerweather, Professor of International Business in the Graduate School of Business Administration, New York University, favours the continentalist approach. He writes that the evidence gathered by those who have studied the matter extensively "fits a generally perceived Canadian view that there is a trade-off between economic benefits of foreign investment and loss of control of national affairs."[23] Professor Fayerweather has undertaken a study of Canadian opinion and predicts that the long-run prospect is for Canada's economic integration with the U.S. since that will meet the desire for a higher standard of living. He concludes:

> My reading of past history and current influences leads me to expect that the main economic and government policy decisions will be governed by the second basic trend: the evolution toward integration. The attitudinal pressures for national identity would be satisfied to a large degree, as they are today, by measures which protect cultural and national identity, along with limited economic measures by which Canadian identity can be preserved with a minimum sacrifice to the standard of living.[24]

The most outspoken supporter of continentalism among academics was the late Canadian economist Harry G. Johnson. Professor Johnson did not mince any words. He referred to the issue of foreign ownership as a "spurious problem." He further asserted: "Insistence that it is a real problem seems to me a piece of hypocrisy perpetrated by commercial greed aiming to exploit the Canadian inferiority complex under the guise of patriotism. . . ."[25] He was not in the least afraid that the identity and independence of Canada would be undermined should its political leadership decide that the best interests of Canada and the U.S. were identical.

The tariffs imposed to protect Canada's secondary industry lead to inefficiency, Johnson claimed. He favoured abolishing the tariffs so that Canada's manufacturing products could be sold on the much larger American market. He called the fear that the removal of tariffs would lead to a decline of Canadian manufacturing "part of the mythology of nationalism," which assumes that a large manufacturing sector protected by tariffs is essential to economic development and national independence. He continued: "Independence, to my mind, and according to both the empirical evidence and the best tradition of the English novel, comes from the enjoyment of a high income; it is hard to see how a nation can be made more independent by lowering its citizens' standard of living and forcing them to earn their livings in occupations at which they are inefficient."[26]

Dismissing two main causes of the nationalists' concern, namely, a high level of imports from the U.S. and the growing U.S. investment in Canada, Johnson argued that "neither imports of American goods nor imports of American capital acquire voting rights in Canada, so Canadian independence as embodied in the sovereignty of Parliament can hardly be threatened that way. . . ." He suggested that what he called the "anti-American sentiment" among Canadians is "closely connected with a certain immaturity in the Canadian national character, expressed in the unwillingness to accept the fact that Canada is, except from the geographical point of view, a small country. Unlike the citizens of other small countries bordering on large countries, Canadians are not prepared to content themselves with the advantages that can be derived from small size, but set themselves the impossible aspiration of equalling the United States, and, still more impossible, of getting the United States to treat them as equals."[27]

Johnson asserted that "far from contributing to the growth of a stronger, more independent, and identity-conscious nation, Canadian nationalism as it has developed in recent years has been diverting Canada into a narrow and garbage-cluttered cul-de-sac."[28]

He rested his defence of complete integration on economic liberalism. Within that context the free market is elevated to the highest authority, economics is viewed as a science where the criterion of efficiency is absolute and a high standard of living becomes the overriding goal. Given this laissez-faire framework, it is not surprising that Johnson considered Canadian nationalism a threat.

Johnson expressed these views in the early 1960s. Since that time our accommodation to U.S. interests has continued in the context of Canada's own commitment to a growing standard of living. Nonetheless, a small but determined band of Canadians has become more vigorous in their opposition to what they call the Canadian sellout.

In Defence of Canadian Autonomy

A number of persons deserve specific mention in terms of their efforts—sometimes against terrific odds—to awaken their fellow Canadians to the danger of losing their nationhood. Notable among these are Walter L. Gordon and Eric Kierans, who have centred their attention on the economic area, and Abraham Rotstein, George Grant and Bruce Hutchison, who have raised searching questions about the very foundation of Canadian society. One could say that the first group is preoccupied with repatriating the Canadian economy, while the second group is aware that a much more fundamental shift of priorities in our entire lifestyle is demanded.

Repatriating the Economy

After World War II, Walter L. Gordon, a Toronto businessman, was one of the first to speak out against the harmful effects of foreign investment in Canada. In the mid-fifties he headed the Royal Commission studying Canada's economic progress. The final report of this Commission hesitantly pointed to some troublesome aspects of foreign ownership and hinted at ways in which the tide might be turned (see above). Gordon joined the Pearson Cabinet in 1963 and as ill-starred Minister of Finance introduced a number of unpopular measures aimed at slowing down the takeover of Canada's industries and resources by Americans. He introduced a controversial 30 per cent tax on the sale of Canadian companies to nonresident firms, which was soon withdrawn in a crossfire of opposition and ridicule. Gordon left the Pearson Cabinet in 1965 and rejoined it in April 1967 until March 1968. He was instrumental in establishing the Watkins Task Force in 1967, which advocated a number of measures to safeguard Canadian industry from foreign ownership. However, he proved to be quite ineffective in persuading Prime Minister Pearson and the other Cabinet members that foreign ownership was an urgent problem.

Gordon wrote three books, *Troubled Canada: The Need for New Domestic Policies* (1961), *A Choice for Canada: Independence or Colonial Status* (1966) and *Storm Signals: New Economic Policies for Canada* (1975), in which he urged the Canadian government and the Canadian people to regain control over their economy. He warned in *A Choice for Canada*:

> Too much of Canadian industry is controlled abroad. Because of this, foreigners, with the help of their Canadian friends and agents, wield far too great an influence, both directly and indirectly, on public policy in Canada. This control and this influence will not be changed by exhortation or by speeches. We have had our fill of both. What is required is not more speeches but action of a specific kind. . . . We still have a choice. We can do the things that are necessary to regain control of our economy and thus maintain our independence. Or we can acquiesce in becoming a colonial dependency of the United States with no future except the hope of eventual absorption.[29]

Writing in the September 1972 issue of *Maclean's* he stated that Canada had only a last chance to survive as a distinct nation. He spelled out his proposals for specific steps to encourage Canadian ownership of Canadian industry. As a long-time member of the Liberal party, he cautioned the government: "If Pierre Trudeau does not announce some major changes in his policies, I expect some of us will decide, on the day of the election, that we must put the future of our country first.''[30]

In his book *Storm Signals*, Gordon presents a plan for recovering control over major sectors of the Canadian economy by buying out the owners of the largest foreign-owned companies. He insists that the method chosen must be fair to the investors, and suggests that as a first step members of parliament adopt a resolution stating that the foreign owners of the larger Canadian subsidiary companies should, over a period of years, sell out to Canadians. He writes that ''larger'' Canadian subsidiary companies be defined as those with assets of $250 million. At the end of 1973 there were 32 of them. All other foreign-owned companies would be left alone until they reached the $250 million mark.

Gordon outlines a five-stage procedure for buying out the foreign owners of the 32 largest companies, as follows:

1. Buying up the companies in the resource sector with assets in excess of $2 billion, over a period of one year or eighteen months. Only Imperial Oil would qualify.
2. The next stage is spread out over three years and applies to companies in the resource sector with assets over $1 billion. This category would include Gulf Oil Canada and Shell Canada.
3. Stage three takes place within five years and applies to companies in the resource sector with assets exceeding $500 million. Six companies would be included.
4. The next step starts within seven years and involves all foreign-owned manufacturing and commercial companies with total assets exceeding $1 billion. This would apply to General Motors, Ford and Anglo-Canadian Telephone.
5. The final stage is spread over ten years and takes in all other foreign-controlled companies with total assets of more than $250 million. This would involve 20 companies.

Gordon estimates that the total cost of this procedure would reach about $15 billion, a figure well within Canada's capabilities. He furthermore wants to restrict foreign share ownership of these companies in the future to 25 per cent with the added stipulation that not more than 10 per cent may be owned by any foreigner or associated group.

In addition, Gordon recommends that Canadian-owned companies be given the advantage of a tax rate 10 per cent below that of other companies and that all government grants should only go to Canadian-controlled companies. He asserts that if his suggestions were implemented, the Canadian economic independence issue would be settled within a decade.[31]

When Gordon introduced the 1963 budget containing a proposed 30 per cent takeover tax on sales of Canadian businesses to nonresidents, Eric Kierans, then Montreal Stock Exchange president, joined the chorus of condemnation. However, in 1966 Kierans reacted angrily to the new U.S. guidelines for American subsidiaries abroad aimed at improving the U.S. balance of payments but jeopardizing Canada's position. In his capacity as Quebec's Acting Minister of Revenue, he wrote the U.S. Secretary of the Treasury, Henry Fowler, protesting the new guidelines. Kierans took strong exception to a speech in which Fowler had argued that U.S. national interests and those of multinational corporations should be reconciled and that the latter had an important role to play in U.S. foreign policy. He concluded his letter: "I am not questioning your right to reduce new direct investment to Canada but I do not believe that you can justify your efforts to direct the reinvestment, dividend and financial policies of Canadian firms. We hope that international companies, unlike armies of occupation, will always have a role to play. To accomplish this, they must conduct themselves as true citizens of the host country."[32]

Speaking to the Toronto Society of Financial Analysts on February 1, 1966, he said in his forthright manner that the American guidelines represented a tightening of the American grasp on our economy that threatened the attainment of our own economic objectives, and they were therefore an infringement of our political sovereignty.

In a discussion of multinational corporations, Kierans described the characteristics of the corporation and particularly its continuity and individuality. Having mastered the limitation of time, the corporation now wishes to overcome the limitation of space and range all over the globe. Kierans mockingly wrote:

> A self-respecting, self-existing, self-acting, self-propelling corporation should be able to go anywhere without being impeded by national governments that may have their own idea about the development and priorities of their economies. . . . With immortality and extension, the corporation would be complete unto itself. Its continued existence everywhere would be assured. Beholden to no other authority it need only get on with the job.[33]

Kierans contests the notion that the interests of the "cosmocorporation" and the national community are identical. He points to the corporation's primary concern with market control and profits, citing from case histories to show that American foreign direct investments have been immensely profitable for these corporations but that this has given rise to serious problems of dependency for the host countries. The developing nations need new technology and capital, but the conditions under which the cosmocorporation transfers them are in many instances harmful and an increasing source of hostility, writes Kierans. In this connection he refers to the U.S. surpluses in merchandise and returns on investments in Latin America, Asia and Africa, to the tune of $4 billion inflow per year from 1968 to 1971.[34] He concludes:

> The cosmocorp thrust will eventually deprive it of any friends —and no institution can continue to exist in an environment of increasing hostility and distrust. Unless the industrialized economies of the world reassess their economic and commercial policies and attitudes toward the less advanced nations, the environment in which the cosmocorp operates will become increasingly unstable. 35

A man of such strong convictions about American ownership, Eric Kierans encountered rough sailing in the Liberal Cabinet like Walter Gordon before him. He grew more and more disenchanted with the continued and stepped-up exploitation of Canadian resources by American companies for the benefit of Americans, short-changing future generations of Canadians. He wrote:

> A generation that deliberately squanders a nation's natural wealth to enhance its own standard of living, to live high off the hog, will have much to answer for. A government that deliberately pursues a policy of selling off the natural wealth of its people to achieve short-run gains in GNP breaks faith with its own future. 36

In April 1971 Kierans left the Trudeau Cabinet because his views about foreign ownership and economic policy collided with Trudeau's and those of the majority of the Cabinet members.

The Committee for an Independent Canada

By the late 1960s the concern over the continuing expansion of American ownership of major segments of the Canadian economy had become more prominent. Abraham Rotstein vigorously pursued this theme on the pages of *The Canadian Forum*. Out of this renewed sense of uneasiness over Canada's nationhood a new organization emerged in 1970, the Committee for an Independent Canada (CIC). Walter Gordon, Peter C. Newman, Jack McClelland, Eddie Goodman, Mel Hurtig and Abraham Rotstein were among the founding members.

The Committee is nonpartisan and seeks to create public awareness of the threat to Canada's independence resulting from the takeover of Canada's industry by foreign—mostly American—multinational corporations. It addressed a petition to Prime Minister Trudeau with 170,000 signatures in support of a more Canadian-oriented policy respecting development and ownership of Canada's economic resources. In 1972 the Committee presented its first publication to the Canadian public, *Independence—the Canadian Challenge*, edited by Abraham Rotstein and Gary Lax. This collection of articles centres on the extent and effect of U.S. power and influence in Canada. As the editors put it: "Taken together they are the prime illustrations of our main theme: that Canadians have lost the power to make key decisions over a significant and growing sector of our economy. If independence is defined as the power to make decisions in the vital areas with which we are concerned, then clearly we have been losing this independence at a rapid rate."[37]

In September 1972 the CIC held a four-day policy conference in Edmonton where a number of policy papers were discussed and adopted dealing with various aspects of foreign influence over Canadian society. The topics included an industrial strategy for Canada, technology, entrepreneurship, energy policy, ownership of land, trade unions, book publishing, televison and radio, film industry, non-Canadian university faculty members and the visual arts. The papers endorsed the recommendations of the Gray Report aimed at reversing the trend toward increasing American control over the Canadian economy.

These papers were published in book form in 1974 under the title *Getting It Back: A Program for Canadian Independence*, again edited by Abraham Rotstein and Gary Lax.[38] The editors explained that the proposed policies were deliberately geared to the mainstream of public opinion in Canada, avoiding appeals to sectarian philosophies or special interests. "We lean to the pragmatic rather than the doctrinaire," wrote the editors.[39] They concluded with this somber warning: "We find the question 'Do you want an independent capitalist Canada or an independent socialist Canada?' somewhat premature. Unless all of us mobilize our energies, there is no assurance that we shall have a genuinely independent Canada of any kind."[40]

The Sellout of Natural Resources

Others have added their voices of discontent over the loss of Canadian initiative and independence in economic matters. This discontent has focused especially on the rapid development of Canadian resources by American-controlled corporations and the export of nonrenewable resources from Canada to the U.S. Major development projects, including the James Bay hydroelectric project and the now abandoned Mackenzie Valley pipeline, have come under vigorous attack. In his book *Sellout: The Giveaway of Canada's Energy Resources* (1973), Philip Sykes, a former Toronto journalist and editor, castigated the Canadian government for failing to protect Canada's long-term interests.[41]

Sellout discusses a work entitled *Economic Development with Environmental Security*[42] which was written by four Dalhousie University professors who assembled a mass of evidence to back their conclusion that Canada's bountiful natural resources of water, gas and oil were being squandered for the sake of short-term gains at the expense of future development in Canada. They studied a proposed development in the Maritimes and five case histories of proposals for the development of Canada's energy resources. The five projects were the Columbia River treaty of 1964; the sale of Alberta's natural gas; the Alberta plan to reverse the flow of rivers from north to south (now abandoned); Manitoba's hydro development on the Churchill River; and Quebec's multi-billion dollar James Bay hydroelectric development. The author of *Sellout* summarized the conclusions reached by the Dalhousie Four as follows:

> Canada, said the Dalhousie Four, is almost always the loser in big energy deals, which are generally undertaken for short-term ends and with get-rich-quick motivations. They are often launched on provincial initiative without serious consideration of the environmental costs or the damage to the national economy. The usual purpose is to service industry in the United States. The involvement of the federal government, the professors found, is "consistently unimposing," even when the constitution provides a clear mandate for action by Ottawa.[43]

Until the summer of 1977, a twenty-seven-member consortium of corporations (Arctic Gas) was preparing to build a huge pipeline (estimated cost $10 billion) to transport Arctic gas along the Mackenzie Valley to southern markets. Mr. Justice Thomas Berger, who conducted a three-year impact study, had recommended to the National Energy Board that no pipeline be built along the Northern Yukon, and that the Mackenzie Valley pipeline construction be delayed for ten years. The NEB rejected Arctic Gas's application, and instead approved a rival pipeline from Alaska through the Yukon to the south. The proposals for these large-scale resource projects and the resulting Berger hearings and report have done much to focus public attention on the destructive nature of resources development, in terms of the lifestyle of the native people as well as the ecological effects. Whether this will result in any fundamental changes in present consumption and industrial development patterns is unclear. Much will depend on those who have to make the decisions, but just as great is the responsibility of the "average Canadian." If there are any still ignorant of these issues—as unfortunately many are—it is not the fault of a number of articulate, concerned and hard-working Canadians who have spelled out the critical dilemma Canada now faces.

Rotstein and the Precarious Homestead

Abraham Rotstein has made an important contribution to the debate on Canada's nationhood. His book *The Precarious Homestead* (1973) is a collection of his speeches and articles, many of which first appeared in *The Canadian Forum*.

In 1964 Rotstein entered the debate with a critique of Professor Harry Johnson's liberal economics. Johnson wrote that American capital in Canada did not threaten Canada's political independence since economics and politics are separate. Rotstein replied:

> In the last analysis, it is the market mentality of the economic liberal which is at the core of his political outlook: the market is impersonal and its participants are anonymous buyers and sellers of the factors of production. These factors, even if they are foreign, have no nationality since the market recognizes only quantity and price and the only criterion for judgment is efficiency. Are American capitalists different from Canadian capitalists? Of course not. Are American workers different from Canadian workers? Is anyone in Canada different from anyone in the United States? Not as long as he is regarded merely as a factor of production on the market. But there is no reason to mistake an economic abstraction, useful in analyzing market behaviour, for a political reality.[44]

In the opinion of Rotstein, the Canadian middle class is responsible for selling out much of Canada's resources to the Americans. He writes that no other business class "has presided so gracefully over its own liquidation." He describes the contemporary businessman's mentality in terms of the early homesteader's defence of his plot. "The truculent posture of the Canadian business community when confronted by reformist social and economic legislation is, we would argue, still rooted in the proprietary imperatives of a homesteading mentality."[45] The question is, How can we overcome this mentality and rezone the homesteads without a paralyzing collision? To begin with, suggests this spokesman for Canadian nationhood, a decentralized form of economic planning should take place through the creation of industry councils for each sector of the economy. Rotstein hopes that these councils would become fresh avenues for business thinking in national terms and provide for the coordination of public and private planning.[46]

Rotstein also takes issue with the other side of this controversy, the Left, which seeks the solution in wholesale nationalization. Rather, Rotstein suggests, we should learn from the Swedish experiment. The key to that understanding is the distinction between the title to property and the functions (or powers) of this property. In other words, the political structures should provide the framework within which economic activity takes place. Therefore, struggle for independence must come first. In the second phase, function should not be transferred from the corporation to the state, but from the corporation to its members. "The critical issue is the devolution of control, the attempt to institute greater democracy at the work place and in the community,"[47] Rotstein asserts.

For this reason Rotstein disagreed with the Waffle Manifesto, a statement adopted by the radical wing of the New Democratic Party (NDP).[48] Furthermore, he took issue with the Manifesto's reaction to the United States. He insisted that there is another America than the one of "militarism abroad and racism at home." He wrote: "A Manifesto which pivots on a reaction to America at a low point in its history is, in my view, not an enduring basis on which to construct the edifice of Canadian independence."[49]

"Americanization" is a worldwide process, Rotstein argues, in the sense that it represents Western man's obsession with industrialization. The multinational corporation has become of paramount significance because it carries the process of industrialization forward on a massive scale. Rotstein writes that the vital national interest is rooted in the major features of twentieth century life; namely technology, the computer and electronics. The new technology exerts great pressure on institutions and human values, but Rotstein counsels against premature despair:

> The essential ingredients of a mature approach to our new environment involve both a fundamental shift in our political values in recognition of the inexorable nature of technological interdependence, and a more conscious and deliberate attempt to protect the human character of our institutional and cultural endowment. No doubt the cost will have to be paid in terms of some technological efficiency. [50]

He sees the multinational corporation as an obstacle to national existence because of the great web of decision making exercised in favour of the home country and not of the host country. He warns that Canada, with more than half of its manufacturing industry under foreign ownership, is losing control in its own house. Therefore, he advocates regulation of the multinational corporation of a kind that goes beyond the traditional scope. "Instead, the aim should be to restore national control over a much wider range of functions, from research and development policy through to assuring the presence of Canadian personnel at the operating and management levels. The objective of this regulation should be to restore Canadian priorities on a broad front." [51]

In writing about the massiveness of our society, its loss of personal relations even in the teaching situation at the university, Rotstein gropes for certainty in the human condition. Obviously, these are the searchings of a deeply concerned man who senses that despair is just around the corner. He writes:

> The anonymous society must evoke from us a morality and a response appropriate to its complex character, so that meaning and significance can be re-defined in the new setting. The mass society is not amoral and certainly not, in my view, immoral. But the nature of a new faith required to sustain our activities in society, to give them meaning and purpose, has to be boldly examined and re-defined. We will have to create, in this new "tribal world," new myths to sustain us, as ethos, as attitudes, as roads to the future.

Seeing a connection between the fast pace of modern living and the distress of our times, he continues:

> A fear sets in, and a peculiar kind of courage is required. We are bombarded with impressions which the new media of communication fire at us in endless salvoes. We must sort these more quickly, respond instantly, decipher the

urgent from the trivial, the manipulations from the genuine pleas, and pursue the moral intuitions which we cannot relinquish. In an immediate sense we are all, in this new era, *unknown students*. [52]

Even if we fault Rotstein for seeking refuge in the creation of new myths, we can nonetheless sense and appreciate his deep concern, the compassion, the truth in much of what he writes about Canada's surrender to the get-rich-quick approach. Rotstein does us all a service when he tells us to slow down, to think again, to question the wisdom of blindly worshipping "progress" à la technique and economic liberalism.

Marx Revisited

The nationalists of the Left are not plagued by the unsettling questions raised by Abraham Rotstein. In their view, the choice is quite simply between Canada as a socialist nation or Canada as a colony of the United States. They view Canada's history in terms first of British, then of American, exploitation of Canada's people and its vast resources. They have amassed a wealth of evidence to suggest there is a great deal of truth to what they say in criticism of traditional and current economic and industrial development in Canada.

Within the past few years these defenders of Canadian nationhood have worked hard to alert Canadians to the dangers lurking in continentalism. Kari Levitt's *Silent Surrender* (1970) has been gratefully used by the socialists. Melville Watkins, chairman of the Task Force that wrote the Report on foreign ownership and the structure of Canadian industry in 1968, has played a prominent role in this movement. He coauthored the book *Gordon to Watkins to You* in 1970. James Laxer has focused on the energy resources development in his *The Energy Poker Game* (1970) and *Canada's Energy Crisis* (1974). *Close the 49th Parallel, etc.: The Americanization of Canada*, edited by Ian Lumsden (1970), and [*Canada*] *Ltd.: The Political Economy of Dependency*, edited by Robert Laxer (1973), also fit within this category. The last-named book contains a collection of speeches on Canadian economic issues in the context of American ownership and influence in Canada. In addition, members of this group have published material in *Canadian Dimension, The Last Post* and other periodicals.

The picture that unfolds from these writings is a Marxist critique of capitalism. Capitalism is founded on individual liberty and laissez faire. The "open door" policy was the result, and this evolved into a continental system, with the U.S. as the metropolis in charge of the vital controls (capital, management, markets) and Canada as the hinterland peopled by "hewers of wood and drawers of water." This "sellout" was aided and abetted by the Canadian business class anxious to enrich itself and indifferent to the real and long-term welfare of its own nation. The proposed solution of the socialist defenders of Canadian independence: eliminate American ownership and control in Canada and nationalize all industry—at least the "commanding heights" of the economy.

The Waffle Manifesto became the centre of debate at the 1969 Winnipeg convention of the New Democratic Party. The opening statement proclaims: "Our aim as democratic socialists is to build an independent socialist Canada." The authors of the Manifesto consider the very survival of Canada the most urgent issue facing Canadians. This survival is threatened because corporate capitalism is the shaping force in Canada reducing it to a "resource base and consumer market within the American empire." All economic and social ills derive from this basis. "Capitalism must be replaced by socialism, by national planning of investment and by the public ownership of the means of production in the interests of the Canadian people as a whole."[53] The Canadian working class and the trade union movement must play a central role in building an independent socialist Canada. The Manifesto predicts:

> A socialist transformation of society will return to man his sense of humanity, to replace his sense of being a commodity. But a socialist democracy implies man's control of his immediate environment as well, and in any strategy for building socialism, community democracy is as vital as the struggle for electoral success. To that end, socialists must strive for democracy at those levels which most directly affect us all—in our neighbourhoods, our schools, our places of work.[54]

The Manifesto was introduced at the 1969 convention by Mel Watkins as an appeal to the NDP for a more radical kind of politics. David Lewis, then national leader of the NDP, opposed Watkins and defended a more moderately-worded resolution. Watkins and his Wafflers lost by a vote of 499 to 268. For a few years, this group played a prominent role as the radical wing of the Canadian socialists. In 1972 it was expelled from the Ontario NDP and since then its collapse was accelerated by serious internal divisions.[55]

The Marxist concept of the crucial linkage between the productive system and culture plays an important role in this camp. Writing in [*Canada*] *Ltd.,* a collection of articles by socialist authors, Professor John Hutcheson of York University states: "Since social consciousness is primarily determined by 'social existence,' social consciousness in Canada today has been readied for a study of Marxism by the crisis of imperialism and de-industrialization we are now experiencing."[56] Another contributor to this same collection sees the liberal ideology as one that fragments social response, for it asserts the primacy of the individual and his rights. "It creates the wholly self-regarding individual and the despotic social order."[57]

The antidote to liberalism in Hutcheson's words is "a Canadian state controlled by the working people which would serve as an instrument of national liberation."[58] Mel Watkins called for taking control of the state for the purpose of taking power away from the owners of the means of production and giving it to the producers. He summed up his views:

> To do this would be to release the creative energies of the people. We could then begin to move to that humane and democratic society where the working people themselves will directly control the conditions under which they work. Then work, rather than being the oppression that it now is, would become an expression of our humanity.[59]

In discussing the nature of democratic socialism, the authors of *Gordon to Watkins to You* assert that power must be redistributed to ordinary people. They then quote the 1968 May Day Manifesto of the British New Left. Since this statement unequivocally reveals the secular humanism at the heart of modern socialism, it is worthwhile to consider it carefully:

> Our own first position is that all the issues—industrial and political, international and domestic, economic and cultural, humanitarian and radical—are deeply committed; that what we oppose is a political, economic and social system; that what we work for is a different whole society. The problem is one of whole men and women who are now habitually relegated to specialized . . . fields, where the society offers to manage or adjust them by this or that consideration or technique. Against this, we define socialism again as a humanism: a recognition of the social reality of man in all his activities, and of the consequent struggle for the direction of this reality by and for ordinary men and women.[60]

According to the Waffle Manifesto, a socialist transformation of society "will return to man his sense of humanity, to replace his sense of being a commodity." But how is that to be achieved? In Marxist fashion, by wresting the power from the capitalists and giving it to the people. This assumption is exceedingly crucial, for it involves the belief that man's place in society is dependent upon his relationship to the means of production. His social consciousness is determined by his "social existence." Man is master and servant at the same time. He is master when he owns the means of production; yet those means of production are determinative. How can he then be the real master? The Marxists are caught here in the old dilemma of humanism which results from the assumption of human autonomy: man is thought to be autonomous and competent to control nature, but he himself is part of that nature. That is the core of the problem of modern technique. Technique is the means of control (mastery) over nature, but in the process man, too, is tyrannized by his own technique. Even Marx recognized this dilemma and searched for avenues to "the realm of freedom" beyond "the realm of necessity" (technique).

Socialism is an effort to escape oppression by striving for real humanity. To achieve that one must understand the core of man. Who is he? What is he here for? Socialists answer those questions within the same frame of reference from which liberalism emerged. As Bruce Hutchison put it, both systems have "faith in wealth as the universal panacea." Charles Taylor, professor of political science and philosophy at McGill University, has expressed this dilemma as follows:

> Socialism in its present definitions is closely tied up with the economic self-image which it has borrowed from capitalist civilization. Perhaps it would be truer to say that both visions spring from the same civilization, born of the Enlightenment and the growth of industrial society.[61]

The socialists' faith—for that is what it is—makes them overlook the fundamental problems of technique. Their solution is therefore far too simplistic: expel the demon by expelling the Americans. They do not concern themselves much about what is to happen after ownership is restored to Canada and then centralized in the state. All the difficult problems of "humanizing" techniques would still be there. Life cannot be "humanized" by good intentions. Most importantly, the socialist "solution" would eliminate certain significant distinctions between the political and the economic—something which is bound to create other serious distortions. Moreover, a long and tiresome succession of liberating "revolutions" that turned sour should make us suspicious of grand and sweeping solutions.

The foregoing is not to deny that Mel Watkins and his fellow socialists have made many important contributions to a better understanding of our situation. Their critique of the present course of industrialization in Canada, dominated by the goals of American *and Canadian* business interests, often deserves our support. Particularly, their warnings against the reckless exploitation of our resources need to be heeded. The socialists have brought into relief a real problem that calls for an alternative and long-range industrial strategy.

Summary

Since the 1960s the need to impose certain restraints on the operation of multinational corporations has become more obvious to a growing number of people. Central to this issue is the predominant role of American-based multinationals in the world. An important contribution to this discussion came from the French socialist author J.J. Servan-Schreiber. In his book *The American Challenge* he warned against the dangers of the American corporate presence in Europe and prescribed an aggressive series of counter measures aimed at strengthening European industry. He emphasized the imperative of staying in the forefront of technological development and the need for a great deal more cooperation within the European community.

A vigorous debate about this topic took place within the United Nations organization in 1974 on publication of a commissioned report on the multinationals. There appeared to be a consensus among the participants that something in the way of an international agreement on multinational corporations was required. This agreement would cover the most controversial features of these corporations, such as ownership, capital and technology transfer, taxation, marketing and employment. Third World countries underscored the importance of bringing about a more equitable balance of development and wealth in a world now marked by staggering inequalities, but little progress was made in devising an international code of corporate behaviour.

The economic ties between the West and the Third World were profoundly affected by the dramatic price increase imposed by OPEC in late 1973. This altered the capital flow in the world, placing severe stress on the developed countries, but often having repercussions of a tragic nature for the developing countries. The multinational corporations, especially the giant oil companies, were at the centre of the new controversy. The efforts of raw material suppliers in the Third World, for example, the Andean Pact countries, to form a common front against the developed countries did not meet with outstanding success. The contention that multinational corporations are an excellent means of transferring the needed ingredients for industrialization to the Third World has not been convincing in the face of the growing disparity between the developed countries and the Third World.

Within the United States itself, there emerged a growing demand for the introduction of restraints upon the large corporations, many of whom belong to the multinational club. These efforts were further stimulated by startling exposures of corporate illegal activity involving kickbacks, bribes and other corrupt practices. The recommended reforms focused on the imposition of governmental restraints on corporations from the outside, as well as on building a greater measure of accountability or "democratization" into the corporate structure itself. Another set of widely debated policies governing American-based multinationals was aimed at improving the U.S. balance of payments, the national employment picture and export opportunities. Invariably, these protectionist measures would work to the detriment of those countries in which American subsidiaries are located.

The Canadian response to the overwhelming presence of multinational, mostly U.S.-based, corporations has become more critical and articulate since the mid-1960s. Three major reports on foreign ownership in Canada were produced under the auspices of the federal government. All three emphasized the mixed character of foreign ownership and recommended new policies that would enhance Canada's economic and cultural identity. A number of policy changes, aimed at reducing the relative size and importance of foreign-owned corporations, were recommended, but the response of the federal government was lukewarm and resulted in no major changes in policy or direction.

In the private sector the debate about the issue of Canadian nationalism versus our dependency on the United States was stepped up. The Committee for an Independent Canada, established in 1970, played a major role in focusing the attention on Canada's unenviable position and the need for drastic changes. The recommendations emanating from this source centred on ways to repatriate important sectors of the Canadian economy and to recover a greater measure of Canadian cultural autonomy.

The socialists were the most outspoken opponents of what they termed Canada's "hinterland" status. The left wing of the New Democratic Party stridently demanded radical measures via nationalization. They placed the dilemma in the perspective of the class struggle and the need for the working class to assert itself and to attain political power.

Despite this renewed concern about the high level of foreign ownership in the Canadian economy, the measures invoked by the federal government brought about little change, the establishment of the Foreign Investment Review Agency notwithstanding. Where efforts were made to improve Canada's position vis-à-vis the U.S., as in the auto industry, they proved to be less than a complete success.

The recurrent theme in the controversy surrounding multinational corporations concerns their potential and real power to undermine the integrity of the nation-state. It has become quite obvious that a fundamental critique of the very foundations of modern industrial societies is needed.

PART THREE: PROBING FOR THE ROOTS OF THE PROBLEM

Chapter 6
The Power of Technology

Nationalism can only be asserted successfully by an identification with technological advance: but technological advance entails the disappearance of those indigenous differences that give substance to nationalism.[1]

George Grant

The argument against modern tools like the computer is, in the end, an argument against reason itself. Not that a computer is a substitute for reason. Quite the contrary, it is the product of reason and it assists us in the application of reason.[2]

Robert S. McNamara

. . . the natural tendency to think of only one thing at a time is a chief reason why we have failed to understand the environment and have blundered into destroying it.[3]

Barry Commoner

The fresh wave of nationalism, and its attendant criticism of trends in Canada's economic and industrial development, focuses on a number of urgent problems. The domination of important industries by U.S. interests and the accumulative network of U.S. influences that have narrowed the scope of Canada's decision-making possibilities in significant areas do not contribute to a healthy national existence. Such foreign domination limits the freedom of Canada in reviewing its national priorities and in reordering the economic sector in accordance with priorities different from those of the U.S. The fact that these harmful effects have been highlighted in recent years provides a basis for some hope.

Concern about Canada's economic and industrial dependency centres on several major issues. First, the outflow of Canadian wealth (capital) to other countries, mostly the U.S., now seriously impairing Canada's balance of payments; second, the lack of opportunities for initiative and entrepreneurship in Canada; third, the dependence of Canada on U.S. political and economic objectives; fourth, the depletion of nonrenewable Canadian resources, condemning Canada to a perpetually inferior position; fifth, the "under-development" of secondary industry and the "overdevelopment" of the service sector, contributing to high unemployment rates.

All of the recommended reforms attempt to come to grips with these main problem areas. Consequently, the emphasis is invariably on more opportunities for Canadian equity investment, more research, development and entrepreneurship by Canadians, loosening the ties of U.S. political and economic forces and a drastic reduction in the exploitation and export of Canada's natural resources, as well as a stronger manufacturing base.

Closely related to this controversy is the question of the direction and control of technology. Some view the problem of regaining greater control over the Canadian economy in optimistic terms. Others, who probe deeper into the nature of modern society and the central role of technology in such a society, take a much more pessimistic position. In this context it will also be helpful to pay attention to a few non-Canadian authors who have critically analyzed technology and its power in modern society.

The Optimists

A number of nationalists are extremely optimistic about Canada's potential. They harbour no doubt about the possibilities for economic and cultural growth if only Canadians succeed in becoming masters of their own house. They view the U.S. influence in Canada as the roadblock to Canada's independence and greatness. Once that obstacle is eliminated, Canada will be a truly great nation. Walter Gordon speaks in that vein in the introduction to *A Choice for Canada*: "There can be no doubt that coming generations of Canadians have a tremendous future to look forward to, both in the short term and in the decades and centuries ahead, provided we retain our independence." [4]

D.W. Carr, author of *Recovering Canada's Nationhood,* describes Canada's economic potential and holds out the prospect of becoming an example to the rest of the world if only we will assert our initiative and determination. "Such a new Canadian initiative can be supported also by the recent and now increasingly urgent need to break out of the stagnant economic thinking into which many advanced countries of the world have fallen recently—a stagnation which in the past has always led to war at this stage. Canada is one of the few nations which could, by grasping the challenge, not only save herself from being overrun but also lead the world out of an alarmingly dangerous paralysis in economic philosophy."[5]

The group of optimists, which includes the Committee for an Independent Canada, stresses the need for repatriating the Canadian economy. The proposals they put forward are filled with glowing predictions of Canada's future in terms of an ever-rising standard of living, full employment, a favourable balance of payments, and so on. But such predictions betray a lack of appreciation for the depth of the problems that Canada now faces. They are misleading and give rise to great disillusionment if the predicted "progress" does not materialize.

It is unrealistic to assume that Canada can painlessly pull itself free from its deeply rooted entanglement with the U.S. economy, because that entanglement involves much more than many billions of dollars. It concerns an intricate network of management, entrepreneurial and marketing ties, as well as a complex of monetary arrangements and fiscal policies that are quite vulnerable. One does not have to be an expert economist to sense that such a deeply entrenched skein of interdependence cannot be drastically altered without certain hardships and sacrifices—at least in the short run. Even if the U.S. were willing to accept gracefully a full-scale repatriation by Canada, there would be plenty of problems. However, it is quite unlikely that the U.S. government and corporate leadership would react to such a move in the spirit of cooperation.

It would be more realistic to tell the Canadian people that their independence, or better, their national integrity, is at stake, that this integrity is essential for Canada's survival and that we must be prepared to accept, at least initially, a measure of hardship for the sake of maintaining that integrity. There is no doubt that Canada is in a very favourable position because of its immense resources, but if we seriously wish to alter current trends, we had better prepare ourselves for a difficult time. As George Grant writes: "Canada's survival has always required the victory of political courage over immediate and individual economic advantage."[6] If we are unwilling to muster that kind of courage, we may as well reconcile ourselves to more and more integration with the U.S.

The Pessimists

There is a second and even more compelling reason why it is unrealistic to assume that the proposals for asserting Canada's independence can be realized without a drastic change in our lifestyle, and this brings us to a discussion of the position held by those who may be called the pessimists. This position is articulated by George Grant and other critics. These individuals recognize that the earth's resources and, therefore, man's potential are finite and, more fundamentally, that it is an illusion to think that happiness can be found in economic and technical progress. It is important to keep in mind that the growing concern about Canada's nationhood in the light of the overpowering influence of the U.S. coincides with the dawning realization that the god of economic and technological growth has fallen on its face.

George Grant on Progress

George Grant has announced the death of Canada, because, like other Western countries, it has succumbed to worshipping the god of our age: progress through technology.[7] Consequently, "the aspirations of progress have made Canada redundant."[8] He writes that Canadian society accepted the dynamics of technology characterized by rationalism and efficiency. "The dynamism of technology has gradually become the dominant purpose in western civilisation because the most influential men in that civilisation have believed for the last centuries that the mastery of chance was the chief means of improving the race."[9] He calls the pursuit of this dynamic technology a "world-wide religion" and describes Canada as a "state capitalist" satellite of the "broader imperial system," meaning the U.S.[10] He blames Canada's surrender to this system on the new world-wide religion and on Canadian politicians and civil servants who supervised the post-war reconstruction. This reconstruction, writes Grant, was carried on "within the assumption that government action never questioned the ultimate authority of business interests to run the economy."[11] It was not in the interest of the economically powerful to be nationalists after 1940. "Most of them made more money by being the representatives of American capitalism and setting up the branch plants." This should not surprise us, Grant asserts, since capitalism is "a way of life based on the principle that the most important activity is profit making. That activity led the wealthy in the direction of continentalism. They lost nothing essential to the principle of their lives in losing their country."[12]

Nor is it the politicians, businessmen and civil servants alone who are responsible for Canada's collapse. Grant claims the idea of progress underlying that collapse must be seen in the context of man's striving for a universal and equalitarian society, which will be achieved by means of science and its conquest over nature. But this conquest extends over *human* nature as well as nonhuman nature. The scientists' victory in biochemistry and psychology will give the politicians the power to homogenize and universalize. Man will yet conquer and perfect himself. Grant then gives this perceptive summary:

> Modern civilization makes all local cultures anachronistic. Where modern science has achieved its mastery, there is no place for local cultures. It has often been argued that geography and language caused Canada's defeat. But

> behind these there is a necessity that is incomparably more powerful. Our culture floundered on the aspirations of the age of progress. The argument that Canada, a local culture, must disappear can, therefore, be stated in three steps. First, men everywhere move ineluctably toward membership in the universal and homogeneous state. Second, Canadians live next to a society that is the heart of modernity. Third, nearly all Canadians think that modernity is good, so nothing essential distinguishes Canadians from Americans. When they oblate themselves before "the American way of life," they offer themselves on the altar of the reigning Western goddess.[13]

Grant clearly sees the significance and consequence of man's obsession with technique and mastery over nature. He understands enough of the dilemma of our age to realize that superficial nationalism versus Americanism is a deception. He writes that we do not realize the ways in which technology has deprived us "because technique is ourselves."[14] Grant perceives that the Canadian situation is aggravated by the nearness of the American empire, but the foremost responsibility lies with the Canadian people and especially their leaders. The choice was made in favour of what Grant calls "the religion of progress" and it is ultimately that choice which dooms Canadian nationhood. He observes: "Indeed our involvement in the American empire goes deeper than a simple economic and political basis; it depends on the very faith that gives meaning and purpose to the lives of western men. To most Canadians, as public beings, the central cause of motion in their souls is the belief in progress through technique, and that faith is identified with the power and leadership of the English-speaking empire in the world."[15] Grant had hoped for years that

> . . . our ecclesiastical organisations (being the guardians of the beauty of the gospel) might continue to be able to permeate this society with something nobler than the barrenness of technical dynamism. I hoped for this when every piece of evidence before me was saying that it was not true. I could not face the fact that we were living at the end of western Christianity. I could not believe that the only interpretation of Christianity that technological liberalism would allow to survive publicly would be that part of it (e.g., the thought of Teilhard) which played the role of flatterer to modernity.[16]

At the core of modern technology lies man's obsession with the *preeminence* and the *autonomy* of human reason. Related to that is the notion that man can rationally arrive at the truth, which in our time has turned into the belief that man's power over his environment can be achieved through the *rational* use of his technical ability.

Jacques Ellul on Technique

In his book *The Technological Society* Jacques Ellul has painted a sombre picture of modern society. He defines technique as *"the totality of methods rationally arrived at and having absolute efficiency* (for a given stage of development) in *every* field of human activity. Its characteristics are new; the technique of the present has no common measure with that of the past."[17] Ellul views reality as "a combination of determinisms, and freedom consists in overcoming and transcending these determinisms." He asserts that in the modern world "the most dangerous form of determinism is the technological phenomenon."[18]

This author warns us not to think only of machines when we think of technique. Machines are necessary for technical development, but in our time technique has become much more than the use of machines. It has extended into our entire lives as an integrating process. He writes:

> But when technique enters into every area of life, including the human, it ceases to be external to man and becomes his very substance. It is no longer face to face with man but is integrated with him, and it progressively absorbs him. In this respect, technique is radically different from the machine. This transformation, so obvious in modern society, is the result of the fact that technique has become *autonomous*.[19] (Emphasis added.)

Technique in the modern age has become an all-pervasive force affecting every feature of our lives, Ellul asserts. Modern technique has exchanged ends for means; it has become an end in itself. Technique is characterized by rationality, universality and efficiency. In the process of storming the world, technique has destroyed genuine communities and individuality, for the latter stands in the way of an *efficient* ordering of the world. Ellul displays insight into the fact that the development of technique, subject only or mainly to the criterion of efficiency, undermines the quality of human life as it comes to expression in the variety of social structures and relationships such as the work community, the political community, the home and the school.

Nowhere does Ellul see any real alternatives and he provides very little hope for the possibility of renewal. His book offers an impressive array of arguments in support of the position that technique has become autonomous and destructive. The author ranges over every important segment of modern life to show the deadening effects of modern technique. He elaborates on the use of technique in economic, social and political life, including education, medicine, leisure, the media and work, picturing the inexorable march toward a future of well-adjusted robots. Ellul perceptively scrutinizes the so-called human techniques aimed at adapting man to an alien environment. He has harsh criticism for the scientists who tinker with man, yet refuse to assume any responsibility for the whole man, or pretend that they know how man can be "happy" and "well-adjusted."

All modern societies, whether capitalist, fascist or communist, claims Ellul, share the fundamental aspiration of the "good life." All pin their hopes on technique for a solution to current problems in the context of adjusting man to the machine. Every problem is seen as a technical problem demanding an efficient technical solution. It is this necessity that lurks at the centre of the technological society described by Ellul. Even revolt serves as an integrating force in this process of building a completely technicized society. The magazine *Krokodil* serves as the official mouthpiece for criticism of Soviet policy. But it does not provide any possibilities for an alternative lifestyle; it merely functions as a safety valve and thus further reinforces the system.

Ellul shows that the elevation of technique to a commanding role in society has profoundly affected work. Work has been made subservient to the production-consumption cycle. Thus the role of advertising is to create needs and to condition men for their role in what has become a technical process. "The important concern is not the psychic and mental structure of the human being but the uninterrupted flow of any and all goods which invention allows the economy to produce,"[20] Ellul asserts. He agrees that labour unions arose as a great human protest against exploitation, but in all countries they have lost their original character and now are purely technical organizations.

He is aware of the great damage done to workers by the predominance of technique in the service of efficiency and maximum production. Ellul understands that work is an expression of our humanity and that there are no substitutes for meaningful work which puts men in touch with each other and with nature. But everything done within the modern work situation serves to strengthen the bonds of technique and isolate men from each other and from nature. All the contemporary emphasis on man within the work situation has as its aim his adaptation to the machine. "Man is doubtless made more comfortable by techniques of human relations; but these techniques are wholly oriented toward compelling man to submit to forced labor. Machine and productivity are in the driver's seat."[21]

Ellul discusses the utopian dreams about a "golden age" to come, dreamt by those scientists who continue to rely on man's technical powers. They boast of their ability to manipulate and control man's genes and personality. The author scorns the folly of such dreams:

> None of our wise men ever pose the question of the end of all their marvels. The "wherefore" is resolutely passed by. The response which would occur to our contemporaries is: for the sake of happiness. Unfortunately, there is no longer any question of that. One of our best-known specialists in diseases of the nervous system writes: "We will be able to modify man's emotions, desires and thoughts, as we have already done in a rudimentary way with tranquillizers." It will be possible, says our specialist, to produce a conviction or an impression of happiness without any real basis for it. Our man of the golden age, therefore, will be capable of "happiness" amid the worst privations. Why, then, promise us extraordinary comforts, hygiene,

> knowledge, and nourishment if, by simply manipulating our nervous systems, we can be happy without them? The last meager motive we could possibly ascribe to the technical adventure thus vanishes into thin air through the very existence of technique itself.[22]

Robert L. Heilbroner on the Human Prospect

Robert Heilbroner, one of America's outstanding authors on economics and the history of economics, recently added his voice to the chorus of dark forebodings about the future. In 1968 Heilbroner could still write in his book *The Economic Problem* that prospects for a future of abundance and thus a radically altered economics looked very promising. He pinned this hope for ending the age of scarcity on man's technical mastery over nature although he still raised the question whether men "will use their triumph over nature to achieve a much more difficult victory over themselves."[23]

A mere six years later Heilbroner's optimism had vanished. By that time he had written *An Inquiry into the Human Prospect* which is an attempt to explain man's predicament. Therein he ascribes the pall that has fallen on America to the confidence-shaking events of our time, including the Vietnam war and other forms of violence, terror and cruelty that have been crowding in on us. The generation gap and the general loosening of all moral and social restraints have added to the disquieting mood of our times. Furthermore, the loss of assurance in man's rational and technical ability to solve social problems has added a new dimension to modern life, writes Heilbroner. Then there is the growing awareness that man's environment is deteriorating and no longer able to sustain economic growth, long considered to be the basis of all solutions. These disconcerting features are underscored by yet another one which he calls the "civilizational malaise." This civilization which is based on the pursuit of material improvements fails to provide the motivating force for the human spirit. It is this complex of changes in our generation that has brought on Heilbroner's pessimism. He writes:

> The outlook for man, I believe, is painful, difficult, perhaps desperate, and the hope that can be held out for his future prospect seems to be very slim indeed. Thus, to anticipate the conclusions of our inquiry, the answer to whether we can conceive of the future other than as a continuation of the darkness, cruelty, and disorder of the past seems to me to be no; and to the question of whether worse impends, yes.[24]

Distinguishing between the *external* threats and our *internal* capacity to cope with them, Heilbroner lists three major sources of external threats to our existence.First of all, the outlook of a rapid increase of the world population within the next two or three generations presents us with insoluble problems. World population in 1974 was roughly 3.6 billion.

Population growth rates are uneven with faster increases in the underdeveloped world. At the current rate of growth, the total world population will be more than 40 billion one hundred years from now. The Malthusian check of famine and disease will likely intervene, but that only underscores how desperate this situation really is.

In the second place, Heilbroner foresees the threat of nuclear warfare, particularly in the form of blackmail by underdeveloped nations against the industrialized nations.

Thirdly, the modern world is confronted with the prospect of a collapsing environment and depleted resources. Even if the search for new resources were to be successful for a long time to come, and this is very doubtful, mankind would be up against one irremovable obstacle—thermal pollution. All forms of industrial production require the use of energy and all energy emits heat. The limit of our environment for the absorption of heat will be approached within a relatively short time at the *present rate* of growth. According to one study, the earth's temperature will rise by about 50° centigrade in approximately 250 years. The implications of this phenomenon are staggering.

Heilbroner, like Ellul, asserts that science and technology are the "driving forces of our age." It is "their fusion in a civilization that has developed scientific technology in a lopsided manner, giving vent to its disequilibrating or perilous aspects without matching these ill effects with compensating benign technologies or adequate control mechanisms."[25]

In a discussion on the relative importance of the controversy between socialism and capitalism, Heilbroner concludes that both isms are equally beset by the overriding threats of our age. In words reminiscent of Charles Taylor, he reminds us that below the surface differences there is "a substratum of common problems that spring from the industrial civilization of both systems." He continues:

> For industrial civilization achieves its economic success by imposing common values on both its capitalist and socialist variants. There is the value of the self-evident importance of efficiency, with its tendency to subordinate the optimum human scale of things to the optimum technical scale. There is the value of the need to "tame" the environment, with its consequence of an unthinking pillage of nature. There is the value of the priority of production itself, visible in the care both systems lavish on technical virtuosity and the indifference with which both look upon the aesthetic aspects of life. All these values manifest themselves throughout bourgeois and "socialist" styles of life, both lived by the clock, organized by the factory or office, obsessed with material achievements, attuned to highly quantitative modes of thought—in a word, by styles of life that, in contrast with non-industrial civilizations, seem dazzlingly rich in every dimension except that of the cultivation of the human person. The malaise that I believe flickers within our consciousness thus seems to afflict industrial socialist as well as capitalist societies, because it is a malady ultimately rooted in the "imperatives" of a common mode of production.[26]

We need to strive for a static economy, he says, but this would demand of both capitalist and socialist systems that they achieve a just income distribution. In an expanding economy, the income of all can rise, but in a stationary one the lower income population can only raise theirs by diminishing the share of the higher income receivers. Such a redistribution would engender serious social and political conflicts, within either a socialist or a capitalist society.

A radically different future awaits us, Heilbroner predicts. "In place of the long established encouragement of industrial production must come its careful restriction and long-term diminution within society. In place of prodigalities of consumption must come new frugal attitudes."[27] The question is whether such a drastic change will be achieved voluntarily. In Heilbroner's opinion it will take dictatorial power, the kind now used in China, to bring about these vast transformations. He writes:

> Thus in all likelihood we must brace ourselves for the consequences of which we have spoken—the risk of "wars of redistribution" or of "preemptive seizure," the rise of social tensions in the industrialized nations over the division of an ever more slow-growing or even diminishing product, and the prospect of a far more coercive exercise of national power as the means by which we will attempt to bring these disruptive processes under control. From that period of harsh adjustment, I can see no realistic escape.
>
> If then, by the question "Is there hope for man?" we ask whether it is possible to meet the challenges of the future without the payment of a fearful price, the answer must be: No, there is no such hope.[28]

Heilbroner admits that before this prospect "the spirit quails and the will falters," but he has "no intention of sounding a call for moral awakening or for social action on some unrealistic scale."[29] Yet he does not advise us to adopt an attitude of passive resignation. This applies especially to the intellectual elements of Western nations. He admonishes his readers to view these immense problems and threats as challenges that must be overcome. *If* they are overcome, *and only if*, the surviving society will be totally different from the present one; scarce resources will have to be carefully husbanded and production will be drastically reorganized. It will be a transformation that seems to imply the end of the grand factory, the huge office and perhaps the urban complex.

What is Heilbroner's ultimate source of confidence—if such it may be called? Not the spirit of Prometheus—the spirit from which modern man has obtained his driving energy and nervous will. That is what has landed him in his present predicament. Instead Heilbroner turns to another figure of Greek mythology, that of Atlas,

> bearing with endless perseverance the weight of the heavens in his hands. If mankind is to rescue life, it must first preserve the very will to live, and thereby rescue the future from the angry condemnation of the present. The spirit of

> conquest and aspiration will not provide the inspiration it needs for this task. It is the example of Atlas, resolutely bearing his burden, that provides the strength we seek. If, within us, the spirit of Atlas falters, there perishes the determination to preserve humanity at all cost and any cost, forever.—But Atlas is, of course, no other but ourselves. [30]

Is There a Way Out?

It has become somewhat fashionable today to write in the vein of Ellul and Heilbroner. This marks the beginning of a new era. The erstwhile confidence in the onward march of progress in terms of man's mastery over nature is gradually being replaced by new attitudes of caution, doubt and even despair.

The Club of Rome and the Limits to Growth

In 1972 the Club of Rome, a group of experts in both the natural and social sciences, produced *The Limits to Growth,* a book that has been widely discussed. It contains the results of the Club's study on the earth's resources versus the rate of their depletion. This report constitutes a scientific study—with the aid of a "world model" and computers—of five major trends of global concern: accelerating industrialization, rapid population growth, widespread malnutrition, depletion of nonrenewable resources and a deteriorating environment.

The startling conclusion was that if the present growth rate in these five areas continues unchanged, the limits to growth on this planet will be reached within the next one hundred years. The only way to avoid the resultant collapse will be to reduce growth and even establish a condition of ecological and economic stability. This raises profound questions about existing relations between rich and poor nations, for in a stable environment the need for an equitable distribution of income and resources is much more compelling than in a growth-oriented setting. The major problem, as explained by the Club of Rome, lies in the tendency for growth in population to take place exponentially rather than in a linear fashion. (For example, the world population at the present rate of increase will double in a mere thirty years!)

The warning contained in *The Limits to Growth* strikes at the roots of the beliefs underlying our society. The changes required are revolutionary and traumatic. The Club of Rome places the major responsibility for this change on the more developed nations, "not because they have more vision of humanity, but because having propagated the growth syndrome, they are still at the fountainhead of the progress that sustains it." [31]

E.J. Mishan and the Costs of Economic Growth

Another warning against making technological and economic growth the number one aim comes from the eminent British economist E.J. Mishan who published *The Costs of Economic Growth* in 1967.[32] Mishan proceeds to attack the myth that economic growth and human welfare are synonymous. He points to the mounting social costs or "external diseconomies" that have accompanied our headlong rush into an ever-expanding gross national product. He argues that we have many more choices than the present race for more and more. But such an alternative choice demands a break with "growthmania." It requires nothing less than what Mishan calls "a new vision of the purposes of life."[33] He disputes that we are locked into the need for expanding output:

> It is quite possible to arrange things as to produce a good deal fewer gadgets and instead to enjoy more leisure. And, although blasphemous to utter, it is also possible to train fewer scientists and engineers without our perishing from the face of the earth. Nor do we need to capture world markets in the hope of being able to lower costs; or to lower costs in the hope of capturing world markets. We can, while acting as rational beings, deliberately choose to reduce our foreign trade and in some lines, therefore, to produce smaller quantities at a somewhat higher cost. We can even decide to reduce the strains of competition and opt for an easier life. All these choices and many others can be translated into perfectly practicable alternatives whenever public opinion is ready to consider them. [34]

In *The Costs of Economic Growth,* Mishan ranges over many ways in which modern life is restricted and genuine humanity smothered despite fantastic strides in technical achievements—or because of them. In describing these "unmeasurable consequences of economic growth," the author is aware of the central role played by the belief that mankind can find salvation in science. Mishan describes modern science as "some ponderous multi-purpose robot that is powered by its own insatiable curiosity."[35] He understands that there is a direct connection between a repudiation of our faith in God and the growing estrangement among men. By the same token, he believes the revival of faith in God will help people to come closer to one another. The faith in a personal God that enables man to open his innermost heart to his Maker also enables him to open his heart to his fellowman.[36]

Discussing the effects of the modern means of transportation and tourism, Mishan draws the conclusion that "the invention of the private automobile is one of the great disasters to have befallen the human race." He sees that "the motor industry has come to dominate the economy as brazenly as its products dominate our physical environment."[37] He does not despair of the possibilities of an alternative lifestyle, but such would have to be accomplished by a fundamental change in our concept of welfare and our attitude toward economics and technology. It would call for measures that would halt the ruthless encroachment on men and nature. This would involve a "rejection of economic growth as a prior aim of policy," a recognition of "the individual's right to amenity," and "a substantial diversion of investible resources from industry to the task of re-planning our towns and cities."[38]

E.F. Schumacher and an Intermediate Technology

Any discussion of authorities who have spoken against the worship of economic growth and technical progress must include a reference to the late E.F. Schumacher who in 1973 published his *Small Is Beautiful: A Study of Economics As If People Mattered.*[39]

This economist, long associated with the National Coal Board of England as an economic advisor, wrote and lectured extensively on the impact of technology on developing nations. He perceived clearly that the resources of the world as well as man's own nature do not allow a continuation of the present trends in economic and industrial activity that dominate industrialized nations. The root of the current crisis, according to Schumacher, lies in man's preoccupation with production and his attempt to consider as worthless anything that cannot be expressed in monetary values. The result is estrangement among men and between man and nature. He sums up his evaluation of the present situation as follows:

> First, human nature revolts against inhuman technological, organizational, and political patterns, which it experiences as suffocating and debilitating; second, the living environment which supports human life aches and groans and gives signs of partial breakdown; and, third, it is clear to anyone fully knowledgeable in the subject matter that the inroads being made into the world's non-renewable resources, particularly those of fossil fuels, are such that serious bottlenecks and virtual exhaustion loom ahead in the quite foreseeable future.[40]

Changes are needed in two fundamental ways, Schumacher insisted. First of all, we need to turn away from a materialistic lifestyle and to appreciate the true needs of man and his right relationship to nature. Secondly, this new awareness, which Schumacher advised must be derived from the Christian faith, must also lead to "a technology with a human face." This technology, which he defined as "intermediate," must break with the inherently violent and ecologically damaging methods of the technology of mass production. Instead, technology must be as simple as possible, conducive to decentralization, compatible with the laws of ecology, gentle in its use of resources, and designed to serve the human person instead of making him the servant of machines. Schumacher asserted that this intermediate technology is of special importance for developing nations, but it is equally necessary for industrialized nations to adopt this new approach to technique.

This author also made a number of important suggestions regarding the restructuring of the large-scale corporation, something which he considered essential in the needed transformation. He suggested that ownership rights traditionally reserved for the holders of capital be dispersed among many people by the issuance of what he calls shares of the "public hand." Under this plan all privately-held shares would be matched by shares of the public hand, purchased with funds derived from company taxes.

Schumacher was convinced that more than merely technical adjustments must be made. He argued that man's imagined mastery and ruthless exploitation of nature have been challenged by the events of our time. He wrote that instead of man's independence and power, these events proclaim this message:

> "Seek ye *first* the kingdom of God, and all these things [the material things which you also need] shall be *added* unto you." They shall be added, we are told, here on earth where we need them, not simply in an after-life beyond our imagination. . . . It is becoming apparent that there is not only a promise but also a threat in those astonishing words about the kingdom of God—the threat that unless you seek first the kingdom, these other things, which you also need, will cease to be available to you. [41]

Human Responsibility Versus Technological Necessity

The problem of the power of technology outlined above is directly related to the issue of Canada's integrity versus integration with the U.S. Those, such as George Grant and Abraham Rotstein, who emphasize that we must come to grips with technology as well as with Canadian nationalism are right. The question is whether we need to share Jacques Ellul's negative evaluation of technology or whether there are grounds for a more hopeful outlook.

There are many reasons why Ellul's discussion of technique needs to be taken seriously. Technique has indeed become an all-pervasive force in our society and it has contributed to artificiality and to the restriction of life. Ellul's writings demonstrate a keen grasp of the problems of modern society. But his assumption that technique is *inherently* restricting and damaging to genuine human relationships must be disputed.

Ellul is a Christian, and he believes in the possibility of overcoming the necessities of technique, but it appears that he thinks this is only possible by "transcending" technique and finding one's refuge in faith. He does not seem to believe in the possibility of redirecting and restructuring *technique itself*.

It is imperative that we clearly perceive the way man's beliefs have shaped our modern society, dominated by technique. The major belief of Western society is faith in man as a rational and autonomous being who can use his scientific and technological powers to control nature *and in that way find his fulfilment.* Raymond Aron has described this characteristic as follows:

> The exploitation of natural resources has to be recognized as a major characteristic of modern society, without precedent at least as regards quantity. At the same time, this technical mastery expresses a new attitude: the will to dominate the natural environment instead of being dominated by it and, in addition, a concern for measurement, rational organization, and forecasting the future.[42]

Aron perceives the effect of the new attitude on the organization of labour as follows:

> Modern societies are defined first and foremost by their organization of labor; that is, by their relationship to the external world, their use of machinery, the application of scientific methods, and the social and economic consequences of the rationalization of production.[43]

The essential characteristic of modern faith is its assumption of human independence (autonomy). This assumed independence has led to a strange paradox. We have created our own gods but these gods have turned on us and enslaved us instead of liberating us. Commenting on the structure of our society, which he describes as "economistic, rationalistic and technocratic," Bob Goudzwaard, a Dutch economist, shows that it has been determined by a *religious* choice. He writes:

> We, in our western civilization, have first given our trust to the powers of economic growth, science and technique to lead us in all our ways—and we are still following these powers as our infallible guides. But, correspondingly, we have turned *ourselves* into images of these gods, and find these traces of ourselves back in the structures of our present-day, growth-possessed society. For it cannot be denied, that our society displays a powerful *belief* in the full self-sufficient autonomy of economic development as the source of both private and social happiness. Human reason, technical progress and autonomous economic development—behold your gods, who are able to deliver you from any house of bondage and bring you into the promised land of welfare! And now, in our modern cultures, we are confronted with the consequences of this religious choice.[44]

Whereas Ellul places the emphasis on the "necessities" of technique, it is more correct to place the emphasis on man's responsibility and to see that technique is not an autonomous monster but the product of man. In other words, the problem *begins* with man's imagined autonomy.[45]

It should be obvious that the present trend in our society is destructive.

We have mentioned a few outstanding spokesmen who have drawn that conclusion, hoisted the warning flag and either despaired of any solution or issued suggestions for finding a way of escape from the looming disaster. But very few point to the need of thoroughly reassessing man's underlying belief in his self-sufficiency. Yet that is where a genuine alternative has to begin.

Chapter 7
Roadblocks to Renewal

Continentalism had divorced Canadians from their history, crippled their creative capacity, and left them without the power to fashion a new future for themselves. Even the will to defend their independence and protect their national identity had been weakened; they seemed scarcely to be aware of the danger in which they stood.[1]

Donald Creighton

Our social order today is suffering from a sense of futility and insecurity born of the intellectual confusion of a fragmented and largely secular society. We represent the paradox of the wealthy who may be empty; of the learned whose knowledge may bring no enlightenment; of the masters of society who may be timid and afraid.[2]

Vincent Massey

As we have seen in the previous chapter, George Grant darkly predicts the disappearance of the Canadian nation because the people have surrendered to the modern notion of progress and freedom. This perceptive Canadian has understood that man's imagined mastery over nature is self-destructive.

A Cry for the Beloved Country

Another outstanding Canadian who must be mentioned in this context is Bruce Hutchison, longtime journalist-author-historian, who has written extensively, with feeling and insight, about the Canadian people. He has consistently admonished his countrymen for mismanaging their resources and failing to ask themselves some urgent questions.

Two pieces of Hutchison's writings on this subject stand out. In July 1971 *Maclean's* published an "Open Letter" from Hutchison to Prime Minister Trudeau. Here he expressed concern over Canada's future, saying that the country was facing the most wrenching times in its history. Hutchison warned that Canadians are miscalculating their assets and liabilities and inclined to lose themselves in "a queer reaction of combined inferiority and superiority." He wrote: "According to the conventional wisdom, the danger lies mainly in the United States and its latest northward surge of Manifest Destiny. As a final proposition, I venture to assert that we are ignoring the true source of danger and baying off, like bewildered bloodhounds, on a false scent." After reviewing the various layers of upheaval taking place in the United States, Hutchison pointed to the fact that we must face the fundamental questions of our existence.

> What, after all, is life intended for? What is the human creature's appointed place and function in the universe? Why has he distorted and defaulted them? To the truly ultimate questions no answer can come from the politicians, the economists, the scientists or the men of business. None from the practical men of any kind, only from the philosophers.

Hutchison stated that the whole world is being Americanized "in style of living, in uses of gadgets, in hunger for goods and easy, predigested ideas." Yet our nationality is not destined to disappear if we are able to distinguish the gloss from reality. We can take certain measures to retain ownership of our resources and in other ways remain master in our own house. But all these measures will only succeed if we can achieve "broad national agreement within Canada." Hutchison asserted: "The decisive question is clear and simple: How much are we prepared to pay in work, money, goods, and, above all, in wisdom for the privilege of being Canadian?"[3]

In September 1972 Hutchison directed a more urgent message to his fellow Canadians, again in the pages of *Maclean's*. In "The Storming of the World" he called for a drastic change in our attitude toward our environment and its resources. Discussions with leading scientists during a visit to the Massachusetts Institute of Technology impelled Hutchison to alert us to the impending collapse of our environment unless we change our way of life. This truth "makes sad gibberish of our economic folklore, our smug ideologies and, in fact, just about everything we have been taught to believe." Hutchison is convinced that this dilemma is not primarily economic or political, but spiritual, in nature. "The test ahead of us is not a test of our social apparatus but of ourselves." The limits to growth now confronting man "mean that the entire economic imperative and, far more importantly, the psychic foundation on which all societies are built must be demolished, the wisdom and central axiom of the ages reversed." He continues:

> All our plans for a brave new world of peace, abundance and justice are sheer moonshine, since they are built on the assumption of steady, rapid and unlimited economic growth. We have always believed it would perpetually raise our living standards, our consumption of goods, our leisure time. It would abolish poverty, unemployment and inflation. It would dissolve the conflicts of class, end the violence of our Western societies, feed the hungry nations, even give them an affluence like ours, and eventually, under a world government, lead us to the promised land.

But all these assumptions, he adds, have turned out to be dangerous illusions. He wonders how people will react to the new realities and how governments will adjust if they can no longer continue to promise an ever soaring standard of living. Before the new predicament, the ideologies of communism and capitalism fade into irrelevancy. Both systems are committing assault on the earth's limited resources—both embrace the "faith in wealth as the universal panacea." Mankind is experiencing punishment for his crime against the earth. Man must find a new "course," but what is it? Hutchison answers: "This is the transcendent question, as practical as it is moral, and now suddenly more urgent than it has ever been in the past. It asks man to reconsider not merely his routine workaday methods but his place, purpose and destination in a universe of harsh penalties and earned rewards stretching from his terrestrial speck to the farthest star."[4]

Grant and Hutchison deserve much more attention than they have received from their fellow Canadians. They exhort us to discontinue worshipping the god of progress in the mantle of technology and a higher "standard of living." They perceive that this idol, like all idols, has a way of devouring its worshippers. Yet they realize we cannot cast out the demon by expelling the Americans. If these two eminent Canadians provide very few answers, their unsettling questions are a healthy antidote to the suffocating complacency and the easy answers that are still all too common.

Donald Creighton, Canadian historian, long-time professor of history at the University of Toronto, must also be mentioned among those who are deeply troubled about Canada's future. Creighton's switch from an early heady optimism to current despair is remarkable. Writing in 1957 about Canada's postwar evolvement into a self-confident nation taking its place among the free nations within the Commonwealth, the United Nations and the North Atlantic Treaty Organization, Creighton asserted that "the same robust feeling of confidence in the future found expression in Canada's words and deeds as a North American power. Nobody troubled any longer to give serious consideration to the old fear of annexation to the United States."[5] This historian pointed out that Canadian public opinion also showed itself unanimously opposed to the project of a North American commercial union. According to Creighton, a multitude of associations between the two countries "did not weaken Canada's consciousness of her own identity or her belief in her own standards and values." Discussing the growth of Canadian literature and the arts, he confidently claimed that the country "was slowly ceasing to be a submissive province of a larger cultural empire."[6] Canada had come of age, thought Creighton.

However, this same author has since become appalled at the prospect of continentalism. What is worse, Canadians are not even aware of the threats to their existence. Provincial and federal governments alike are often addressing themselves to bogus issues. The federal government, "too intimidated to raise the vital issue of the redivision of legislative powers and too cowed to urge the need of wider federal jurisdiction, busied itself mainly with individual and group rights, language guarantees, and changes in the composition and functions of the Senate—'Senate reform' being one of the stalest and most fraudulent of all exercises in Canadian politics."[7]

All the while, Creighton detects the breakdown of the body of political theory and social and moral philosophy that at one time was common to the whole of British North America. The final disintegration came as the price Canadians paid for rapid economic development: the loss of national identity. Continentalism divorced Canadians from their history and sapped their will to fight for their independence. They became indifferent to their glorious British heritage of constitutional monarchy and representative institutions, wrote Creighton in 1967:

> Canadians were almost incapable of realizing that their great nineteenth-century creations had been lost or destroyed and that they had literally nothing of their own to replace what had irrevocably vanished. They had permitted their government to turn its back on their past and to repudiate their history; and in the bankruptcy of their own national philosophy, they turned instinctively to the nearest available creditor, the United States. . . . Imitation and plagiarism had become deep-seated Canadian instincts; economic and political dependence had grown into a settled way of life. It was only through a great collective effort, in which both English Canadians and French Canadians fully participated, that the nation could have escaped from its mental vassalage and recovered its independent powers of creation and self-determination. But the new dominance of ethnic values in Canadian domestic politics and the resulting outbreak of cultural conflict had destroyed national unity at the moment when it was desperately needed.[8]

In a 1975 article in *Maclean's,*[9] Creighton focused on the far-reaching effects of the energy crisis triggered by the huge increases in the price of crude oil. Too long Canada had turned a blind eye to reality. Canadians had unthinkingly joined the race for an ever higher standard of living and a greater dependence on the export of resources. Creighton wrote that the Canadian people and their governments have been afflicted by "growth-mania." This has resulted in a rapid depletion of readily available resources, a grossly expanded government bureaucracy and a swift increase in the supply of money. Short-run policies have left Canadian governments hesitantly limping between fighting the twin evils of inflation and unemployment. In the process, Canadians have sold their birthright to the Americans. Creighton said: "Canada was like a spendthrift who had run through his own inheritance and had engaged himself as a permanently indentured servant to a very hard-up master." In the face of this dependency and the loss of national vigour, he predicts a difficult road ahead: "A very grim future awaits the elaborate urban civilization which has grown up in Canada during the past 30 years."[10]

Though we might like to dismiss these dire predictions as undue pessimism, it would be folly for us to disregard the warnings of this noted Canadian historian.

Canada's Vertical Mosaic

Since it first appeared in 1965, *The Vertical Mosaic,* John Porter's study of Canadian society, has been hailed as a milestone in Canadian sociology.[11] James Heap, a Canadian sociologist, claimed that with this volume "sociology fully arrived as a major discipline in Canada. . . . It has become more than a major text in sociology. Its wide and continued use by political scientists and historians marks it as the major social scientific work of the sixties."[12]

Canada is not a genuine democracy for there is no true equality of all people, Porter insists. On the basis of extensive statistical information and his concept of class and power, he concludes that power in Canadian society is concentrated in a relatively closed and small group of elite. This group maintains its privileged position by means of ready access to superior education, a disproportionate share of income and wealth, kinship and friendship ties and by means of an interlocking web of functions in business, politics, higher education and the media. "Canada . . . has a long way to go to become in any sense a thoroughgoing democracy."[13]

Porter demonstrates that income distribution in Canada is grossly unequal.[14] In 1955, 74 per cent of all income recipients received less than $4,000 per year while 2.2 per cent received $10,000 and over. Higher education was much more readily available to those in the top income levels. He found a heavy concentration of corporate power in a few hands, singling out 183 "dominant corporations" which controlled a disproportional share of the country's wealth. At the head of the corporations were 985 men whom Porter designated as the country's elite. Through interlocking directorships and a self-perpetuating power base, this elite has access to the vital areas including politics and the media.

Using a pragmatic concept of value systems, this sociologist describes beliefs and values in terms of an evolutionary social process. He is a vigorous advocate of equality of opportunity but is pessimistic about the prospect of change in the face of opposition on the part of the elite, and apathy and withdrawal on the part of the disadvantaged. He concludes his lengthy book with this essentially pessimistic finding:

> Given the complexities of modern societies it is unlikely that widespread participation can develop without very great changes and institutional experimentation. If power and decision-making must always rest with elite groups, there can at least be open recruitment from all classes into the elites.
>
> Canada is a new society, and should have had great opportunities for in-

> stitutional innovation, but so far it has been incapable of taking a lead in the changes and experimentation necessary for more democratic industrial societies. A fragmented political structure, a lack of upward mobility into its elite and higher occupational levels, and the absence of a clearly articulated system of values, stemming from a charter myth or based in an indigenous ideology, are some of the reasons for this retardation. [15]

In 1975 Wallace Clement of Carleton University, Ottawa, wrote *The Canadian Corporate Elite: An Analysis of Economic Power,* in which he continues and deepens the theme of Porter's earlier study.[16] The basic values underlying the book "are contained within the idea of democracy." He is critical of the freedom of liberal democracies "which must, however, be set within the context of basic inequalities," but he is hopeful that the inequalities now present can be removed in the future society.[17]

Focusing on the existence of elites, Clement defines them as "a set of uppermost positions within any given institutional sphere that is arranged in a definite hierarchy." An elite to be a social group "requires that its structure be specified, that members of the group interact and are related to one another sufficiently to say they exhibit solidarity, cohesiveness, coordination and consciousness of kind."[18] Clement holds that the Canadian corporate elite meets these conditions of class on the basis of ownership and control of capital and other resources. The perpetuation of this class is accomplished by accessibility on the part of members of the same class and the lack of such accessibility on the part of others. Clement distinguishes among national or indigenous elites, comprador elites who operate the branch plants of foreign-based corporations and parasite elites who are the heads of multinational corporations outside the host country.

Clement classifies corporations as dominant on the basis of assets greater than $250 million and annual income in excess of $50 million. Within this group there is a high degree of oligopoly. In 1972 there were 113 such dominant corporations with a total of 1,454 directorships held by Canadian residents and another 301 held outside Canada.[19]

The criteria for dominant size used by this author differ from those of Porter; hence the categories chosen by each are not comparable. But the trend toward larger size through mergers is obvious—41 of the 183 corporations identified by Porter as dominant had been reduced to 17 by 1972 through mergers and acquisitions.

The Canadian Corporate Elite contains a wealth of statistical information to demonstrate the close integration of the Canadian elite, indicating the continuous growth of concentrated power among those in the corporate and media elite as well as those in other leadership positions, including the political. Clement underscores the importance of the banks and other financial institutions in the decision-making processes related to investment, production and even lifestyle. He detects a direct relationship between the Canadian elite and the threat to Canadian nationhood, since the existing elite is subservient to U.S. interests.

In discussing the role of the Canadian financial elite, Clement writes:

> . . . the Canadian component must commit itself to the continental context to remain strong. In the meantime, indigenous industrial forces are restrained, their mobility limited, and the independence of the Canadian nation-state bypassed. The power of the indigenous commercial elite and the foreign industrial elite reinforce one another in the continental context. [20]

Clement argues that the pluralists' defence of Canadian democracy is spurious because the state allies itself with the interests of the dominant groups thus perpetuating existing inequalities. Arrangements between public and private power result in benefits to those who are able to demand the benefits, that is, the already powerful. He concludes, therefore, that Canada has not fulfilled its promise of equality and will not do so as long as corporate power is allowed to remain in its current concentrated stage.

It should be kept in mind that Clement is guided by an essentially Marxist concept of class in his evaluation of Canadian society.

A third book dealing with the elite in Canada is *The Canadian Establishment,* Peter C. Newman's bestseller.[21] Although Newman's style is much more casual than that of Porter and Clement, he also takes issue with the concentration of wealth and power in Canada. The author provides fascinating background information on the most important members of Canada's elite, who have cheerfully assisted in undermining Canada as a viable national community. He pictures a smug and wealthy establishment lost in the pursuit of money and power, committed to what Newman calls "the theology of free enterprise."[22] He elaborates on the interlocking ties between the corporate elite, singling out some 1000 persons as those who dominate our nation's development often behind closed boardroom doors.

Newman does not present a simple black-and-white dilemma of capitalism versus the working class. He detects changes in the wind. The old bastions of power and privilege are swaying. Newman envisions the rise of new forces and a shift in the old demarcation lines, for example, with respect to the conflict between labour and management and the traditional alliance between big business and government.

It is obvious from the findings of the three authors mentioned above that certain characteristics of Canadian society, particularly its often hidden elitism involving great disparities of money and power, stand in the way of a wholesome and open development of that society. These obstacles to a just society are reinforced by the preponderant place of the large (multinational) corporations committed to the narrow goals of commercial aggrandizement.

The New Technocrats

Canada, like other industrialized nations, is increasingly recognizing the central role of science, and its application, in politics. The Science Council of Canada was established in 1966 as a Crown corporation charged with assessing Canada's scientific and technological resources, requirements and potential, and acting in an advisory capacity to the federal government. It is involved in research and development and concerned with the use of science and technology in respect to Canada's social and economic problems.[23] The latter task reflects the phenomenon so well described by Jacques Ellul, who has argued that the integration of science and society inevitably leads to uniformity and a loss of freedom. The question we must consider is whether Ellul's pessimistic evaluation applies to Canada.

The attitude of those involved in the Science Council of Canada reveals a certain shift in emphasis on the surface but a continuation, and even a deepening, of the traditional faith in science as the avenue of liberation and hope for mankind. In 1967, a special committee on science policy was formed "to consider and report on the science policy of the Federal Government with the object of appraising its priorities, its budget and its efficiency in the light of the experience of other industrialized countries and of the requirements of the new scientific age." This committee was headed by Senator Maurice Lamontagne. Its findings are contained in a three-volume report, *A Science Policy for Canada.* Chapter Two is devoted to a discussion of the challenges and opportunities for science and technology. In that context, the report draws attention to the dark side of technology and its threat to man and his environment. The various aspects of that threat, in terms of pollution, depletion of resources, inequality on a world scale and human life itself, are described to underscore the point that early optimistic expectations of unlimited growth and innovation were deceptive. A reassessment of technology and innovation is advocated.

The report speaks of the need to "invent our future," and it asserts that we "must learn to design and manage the public institutions associated with science and technology more effectively; we must overcome the time lags and inertia that characterize almost all institutions, these factors that conspire to deflect institutional concern from the problems of today and tomorrow to problems that are already embalmed by history."[24]

In considering the relationship between scientists and society at large, the report rejects the notion that scientists should be left completely free, but it argues for the need to establish close links between scientists and politicians. Scientists have to accept that "most research activities have become political in the best sense of that word,'' and therefore politicians and scientists must learn to become partners. The report describes this partnership as follows:

> They must not only live together but work together and help each other to serve society better. It can be a most rewarding challenge for the scientist with his new responsibilities to integrate himself into society. The researcher will of course have to remain a true scientist but he will also become a servant of the public with important social functions.[25]

In the concluding part of this discussion on the role of scientists and politicians,[26] the report simply states that ''it has become a major responsibility of government in this age of the scientific revolution to ensure that society gets the maximum benefits from science and technology at a minimum cost.'' Therefore, the report argues, the government needs not only science policies by sectors, but also ''the macroscopic approach that only a coherent overall science policy can provide.'' This general science policy is said to require a system of control calling for the application of systems analysis. This is urgent because there are still problems to be solved resulting from our earlier failure to meet the initial objectives of our national research and development effort; at the same time we must meet new objectives and new needs arising from ''the challenges and opportunities of the affluent society and the permanent technological revolution.''

The report then describes the ''first generation of science policy'' in the Western world as being centred around national defence and industrial innovation to promote economic growth. The new direction in science policies, the ''second generation science policy,'' must be centred around the good life rather than the ''goods life.'' Our national science efforts must be so reorganized that science can make ''its full contribution to the solution of the social problems that will otherwise soon cripple our society.'' The report lists a number of serious social problems, including student unrest, inadequate housing, overcrowded cities, poverty and disease, and acknowledges that we do not even understand the true nature, and the real dimensions, of most of these difficulties. But the hope of overcoming this failure is placed in research and development activities in these crucial sectors, so that we can meet our economic objectives more effectively and also face our mounting social problems.

The uncritical acceptance of a number of key assumptions in this report is striking, including the assumptions of the affluent society and the permanent technological revolution. Both of these assumptions are fraught with unanswered questions and inherent contradictions. Further, if we do not understand the true nature of most of the difficulties now facing us, then how do we know that the presuppositions underlying the affluent society and the permanent technological revolution themselves must not be fundamentally challenged?

A second organization involved in analyzing the direction of Canadian society is the Economic Council of Canada (ECC), established in 1963 for the purpose of assessing medium- and long-term economic prospects in relation to the growth potential of the Canadian economy. In its *Ninth Annual Review* it published a revised set of what it calls indicative targets. The Council increasingly turned to a more integrated system of analysis assisted by the Canadian Disaggregated Interdepartmental Econometric project (CANDIDE) which enables economists to construct different computerized models of the Canadian economy for the purpose of predicting future trends.

The Council's *Eleventh Annual Review* (1974) is entitled *Economic Targets and Social Indicators.* It explains that previously the measures most frequently used to gauge the state of our society have been economic, such as growth, real output per person employed and price indexes. But the Review continues by pointing out that these measures do not adequately reflect many of the major dimensions of our society. The concerns of society have greatly broadened and now include the concept of overall well-being. The Review states:

> To take account of these other concerns, there is a need for a broader framework within which it should be possible to say something concrete, from the viewpoint of overall well-being, about the ultimate ends of the socio-economic activity of the nation, the means to achieve these ends, and the degree to which they are being achieved. Ideally, one would like to be able to treat the social system in an integrated way. However, the capacity to do this implies the existance of an overall model or theory of the social system. In fact, although there are a number of approaches to conceptualizing a general social system theory, none of these has yet been developed to a level that would permit a simultaneous comprehensive examination of the impact of particular activities on all facets of the social system. Such a model—which would make possible a form of "social accounting"—cannot even be said to be on the horizon, in any practical sense.[27]

Despite the absence of an "overall model or theory of the social system," the Council believes that a wider (than the economic) perspective is needed and it suggests that this can be approached via "social indicators." This broader framework, or conceptual approach, involves first "a delineation of society's basic goals and the division of the system into areas of social concern." These areas may be considered individually, for the purpose of better understanding the internal processes and of developing indicators that measure both the state of, and the changes in, these areas. The major areas of concern are listed as follows:[28]

1. individual rights and responsibilities (legal rights, including security of life and property; and participation in public decision-making)

2. social rights and national identity (domestic social rights, including the protection of group rights; and international relations, including defence)
3. health (positive health, morbidity, and mortality)
4. command over knowledge and skills (basic and higher education, other training, artistic creativity, research and development, and information networks)
5. the natural environment (air, water, and soil)
6. the man-made environment (social, including leisure; and physical, both rural and urban, the latter including housing, land use, and transportation)
7. employment (market for labour, labour-management relations, job security and satisfaction, and occupational mobility)
8. the production and consumption of final goods and services
9. financial status (income and assets)

In considering society's basic goals, the Review asserts[29] that "each individual has certain needs, and these range from the most fundamental, such as survival, to the more complex psychological ones, such as self-realization." These needs can be restated in terms of two basic goals, well-being and equity. "Well-being" refers to the extent to which the various needs are met; "equity" refers to an appropriate distribution of well-being among members of society. Because these goals are considered to be too general, a more detailed discussion of the social system and its objectives is required. In the absence of an operational social system theory, all socioeconomic activities cannot be treated in an integrated fashion; hence the need to subdivide the social system into the main areas of concern shown above.

It is not the intent to deal extensively with the conceptual framework of the Economic Council or with its findings, but rather to draw attention to the terms and concepts, such as *social system,* a *model* or *theory* of such a system, *processes, measuring, the ultimate ends of society's activities, interactions, inputs, outputs, feedbacks,* all of which are generously sprinkled through the Council's Review. This terminology bespeaks a mechanistic concept of human society that involves the reduction of man and society to objects of quantifiable measurement and analysis. Inherent in this is an attempt to squeeze society into a model that can be *understood* and *guided* in terms of an automated (self-contained and self-adjusting) mechanism. It is the language of the social engineer who wants to "plan the future" and program the kind of society that Jacques Ellul, George Grant and others have warned us against.

The approach of the Economic Council involves the acceptance of systems analysis, a methodology that grew out of the operations research work during World War II. The following definition of this method is provided in a special study prepared for the ECC in 1968 by Andrew H. Wilson:

> The systems concept is primarily a way of thinking about the job of managing. It provides a framework for visualizing internal and external environmental

> factors as an integrated whole. It allows recognition of the proper place and function of subsystems. The systems within which business must operate are necessarily complex. However, management via systems concepts fosters a way of thinking which, on the one hand, helps to dissolve some of the complexity and, on the other hand, helps the manager recognize the nature of the complex problems and thereby operate within the perceived environment. It is important to recognize the integrated nature of specific systems.
>
> . . . But it is also important to recognize that business systems are a part of larger systems—possibly industry-wide, or including several, maybe many, companies and/or industries, or even society as a whole.[30]

Two things must be discerned. In the first place, the systems concept as defined here is an attempt to create a model of society after having already discarded the belief in a created and orderly structure of reality subject to the law of the Creator. Any concept of a *given normativity,* that is, one that comes from outside of man, is lost.

In the second place, systems analysis has a number of major parallels with the older and less ambitious scientific management methods. It, too, seeks to construct a technique of control on the basis of rational analysis and efficient organization. It is the old elitism in a new garb; and because of its inclusive and systematic character it is even more liable to move us into the direction of a collectivistic society whose outlines are vividly pictured by George Orwell in his *1984*.[31] Because of its essentially elitist and scientific character, systems analysis stands in the way of genuine personhood and wholesome, open interpersonal relationships.

The question is whether this trend can be headed off by counter forces. Regrettably, such counter forces are not powerfully present in our midst. Further, the "scientific method" at the core of the systems approach has its own built-in defence. The prevailing notion of science and the manner of its integration in society will not allow for setting limits to the scientists' ambition. How can the nonexpert question the wisdom of the expert, especially when the former has been deprived of a coherent, alternative perspective that provides him with the needed conviction and courage to stand against a powerful current. This is how Andrew Wilson views the relationships between engineers and scientists on the one hand and nonexperts on the other:

> While engineers and scientists may now have a new and unaccustomed duty to make known the hopes, opportunities and challenges of their work, they also have a duty to explain their past work in ways intelligible to non-expert but interested members of the general public. By the same token, however, these same non-expert but interested people must become increasingly familiar with the background to the problems involved in the generation and application of science and technology. On the other hand, the non-experts should become involved as little as possible in what are essentially scientific or technical judgments.[32]

Thus engineers and scientists are spared the trouble of meddling by people who do not know what they are talking about. Note that this is done in the name of "essentially scientific or technical judgments," that is, judgments that are value-free and neutral. But the presuppositions and consequences of technical and scientific decisions are not neutral and value-free. Moreover, what happens in this scheme to the old ideal of democracy, and the distinctive *political* responsibility of the politician? The latter's task of governing can never be reduced to scientific and technical expertise.

Some of the answers to the question of the relationship between the politician and the technical expert are provided by Walter Stewart, contributing editor of *Maclean's,* in his 1972 book entitled *Shrug: Trudeau in Power.*[33] Stewart gives a critical account of the "Trudeaumania" that swept Canada in 1968. He shows that the grand promises of participatory government and all the other slogans of the campaign amounted to window dressing. There was little participation by the ordinary citizen, and the promises of a more accessible government did not materialize. According to Stewart, Pierre Trudeau set out to downgrade the role of parliament, and he deliberately replaced those advisers, like his cabinet minister Eric Kierans, who were seen to disagree with his policies. Trudeau's biting style and short temper gave rise to this outburst against critics of a government proposal, Rule 75, that provided for setting a time limit on debates in the House of Commons:

> I think we should encourage members of the opposition to leave . . . every time they do, the I.Q. of this House rises considerably. . . . When they get home, when they get out of Parliament, when they are fifty yards from Parliament Hill, they are no longer Honourable Members. They are just nobodies.[34]

Under Trudeau's leadership, the work of the members of parliament may have been streamlined and reorganized with a view to efficiency and speed. But the overall impact of the changes is a transfer of power from parliament, and even the Cabinet, to an in-group of the Cabinet, in association with another circle of powerful advisers whom Stewart calls "the Supergroup." The result has been a loss of morale among the career men who do not fit within this close-knit and powerful circle. Trudeau at times has even ignored Cabinet members and deferred to the advice of the Supergroup. Stewart quotes a number of bureaucrats who describe the transfer of power to the new advisers. One who left his government position put it this way:

> You get this feeling of why should you knock yourself out on this or that subject, because somebody else will make the decision anyway. It's a soul-

> destroying kind of thing. You didn't come to Ottawa for this. It's not just the job, the feeling you get is not that we're developing a bad government, but a tough, hard, ruthless, heartless government that doesn't seem to be weakened by any streak of humanity. . . . It's the de Gaulle fist in the Kennedy glove.[35]

Stewart's book also describes the new trend toward sophisticated decision making by the Prime Minister and his advisers. Marc Lalonde, formerly the Prime Minister's Principal Secretary and Minister of National Health and Welfare, is pictured as the most powerful man within the group of Trudeau's advisers, whose job amounted to being Assistant Prime Minister. He once told a *Time* magazine reporter, "Technology means the systematic application of scientific or other organized knowledge to practical tasks. That's what we are trying to achieve: the ability to apply reason to broad social and economic problems."[36]

Trudeau's commitment to rationalism and a functionalistic approach to politics was unequivocally expressed in a speech presented in 1964. Contrasting emotionalism with rationalism in a discussion about nationalism, he stated:

> In the world of tomorrow, the expression "banana republic" will not refer to independent fruit-growing nations but to countries where formal independence has been given priority over the cybernetic revolution. In such a world, the state—if it is not to be outdistanced by its rivals—will need political instruments which are sharper, stronger, and more finely controlled than anything based on mere emotionalism: such tools will be made up of advanced technology and scientific investigation as applied to the fields of law, economics, social psychology, international affairs, and other areas of human relations; in short, if not a pure product of reason, the political tools of the future will be designed and appraised by more rational standards than anything we are currently using in Canada today.
>
> Let us hasten to add that I am not predicting which way Canada will turn. But because it seems obvious to me that nationalism—and of course I mean the Canadian as well as the Quebec variety—has put her on a collision course, I am suggesting that cold, unemotional rationality can still save the ship.[37]

In predicting the outcome of the 1972 election, Stewart put his finger on a sore spot when he explained that Trudeau would win not because he had done well in office "but because of other factors, including his own strong image in an age that clamours for strong men, the lack of a viable alternative, and a general and lamentable ignorance about exactly what has happened to government in Canada since June 1968."[38]

Stewart's critical evaluation of Pierre Trudeau's leadership and performance during his first years as prime minister needs to be balanced against later developments. A more favourable evaluation of Trudeau after the 1972 and 1974 elections by a number of observers, especially George Radwanski in his 1978 book *Trudeau*, should be taken into account. Trudeau has changed in some ways, particularly with respect to his reliance on a broader base of advisers and assistants. Furthermore, when criticising Trudeau, we should also keep in mind that he forcefully warned against the pursuit of an ever-rising standard of living. In this connection his Duke University speech of May 1974 and his subsequent speeches dealing with the need for wage and price controls are important.

Stewart, who spent seven years in Ottawa as a political journalist, gives low marks to the media men who report the political events and developments. To anyone who still harbours some illusion about an alert and independent press as a bulwark against an all-powerful state, Stewart's description of an intimidated and dependent Ottawa Press Gallery is, to say the least, discomfiting. All the trends of news management, including friendly chats, subtle threats, opening or closing the sources of information to keep reporters in line, are employed to make the government look favourable. Unfortunately, in Stewart's opinion, the watchdogs of democracy have happily colluded in this taming of the press.[39]

Stewart fails to deal with the underlying reasons for these trends, because he considers them primarily in terms of personalities and style. He does not seem to appreciate that at bottom these phenomena are related to the crisis of meaning that has occurred in Western civilization as a result of the hammerblows of an insistent rationalism. What began as rationalism has increasingly turned into a cynical pragmatism that systematically attempts to strip down all issues to details of technique and expediency. The breakdown of Canadian politics can only be *understood* and *challenged* on the basis of a radically different view of reality from the one now underlying Western civilization. Although he treats the sickness of Canadian politics in a somewhat superficial manner, Stewart alerts us to certain destructive features of modern politics.

Donald Smiley, Professor of Political Science at Erindale College, University of Toronto, has also raised his voice against the direction of Canadian politics. In "The Managed Mosaic,"[40] an article written in response to George Woodcock's defence of the anarchist position, Smiley asserts that the evidences of the new direction, that is, viewing politics in terms of cybernetics, are everywhere. He refers to the influence of those with a systems-management orientation among Trudeau's advisers; the emphasis on rationalized procedures for policy making in the Cabinet and the federal bureaucracy; the centralization of information functions in Information Canada (now disbanded); the government-sponsored survey research in popular attitudes; and federal sponsorship of public policy research. Smiley detects in current trends a shift away from a genuine Canadian pluralism; he describes the emerging society as a *managed* mosaic. He calls for rethinking the limits of legitimate state power, and he laments the scarcity of philosophic treatments of human rights.

Smiley shows insight into both the deceptive nature of what today passes for freedom, and the manner in which hedonism can become a correlative of tyranny—although that possibility may strike some as absurd. He writes: "We are concerned with individual privacy, and strident expressions of 'possessive individualism' call for a lifting of the restrictions on our freedom to bemuse ourselves with alcohol or drugs and for abortions on demand. But such privatization is no barrier to tyranny, and a rational tyrant would work towards assuring that his subjects were so satisfied with the purely private aspects of their lives that they would be dissuaded from autonomous social and political activity challenging his power."[41]

The traditional symbiotic relationship between government and private economic enterprise is now being supplemented by a similar relationship between the political and the social, Smiley argues. "The euphemism is 'partnership' but in such a relation, government, almost by its nature, is dominant." He then sketches three areas where a program of pluralist reform must begin.

First, there is the need to redress the balance of power between the House of Commons and the government. Smiley warns that when the House is true to its task, it cannot be "part of a feedback loop in a communications system." He views the role of the House in terms of an obstructive role because "in some critical circumstances resistance to government is the ultimate safeguard of freedom." Second, Smiley pleads for the destruction of the monolithic nature of provincial systems of public education. "Education must be high on the pluralist agenda." Third, the role of the private family farm must be safeguarded against the encroachment of corporate-type, integrated agricultural enterprises. The three areas he singles out are important in the fight for establishing a pluralist society—something which must be done if Canadian society is to escape the pitfalls of collectivism and tyranny.[42]

The drift toward a homogenized society, the loss of distinctions between the political, social and economic, the emergence of a new breed of pragmatic and systems-oriented "managers" in governments as well as in all other major areas, the general loss of integrity and morality are all very much evident. There is reason to fear that the kind of society described by Erich Fromm is also emerging in Canada:

> A specter is stalking in our midst whom only a few see with clarity. It is not the old ghost of communism or fascism. It is a new specter: a completely mechanized society, devoted to maximal material output and consumption, directed by computers; and in this social process, man himself is being transformed into a part of the total machine, well fed and entertained, yet passive, unalive, and with little feeling. With the victory of the new society, individualism and privacy will have disappeared; feelings toward others will be engineered by psychological conditioning and other devices, or drugs which also serve a new kind of introspective experience.[43]

Even more serious is that there appears to be little critical awareness of the real condition, and even less insight about a concrete, radical—in the sense of going to the root of the malaise—and viable alternative. It is in the context of the phenomena discussed here that we must take a fresh look at the question of Canadian nationhood.

If we are to regain our independence in relation to the U.S., the Canadian government must obviously play an important role, especially with respect to the development of science and technology and the framing of an overall economic policy. At the same time, we are confronted with the danger of a dominating government aided by the tools of modern technology. Is this a vicious circle from which we cannot escape? Is George Grant right after all when he sums up this terrible dilemma of our time: "Nationalism can only be asserted successfully by an identification with technological advance; but technological advance entails the disappearance of those indigenous differences that give substance to nationalism"?[44]

It should be abundantly evident that foreign ownership in itself is unimportant compared with the other, more fundamental issues that concern the meaning, direction and content of our lives. In terms of priorities, it is the assumption regarding the purpose of our lives, so widely accepted both in the U.S. and Canada, that must first of all be challenged. As long as we continue to operate on this assumption, even regaining complete independence from the U.S. would make little difference to us. If we recover more control, yet blithely continue in our current way of life, our society will remain unchanged. That is George Grant's message, and unless the dilemma he poses is confronted courageously and with insight, we will find ourselves compelled to join him in his lament for Canada.

The Crucial Role of Labour

It is self-evident that any attempt to reform the corporate structure requires vigorous government action as well as the participation and cooperation of the labour movement. In evaluating that possibility it is helpful to review the state of collective bargaining structures and practices in Canada.

The most important characteristic of "collective bargaining" is the assumption that labour and management are adversaries. They are seen as two opponents who slug it out with each other, while the collective agreement describes the terms of a temporary armistice. Management is anxious to show as high a profit as possible on behalf of the shareholders, whereas union leaders try to get as high a wage rate as possible for their members. What the one gains, the other loses in this zero sum game. In keeping with the spirit of capitalism, the dollars-and-cents side of the labour-management relationship has become dominant. Consequently, the even more important underlying issues surrounding work itself are neglected.

Labour unions generally are not bothering to explore ways to overcome the curse of fragmented and boring jobs, nor does management show much interest in that approach. As a result, labour-management relations are conducted within the context of an economic power struggle. The 1968 *Report of the Task Force on Labour Relations,* compiled under the chairmanship of Professor H.D. Woods of the McGill University School of Industrial Relations, boldly stated: "One cannot assume a correlation between the results of collective bargaining and any particular concept of equity. Collective bargaining is basically a power struggle; the outcome is more a reflection of the relative economic positions of the protagonists than of the merits of their claims and counterclaims in terms of some standard of equity."[45] In 1972, Ed Finn, public relations director of the Canadian Brotherhood of Railway, Transport and General Workers Union, sounded a similar note in the *Toronto Star* when he stated that it would be foolish for unions not to exercise their power through the strike weapon, because "power, after all, is really what collective bargaining in Canada is all about, not justice, or ability, or merit, but naked power."

Unfortunately, this diagnosis is by and large correct and forms the most important reason for the worsening crisis in labour-management relations. To reduce human relationships to mere power struggles inevitably leads to a loss of realistic perspective despite the illusion of being hard-nosed and practical. Real practicality begins with wisdom, humility and justice.

It is obvious that reducing labour-management relations to a cynical struggle for power has aggravated the problems surrounding work within the confines of modern corporations. Union leaders who view their role as "managers of discontent" have no time and energy left to apply to the difficult task of restructuring fragmented and meaningless, that is, demeaning, jobs into meaningful and rewarding tasks in which a sense of community can be experienced. What is worse, these union leaders soon have a vested interest in perpetuating the adversary style. The Task Force on Labour Relations commented on this phenomenon and pointed out that collective bargaining is not suited to deal with the problems of job dissatisfaction and alienation from work. The Report refers to the rigidity of the collective bargaining rules as one reason for this failure. It asserts that unions have failed to recognize the magnitude of this problem. Furthermore, it states that increased wages to provide for "a good life off the job" will not adequately compensate for the emptiness of many jobs.[46] A more damning analysis of collective bargaining in Canada could hardly be given, but little attention was paid to this part of the Report and there certainly was no determined effort to tackle the problem areas singled out by the Task Force.[47]

The symptoms of the crisis in labour relations—which must be seen as part of the fundamental crisis of our society in general—are:

- the increasing resort to strikes with the resulting interruption of essential public services
- fragmentation of the collective bargaining system
- monopoly control over jobs through compulsory unionism
- a disregard for law and defiance of the courts
- exorbitant wage increases gained by strong unions, while nonorganized workers or those employed in economically weak sectors are receiving low wages
- inflation
- corruption and violence

The problem of violence in labour relations again surfaced a few years ago in the Cliche Commission's investigation of the construction industry in Quebec and, on a smaller scale, in the Waisberg Commission's investigation into violence and corruption in certain sectors of the construction industry in Ottawa, Toronto and Hamilton. These investigations uncovered an alarming degree of corruption involving union officials, employers and, in the case of Quebec, government officials, with incidents of bombings, shootings, beatings, sabotage, blackmail, loansharking and payoffs on a staggering scale. The Canadian strike record is deplorable. In 1976, more than 11 million man-days were lost due to strikes and lockouts, giving Canada the worst record of all industrialized Western countries.[48] Fortunately, statistics for 1977 showed a 70 per cent decrease in time lost in Canada due to strikes and lockouts.

On October 14, 1975, the federal government imposed a framework of price and wage controls, administered by the Anti-Inflation Board, in an effort to reduce inflation, which had climbed to 11 per cent in 1975. In defending this new policy, Prime Minister Trudeau called for a drastic reappraisal of values and a lessening of our collective demand on the economy. Both labour and managment reacted with hostility to the Prime Minister's appeal and began an unrelenting campaign against the controls program. Labour depicted it as a frontal attack on free collective bargaining and a step towards the corporatist society.[49] Management opposed the controls as a violation of the free market.

The Canadian Labour Congress staged a one-day general strike on October 14, 1976, and called for a tri-partite redistribution of equal power among government, business and labour.[50] In the face of increasing disagreement about tri-partism within the CLC and strong opposition without, the CLC quietly dropped this ambitious program. In November 1977, the federal government announced the phasing out of the wage and price controls. This took effect on April 14, 1978, after which the task of "monitoring" changes in wages and prices was given to the Economic Council of Canada. Previously, the government had unsuccessfully attempted to arrive at a consensus about self-imposed restraints among the major sectors of the economy. While the controls program was being dismantled, inflation edged upward again. (It had been reduced to 6 per cent in 1976, but it rose again to 9 per cent by the end of 1977.) Nonetheless, while admitting that inflation had not been beaten, the federal government insisted that the restraint program had helped to generate new anti-inflation attitudes.

A more normative development of labour-management relations would entail rejecting the adversary method and accepting the notion that the enterprise is a work community consisting of different participants who are involved in a cooperative venture in providing goods and services for the well-being of others. The activities of unions, grabbing monopoly power and using this at the expense of other sectors, should be curtailed by law. Workers and unions, who are now excluded from responsibility within the enterprise and treated as outsiders, should be recognized as participants within the enterprise and included in decision making at the highest level. To put it boldly: unions should relinquish their adversary role and assume a more positive and coresponsible role within the enterprise, as well as within the economy as a whole.

Furthermore, fragmented collective bargaining must be replaced by industry-wide agreements. As collective bargaining now functions, this change would give unions a complete monopoly over jobs. That would be undesirable in a society striving for greater distribution of responsibility; therefore, industry-wide bargaining would have to be accompanied by provisions for the participation of alternative unions and for freedom of choice among the workers. The public interest must be represented by other than the spokesmen for management and labour in the settling of collective agreements. A labour court, or its equivalent, should be established to settle disputes for the same reason that civil disputes are settled in courts. A coherent and unified incomes policy must be adopted with the aim to raise incomes of those at the bottom of the scale through wage increases, tax cuts, minimum wage legislation and public assistance. Perhaps most important of all, drastic changes must be introduced to improve the organization of work so that it can provide challenge, satisfaction and fellowship for the workers.

It is obvious that these proposed reforms would require more than mere structural changes. *They require different priorities and a different goal for our economic activities.* Economic growth must be downgraded from the predominant place of influence to a place of secondary importance, and a profoundly different understanding of the task of management, labour unions and the government is needed.

Many will consider the reforms so cursorily mentioned here hopelessly "idealistic" and naive.[51] They are ready to give in to the trend toward more confrontation, more breakdown, more inequity and more ruthless manipulation of power.[52] There are others who believe there is no way to avoid the complete collapse of our democratic society. Simply repeating these predictions is an empty exercise. It is more constructive to underscore the possibilities for renewal and restructuration through an imaginative approach to the problems.

The Dilemma of Democracy

There are many who conclude that democracy is doomed because it is beleaguered by a host of conflicting pressures that cannot be reconciled. Among others, Arnold Toynbee, the late British historian, warned that Western democracies cannot survive because of the collision between the revolution of rising expectations and the limits of the world's resources. He predicted a period of unprecedented social and political conflict that will be followed by an authoritarian regime in all developed countries.[53]

It is obviously impossible to do justice to the subject of democracy in this chapter, but it is possible to comment briefly on some of the problems underlying modern democracies, especially with respect to the notions of freedom and equality. The term *democracy* is largely meaningless because it implies many different things to different people. It is used to defend individual freedom, as well as dictatorship (by the majority or the minority), and the two are mutually exclusive. Because of the confusion of tongues, it is necessary to spell out the intended interpretation by articulating one's perspective and commitment.

The roots of modern democracy are varied. They include Christian and non-Christian influences. But it is safe to say that at present the non-Christian influences are all-powerful, especially the belief in man's autonomy. In the context of this major premise all the minor ones can be understood. This notion of human autonomy or freedom gives rise to a number of internal contradictions, especially when it is paired with the other pole of democratic thought; namely, equality. For if I am autonomous and free, the free pursuit of my interests may well lead to great inequality. This is one of the inherent contradictions of political liberalism. To be sure, it is sometimes argued that equality should apply to equality in conditions and not to equality in results. However, inequality in results will sooner or later lead to inequality in conditions.

Perhaps the most profound problem faced by the believers in human autonomy concerns the basis of political authority; for if man is free, why should he acknowledge any authority over him? A number of different attempts have been made to square authority with freedom, including those of Locke and Rousseau with their concept of the social contract. But the tensions between the two poles remain. The most drastic resolution of this problem in this century was undertaken by Lenin. Once he obtained a position of mastery in the Russian revolution of 1917, he pursued only one aim—power—and he did it with a ruthlessness equalling that of the cruelest despot of any age. Stalin and Hitler followed in Lenin's footsteps. Thus millions of people were sacrificed to the ambitions of men who understood that the time was ripe for the coming of the man of power predicted by Friedrich Nietzsche (1844-1900), that great German philosopher who announced the death of God and the advent of nihilism.

The liberal democracies have pursued a different road by emphasizing individual liberty and reason as the basis of democracy. But at one fundamental point they do not differ from the dictatorships, namely, with respect to the belief that social reality is a result of man's autonomous action.[54] This in turn has led to the notion that *social reality can be ordered by man's rational power*—the latter increasingly has come to mean man's scientific, technical power over the world, and over other men as well. Democracy was identified with rationality. These sentiments were succinctly expressed by Pierre Elliott Trudeau in a paper presented to the Canadian Political Science Association and the Association of Canadian Law Teachers in 1964:

> Thus there is some hope that in advanced societies, the glue of nationalism will become as obsolete as the divine right of kings; the title of the state to govern and the extent of its authority will be conditional upon rational justification; a people's consensus based on reason will supply the cohesive force that societies require; and politics both within and without the state will follow a much more functional approach to the problems of government. If politicians must bring emotions into the act, let them get emotional about functionalism!
>
> The rise of reason in politics is an advance of law; for is not law an attempt to regulate the conduct of men in society rationally rather than emotionally? It appears then that a political order based on federalism is an order based on law. And there will flow more good than evil from the present tribulations of federalism if they serve to equip lawyers, social scientists, and politicians with the tools required to build societies of men ordered by reason.[55]

Three things have happened that have profoundly affected modern rationalism. In the first place, contemporary humanism—or that segment of it that has maintained its rationalist basis—has undergone a deepseated crisis of certainty. Existentialism is a powerful counterforce over against the old, self-assured humanism priding itself on its scientific and universal basis. The existentialists understood that this worship of science would mean the destruction of the individual and of freedom. Hence their new emphasis on individual experience—even if that means a confrontation with nothingness and absurdity.

In the second place, humanism has experienced so many shattered dreams and broken promises that the early optimism has evaporated. The faith in progress was smashed by the violence, brutality and ignorance of the twentieth century, epitomized by the gas chambers of Auschwitz.

More recently, men have starkly encountered their own finitude in that of nature. Both realities have contributed to the dawning realization that the old aspirations of progress have to be abandoned. But since that belief in progress based on unlimited scientific power was the mainstay of an entire culture, its abandonment has created a vacuum that has not yet been filled.

A third phenomenon in this context is the rise of a new pragmatism that asks no questions as to the why of things but is totally absorbed in the how. The new powerholders, backed by organization and technology, are the bearers of this pragmatism. But their power is devoid of a moral basis and leads to the inner collapse of politics.

The three phenomena briefly mentioned here are evident in Canada, especially the third. Politics, for example, has been largely reduced to techniques—techniques of winning at the polls, of administration, and of gaining popular support by exploiting the modern mass communication media in the same way that advertisers of automobiles and cornflakes do. This is how the Canadian party system has been described:

> The parties deceive the public, but so do propagandists of every kind. The deception does not often arise from cynicism but rather from zest for the game itself, a general human trait. It may be said generally in conclusion that the evils in the party system are not peculiar to it but are the outcome of general human frailties. Indeed, it is hard to see how the parties that must woo the electorate with success can do other than reflect its virtues and its vices. Perhaps it is people as much as institutions that need to be reformed.[56]

The dilemma of modern democracy is centred on its lack of a moral basis, that is, the absence of norms, giving rise to a remarkable paradox. On the one hand, we detect evidence of dissolution all around us, for example, in the crisis of authority, the decline of integrity and trust, and in the rise of corruption and violence. On the other hand, a growing number of restraints are imposed on people's range of choices in ordering their own lives. Thus we see the two poles of license and compulsion at war with each other in our society. There is nothing new about the existence of these extremes. What is new is their magnitude, and our failure to cope with them in terms of a coherent and trustworthy norm for political life.

The anarchists have discerned the dark side of the nation-state and their response is total rejection. They believe that the nation-state is evil *per se* and must make way for loosely-joined cooperative relationships, preferably in small, local communities. The case of the anarchist ideal has been eloquently made by George Woodcock, the acknowledged Canadian spokesman for that position. In his "A Plea for the Anti-Nation," published in *Nationalism or Local Control,* Woodcock argues that the new nationalism, in a Canada striving for independence from the U.S., contains the seed of a narrow and dangerous chauvinism.[57] He advocates that Canada become the "anti-nation," that is, a federation of decision-making groups in which a minimum of remote control would be coupled with the maximization of responsibility through participation. He asserts that "any decision of any kind that affects only a local group must be reached by that group alone, and by consensus if possible."

Woodcock is hopeful that participation and the socialization of the sources of wealth would reduce conflicts of interest. He writes: "Today we conduct political life by means of coercion and confrontation. In a post-national world we shall have to conduct it by co-operation, consensus, and participation, and to devise the means to make this possible involves a profound reconsideration of political structures and political goals alike."[58] He knows that there is a close relationship between the modern nation-state and technology, between bureaucracy and technology, and he welcomes a lessening of our reliance on the nonrenewable resources and a consequent lowering of our material prosperity. He also believes that Canada must follow the anarchist course of a loose federalism for Quebec to remain within the Canadian nation.

Woodcock's concept of the anti-nation is based on a shaky foundation and characterized by certain inconsistencies. For example, he writes that any decision that affects only a local group must be reached by that group alone and by consensus, if possible. In the first place, decisions that affect only local groups are likely to be the most trivial ones. Many individual and group decisions have consequences that extend beyond the bounds of that particular group or individual. For example, the decision by Vancouver grainhandlers to strike for higher wages deprived starving people in Bangladesh of desperately needed wheat. Someone must make the decision about the price of oil in Canada, but that decision affects all Canadians. Life is made up of a host of such interdependent situations where decisions are not limited to local effects. Secondly, Woodcock hopes for consensus if possible, but he does not spell out what happens in the absence of such consensus. Yet, provisions must be made for such eventualities, or stagnation will result. The latter can just as well give rise to social tensions and injustice as the wrong kind of dynamic development. Furthermore, Woodcock depends on the "socialization of wealth," as a means to reduce social conflict. But this kind of socialization presumes the existence of a powerful and determined central government.

These and other inconsistencies have been articulated by various respondents to Woodcock's article, and many of them score significant points against the proposal to change Canada into an anti-nation. However, none of the contributors to *Nationalism or Local Control* question the central idea of anarchism. This same idea is found in Marxism and liberalism. Underlying all three philosophies is the belief that people can order the structures of their society as they see fit without any reference to a transcendent norm and that the only criterion for such a structure is its practicality. Mao Tse-tung was expressing the radically secularized view of life that underlies both the democratic and communist cultures with this terse statement: "There is no 'ism' in the world that transcends utilitarian considerations."[59]

Chapter 8
Prospects for Renewal

Behind the problem of politics, in the present age, lies the problem of man, and this is what makes all thinking about contemporary problems so thorny and difficult. The intellectual collapse that occurred in this country after the decade of the 1930's, when our intellectuals had been able to submerge themselves totally in a program of political action, shows that philosophy can no longer be considered a mere appendage to politics. On the contrary, anyone who wishes to meddle in politics today had better come to some prior conclusions as to what man is and what, in the end, human life is all about. I say "in the end" deliberately because the neglect of first and of last things does not—as so-called "practical" people hope—go unpunished, but has a disastrous way of coming in the back door and upsetting everything. The speeches of our politicians show no recognition of this; and yet in the hands of these men, on both sides of the Atlantic, lies the catastrophic power of atomic energy. [1]

William Barrett

Everywhere in the industrialized world one detects an atmosphere marked by uncertainty, tension and violence. Confusion about the true nature of our humanness lies at the core of that crisis. This lack of insight cannot be compensated for in any way. The current attempts to remould man and society in terms of a preconceived model, derived from a mixture of the physical and the social sciences, in no way escapes that vacuum but violates the true nature of man.

A Plea for an Open Society

The nation-state is a significant institution in our time, and politics plays an important role in the shaping of our society.

The Scriptures are very clear in showing that the authority of government—which concretely means the current Canadian government—is instituted by God for the purpose of doing justice to all the people (see, for example, Romans 13). The state therefore always has a specific focus and, because it is called to do justice, it must seek to establish those conditions in society within which persons and social structures can function effectively. The Bible teaches that every person is an image bearer of God and all societal relationships are God-given structures, or channels, for the unfolding and opening up of life.

In this context, Bernard Zylstra, professor of political theory, said in a 1973 magazine article that human rights are not founded in an inherent dignity of human personality but in the dignity with which man is endowed by the Creator:

> This dignity, first and foremost, is to be God's imager on earth. This divinely endowed dignity requires a recognition of man's unique place and responsibility in society. In the light of this dignity as God's imager we can say that man transcends all social structures. He may not be enclosed in or enslaved by any institution.

Elaborating on the Biblical concept of justice, Zylstra continued:

> . . . the norm of justice requires a social order in which men can express themselves as God's imagers. To put it in different words: the norm of justice requires social space for human personality. By personality I then mean the human self whose calling lies in love of God and love of fellowman. That calling entails the realization of a multiplicity of tasks in history. Justice therefore also requires societal space for man's cultural tasks. Moreover, the realization of man's central calling also entails the establishment of social institutions, like marriage, the family, schools, industries, and the like. Hence justice requires societal space for these institutions as long as they contribute to [a] meaningful, [a] harmonious, and an opened up human existence.[2]

In light of the state's inclination to seek power for its own sake, and therefore to side with the powerful, it is very tempting to oppose the state *per se* and to side with those who insist that the best government is the least government. But the only effective antidote against the wrong use of political power is the renewal of politics by subjecting the use of political power to the realization of justice. In this perspective we can accept political authority as legitimate. In a democratic state, citizens have the opportunity and duty to help shape the political life of the nation *in a normative direction*. They cannot perform their duty properly if they have no viable norms by which to judge political action.

Democracy is invariably linked with equality. But this concept is beset by a host of conflicting interpretations. The Bible teaches that there is a fundamental equality of all men before the face of God (e.g., see Gal. 3:28); at the same time it shows that there is immense variety in all of creation, also in terms of the variety of tasks that must be performed in society. Inequality is therefore not evil *per se* although it often results from the abuse of power. It can and does result from differentiation and variety in tasks, authority, responsibility and positions that reflect the richness and multifaceted character of God's creation in its historical unfolding. This variety is clearly demonstrated by Paul in his letter to the Corinthians. In I Corinthians 12 he compares the community with the human body that is made up of different parts, yet all function to advance the well-being of the whole—each making its own distinctive contribution such as that of the eyes, ears, hands and feet. This is a beautiful description of how mankind is to function. Immediately after this Paul points out that the most important requirement for human relationships is that they be cemented by love.

Much of the inequality we encounter today, in Canadian society as elsewhere, does not reflect the variety Paul refers to but, instead, results from a selfish use of privilege and power. The prevailing stark inequalities in income, wealth, authority, responsibility and opportunities for opening up our lives are unjust and must be opposed. Specifically, it is unjust

- that, in 1973, 11.4 per cent of Canadian families had incomes below the poverty level (Economic Council of Canada figures), whereas the rich received a grossly disproportionate amount of income;
- that many workers are forced to perform boring and demeaning jobs whereas all of the important decisions are made by a handful of people at the top;
- that some live in squalor while others inhabit extravagant homes and wallow in luxury;
- that the economy is dominated by a relatively few giant corporations, whereas most people are forced into a position of dependency with respect to this power;
- that some have ready access to an education, which sometimes they don't even value, whereas others are deprived of an education although they have the ability and desire for academic work;
- that some get rich on land speculation, whereas others consequently cannot buy a house of their own and are forced to live in apartments not designed with an eye to the needs of families.

There are any number of instances of inequalities that are patently unjust and demand action by the state as the administrator of public justice. The state must take action not to make itself the dominant institution, but to ensure that persons in their societal relationships (e.g., families, schools, business enterprises, unions and associations of artists) are better enabled to perform their respective tasks.

How can state dictatorship (or any other kind of dictatorship sometimes under the umbrella of majority rule) be avoided? In exploring this problem, Kenneth D. McRea, professor of political science at Carleton University, observes:

> The ultimate source of these shortcomings lies not so much in any specific institutional arrangements as in attitudes rooted deeply in the Canadian political culture, attitudes that fail to comprehend the meaning of a plural society. . . . As long as English Canadians remain majority-minded, many French Canadians will find their most effective response in an increasingly autonomous Quebec. This majoritarian attitude on both sides, I suggest, is the Achilles heel of the Canadian political system. It is the *damnosa hereditas*

> of the Anglo-American democracy and Lockean political theory and liberal society. . . . [3]

McRea puts his finger on the trouble spot; at the same time he suggests that this problem can be overcome in an open society. An open society is one that has a plurality of religious communities and societal structures. Pluralism then is the crucial issue with respect to the future of our society.

A free society can only flourish in an atmosphere where differences are freely acknowledged and respected, that is, where there is social, economic and political space for the development of different lifestyles. For this reason we must be alert to others who also favour a plurality of social structures, whatever their perspectives may be. Gad Horowitz of the University of Toronto comments on this issue in a review of John Porter's *The Vertical Mosaic:*

> The development of an English Canadian national identity does not require that we impose a single set of social and political values on our society. The United States is not the only model of a nation. Most countries manage to combine national identity with ideological diversity. Our terrified equation of nationality with uniformity is irrational. [4]

In this context, the comments about "the dialogue society" by Charles Taylor are significant. Taylor detects a decline of "public meanings," that is, firmly held convictions of reality, commonly accepted, and warns against an artificial substitute (totalitarianism). He envisages that a dialogue society would offer hope of ending the tyranny of technique and what he calls "the fetishism of the machine." He writes:

> This society would start from the fact of pluralism, from the fact that we are of many different faiths, beliefs, and moralities; but it would also start from the fact that we are all less satisfied and dogmatic in our possession of the truth; that we are all therefore in some way searchers; and that the fact of pluralism has entered into the very content of our varied beliefs so that we are already in dialogue within ourselves with the ideas of others. [5]

We need a new definition of toleration that goes beyond John Locke's conception of a rationality that binds men together in the social contract. The state is called upon to establish a unity that can accommodate a variety of religious and cultural influences in the social fabric—also in the representation organs of the state itself. We should have no illusion about our present situation. It will require a conscious and determined effort to reverse the current trends. We must be on our guard against the new tyranny, a tyranny that is nourished by the belief in a common rationality. This faith has provided a massive blind spot on the part of its adherents who in the name of neutrality impose their concept of a social order on everyone. This phenomenon is also related to the problems surrounding the structure and role of the business corporations.

But there are two additional areas where the same thing is immediately evident, namely, education and employment. The public school is considered to be the school for all people because it is thought to be religiously neutral. The equal rights of parents who choose to nurture their children on a different basis from the one underlying the public school system —and that basis is at bottom religious in nature—are not recognized. Similarly, all workers covered by a closed or union shop agreement are forced to belong to a union despite the fact that some of them cannot in good conscience endorse the beliefs underlying that particular union.

In a 1967 ruling on a worker's refusal to support the United Steelworkers of America because his Christian belief clashed with the beliefs and practices of the union, Mr. Justice Bora Laskin of the Ontario Court of Appeal stated:

> I find nothing admirable in the applicant's stand. Our society secures to every one the right to adhere to a religion of his choice and to hold to a self-determined political creed. It does not, however, give liberty to insist on religious convictions or political creed or both in contexts which the law does not regard as relevant to their free enjoyment and as a ground for thwarting agreements binding on all irrespective of religious or political persuasion. [6]

Mr. Justice Laskin here speaks in the tradition of the majoritarian principle. But the assumption underlying his opinion, namely, that society decides what is relevant to the free enjoyment of religious conviction, is clearly related to the faith in the universality of the rule of reason.[7] The only way the compulsion inherent in this position can be overcome is to substitute the principle of plurality for the majoritarian one. This means the state when involved in cultural spheres that are not political in nature (family, school, university, trade unions, professional organizations, and so on) must respect and create legal space for the *different* basic commitments that shape the direction of these spheres.

The acceptance of this principle of plurality is indispensable for an open society. This requires a recognition of the equal legitimacy of various communities held together by a bond of faith, whether that faith be Christian, Marxist, socialist or liberal democratic. Such recognition would call for an admission that one's own commitment cannot be considered valid for everyone. In other words, it would require the recognition that all men are ordering their lives around some central belief about the nature of reality, a belief that is religious insofar as it pertains to man's innermost conviction regarding himself and his relationship to the rest of reality.

Everyone has to make some decision about the core questions of his existence. In making those decisions, no one is purely rational and value-free. Before the rationalist embraces rationalism, he has to make some prescientific assumptions about himself and the "light of reason" within him. This is an act of faith—as much as the Christian's acceptance of the reliability and authority of the Scriptures. Our society is closed in one important respect because those who do not accept the "light of reason" as their final guide are dismissed as *sectarians* whose "peculiar" beliefs may be adhered to in church and synagogue as long as they do not affect the public order—that is, an "order" in which production and consumption are given preeminence. Only the rationalists are allowed to carry their beliefs into the public arena. The limits to "toleration" in our society are therefore clear. These limits are not constitutionally spelled out; they are the underlying, often unspoken, assumptions of our "closed" society.

Over against the "closed" society we propose an "opened" society, on these fronts. In the first place, we suggest that a variety of religious and cultural convictions within a single nation should be given room for self-expression in the social order. To be sure, this will require compromises. Therefore, within the political process, a new system of representation is needed, so that our legislative bodies will more adequately represent the citizenry.

In the second place, we propose that in the borderline area between the state and the nonstate sectors of society the religious or commitment plurality within the citizenry be recognized by the state in its expenditure of public funds. For instance, the monopoly of the public school in most provinces should be abolished, to make room for a plurality of school systems, all justly supported by tax monies.

In the third place, we suggest that the symbiosis between the state and the industrial sector, notably the giant multinationals, is today the most significant violation of the principle of societal plurality. In addition the non-industrial spheres of our culture are either commercialized (for instance, the media) or monetized (for instance, the professions). Therefore, a third step toward a more open society will require a limitation of the impact of the corporate sector upon the rest of society. This limitation can only be accomplished if the present symbiosis of special cooperation and privilege between state and industry is dismantled.

A new view of man must give rise to a new view of the social order, and that, in turn, must give rise to a new politics and economics.

Is There a Normative View of the Corporation?

In evaluating the multitude of proposals put forward for reforming the corporation, it is essential to keep in mind the driving, culture-shaping belief that now undergirds economic activity in general and the corporations in particular.

The driving force of the corporations is derived from a secular, that is, non-Christian, motive that was introduced into Western society via the Renaissance and the Enlightenment. *The core of this belief is the notion that man is in effect his own lawgiver.* Crane Brinton, an American historian, describes the faith of the modern era as a rationalism that "tends then to banish God and the supernatural from the universe. It has left only the natural, which the rationalist holds to be ultimately understandable, almost always by what most of us know as the methods of scientific investigation. Historically, the growth of scientific knowledge, the ever more skillful use of scientific methods, is closely tied with the growth of the rationalist attitude toward the universe, with the rationalist cosmology."[8]

Science and technology became the means to mastery over nature. The Industrial Revolution was the beginning of a relentless assault on nature and, in the 1920s, led to the emergence of the first mass-producing and mass-consuming society in the U.S. The large joint stock companies were designed to amass capital, labour and managerial skills and they now dominate the economy of the developed countries—often in overpowering ways. The corporations, however, have by and large pursued their ambition with single-minded devotion to growth, technical innovation and profits. *They have become organizers of human effort on a vast scale, but in doing so they have had little or no regard for man as a servant of God,* made in His image for fellowship with his neighbour, enjoying and using the resources of the world as possibilities for human development and enrichment.

One of the first things that we notice about the large business corporation is the contradiction between its internal discipline and rigidity, and the belief in self-realization and autonomy so powerfully at work in our society.[9] More and more it is accepted that all restraints and norms are obstacles to freedom and, therefore, to genuine humanity. Freedom is to do as you please; anything goes. Modern advertising is an expression of that all-pervasive belief, and it has perfected the art of subtle manipulation and suggestion for the sake of increased sales and economic growth. The message coming through advertising (and other media) is that happiness consists of consuming and enjoying the vast array of goods and services made available by the mass production system. Politics and economics are now firmly hitched to the wagon of an endlessly rising GNP because that is the way to greater happiness.

The freedom of "the good life" promised through consumption contrasts sharply with the discipline exacted in production. Here the worker experiences control, rigidity, uniformity and often utter boredom. This disjunction between work and the rest of life has been a major source of confusion and even disintegration. Many attempts are made to bridge this gap, but these attempts are bound to fail as long as the very foundations of "the good life" and the modern system of production are not radically altered.

A Christian critique and evaluation must begin with the acknowledgement that man is created to serve God and that God has given His revelation so that men might know how to perform that service. To be sure, sin has entered the world and has caused disharmony, injustice and oppression. But in Christ man is again restored to a place of responsibility in creation. Another word for that responsibility is calling, or office. Man holds an office in relation to his Maker that requires of him a life dedicated in its entirety to joyful service. Furthermore, man is related to his fellowmen in a multiplicity of ways ranging from the intimate ties of kinship (family and marriage), to the much looser ties of voluntary organizations, down to the fleeting encounters of everyday life such as those that happen on a train. Finally, man is directly related to the rest of the created world in the sense that God made the world for mankind's use. The earth's resources must therefore be seen as a means for human development. In this threefold relationship, namely, man to God, to his fellowmen and to the world, man is first of all a responsible being, subject to the command to love God above all and one's neighbour as oneself.

The foregoing implies that man's relationship to God is all-embracing and absolute. Therefore, man's primary and all-inclusive allegiance is to his Creator. From this follows that all interhuman relations are limited and defined. No one societal relationship may claim a person's life in its entirety. On the contrary, men are involved in a variety of relationships *simultaneously* but in *different ways.* For example, a person is a father or mother (or child) of a family, a member of a church, teacher (or pupil) in a school, citizen of a nation, employee of a corporation, member of a labour union and a political party.

Within all these societal structures we experience *internal* relationships of an *authority-subordinate* character. Parents have authority over their children, managers over employees and governments over citizens. This authority relationship deteriorates into oppression and abuse, unless those in authority are guided by the norms that hold for the exercise of that authority. These norms have to be realized in different ways in the various structures but they must all aim at providing maximum opportunities for exercising responsibility on the part of everyone. In other words, those in authority must respect and reckon with the *calling* or *office* of those under authority. There must be a proper balance between authority and freedom within each societal structure with a view toward opening up and enriching the lives of all people within such structures.

The *external* relationships of the various societal structures are *coordinate* and not subordinate in character. Although in the everyday affairs of people there is much interaction and a great deal of interdependence among the various structures, there is something specific, something that is unique to each societal structuration. (For example, while the church may have a legal side to its existence, it is the one structure that functions as a community of worshippers.) Each structure has its own sphere of competence, its own inner makeup that cannot be reduced to that of another. This principle is usually referred to as the principle of *sphere sovereignty.*[10]

This term is subject to misunderstanding in that it may give the impression that each sphere is completely autonomous. On the contrary, while each structure is sovereign within its own sphere, this sovereignty must be understood as subject to certain God-given norms for the maintenance of life. The recognition of the principle of sphere sovereignty provides a bulwark against all forms of anarchy and tyranny.

Sphere sovereignty implies that freedom cannot be adequately safeguarded on the basis of individual freedom alone, but must be anchored in the freedom of societal structures. As Hendrik Van Riessen, Dutch professor of philosophy and author, has pointed out, the struggle against totalitarianism is nearly always hopeless from the outset without such anchorage.[11]

With respect to both the proper balance between authority and freedom (internal relations) and sphere sovereignty (external relations), it is safe to say that modern society has not developed in keeping with Christian norms. Obvious distortions and abuses have resulted and these in turn have given rise to *two conflicting views* of society.

First, there is the position of those who tend to consider individual freedom in an absolute manner. To them freedom means especially freedom to engage in economic life, that is, the freedom of the marketplace. This one-sided view has led to freedom on the part of those who managed to get hold of, and keep, the reins of power. They were "successful" and came to the top. On the other side were those who had very little or no economic power and they suffered the consequences. The strange thing is that those who proclaimed individual freedom did not worry much about the fact that many had no freedom at all but were subordinated to powerful economic forces over which they had no control. To square theory (individual freedom) with practice (a loss of freedom on the part of the powerless and the propertyless), men resorted to the theories of evolution and the survival of the fittest.

These ideas became especially influential in North America and served to justify an immense concentration of economic power and wealth. Vast economic empires, that is, large-scale corporations, evolved rapidly, and economics and profits were elevated to all-consuming goals. Consequently, people were reduced to factors of production, to objects that can be subordinated to the interests of the corporations. This has had devastating effects on the manner in which work has been organized and resources exploited. A system of ever-growing production was considered the sure way to achieve the abundant life, and both men and natural resources were simply seen as factors of production.

Progress was identified with an increased control over nature and a rising level of material goods. Because they enabled men to exercise more control, science and technique came to be seen as the keys to progress and genuine emancipation. It should be noted that this concept of human progress is entirely founded on the things of this world; it is fundamentally secular. Unfortunately, Christianity's response to this powerful culture-shaping force has been largely confused, ineffective or absent. By some strange reasoning, one segment of Christianity began to identify this liberal ideology, or capitalism, with the Christian way of life.[12] But it could only do so after the Scriptural revelation regarding man's place in creation as God's servant became thoroughly beclouded by the forces of secularism, particularly scientism and materialism.

In the second place, there are those whose reaction to liberal ideology and concentrated economic power has been prompted by Marxist thought. Labour unions also arose in reaction to liberal ideology and practice. Although Marxism has not flourished in Canada and the U.S., in some ways the reaction from this side is most important. Both of these responses will be considered in the section on authority.

A third phenomenon must be mentioned. Public policy in Canada has adopted the goal of balancing various countervailing forces. Welfare economics has become the tool in the hands of governments to bring about a redistribution of wealth and a measure of economic security. Full employment and social security are the objectives ardently pursued. In this process a host of administrative agencies and programs are established. Bureaucratic power has proliferated, but poverty and insecurity are not eliminated.[13]

There are numerous forces at work that tend to reduce persons to objects to be categorized and moulded for the sake of an efficient and orderly administration. Though there is much talk about democracy and participation, a trend toward uniformity, anonymity and, consequently, personal insignificance prevails. Meanwhile, the propaganda machine grinds on, elections are held with much fanfare, but politics is largely devoid of debates about clearly articulated political options and genuine involvement. The influence of pragmatism is prominent in this development. The result is that significant distinctions between governments, business enterprises, political parties and labour unions—to name four significant entities—are blurring. Particularly with respect to the state and the business enterprise, crucial distinctions are erased. We are more and more drifting toward what Bob Goudzwaard calls "economic corporatism." He signals the transition from the conventional capitalism to the new form of corporatism

> in which industrial concerns themselves are the controlling suppliers and owners of their capital resources; where these concerns can choose their own goals in an autonomous manner beyond the effective control of any outside influence; and where they are sufficiently powerful to shift competition to the safer areas of technical innovation and consumer management. This system can be described as economic *corporatism* because it has the support of political power. There is here a co-partnership with the state which conforms to and financially supports the major goals of economic growth and technological progress. A monolithic structure is rising in our midst.[14]

A renewal of society requires maintaining the crucial distinction between the state and the business corporation. The task of the state is to administer public justice so that life can unfold harmoniously and that people are enabled to open up their lives in response to their office as image bearers of God. In case one sector of society obtains too much power so that other sectors or persons are hindered in their life possibilities, the state has the task to intervene. It is self-evident that in a modern, complex society it is no easy matter to define exactly what the state must do in a given situation. But it does help immensely to understand that the norm for the state is public justice aimed at furthering the possibilities for a normative unfolding of the various societal relationships. For example, if the business corporations usurp power, the state is called to restrain that power and push it back to its legitimate boundaries. That is why economic corporatism is a dangerous and anti-normative phenomenon.

The norm for a business enterprise as an economically qualified societal structure is *stewardship*. This must be the key guideline in all its activities. The realization of the norm of stewardship entails a careful use and allocation of natural resources, labour, managerial talent, capital, etc., so that an *economic surplus* is attained as a result of economic productive activity. This economic surplus can be measured in a financial manner in terms of *profit*. But as soon as we mention the word *profit*, a warning is in order because of the loaded history of that term. A business enterprise must respond to a broader variety of social norms than merely the economic; it must take into consideration a broader variety of interests than merely the financial yardstick of profit. A business enterprise—also a multinational corporation—must take into account the interests of investors, but also the interests of the suppliers of natural resources, of the workers, of the consumers, and of persons and social structures—especially families—that are directly or indirectly affected by the enterprise's productive activity. An economic enterprise is never closed off from its social environment and the slogan of "free enterprise" should not blind us to this fact. An economic enterprise must display its own normative structuration—"sphere sovereignty"—in the context of societal interdependence and intertwinement. This complexity constantly calls for a normative weighing or balancing of various possibilities that demand a choice.

A long-range pattern of choice reveals the underlying value-system of the decision makers in industry and the economy. For example, saying that industry exists for profit reveals a specific value-system: it indicates the absolutization of the monetary aspect of industry. To be sure, profits are necessary in industry, for without profits an industry cannot continue to exist. This is the case in both a capitalistic and a communistic social order. But *making a profit* is, by itself, not at all indicative that an enterprise is guided by the norm of stewardship, and the other social norms that are to structure industrial production. For *making a profit* can simply mean the *accumulation of capital* for the benefit of the particular industry itself, or for the investors, or for excessively salaried management personnel. Such a profit may well have been made at the expense of the suppliers of natural resources (especially when these come from the underdeveloped world), of the workers at the assembly line or the consumers. The singleminded pursuit of profits and economic growth jeopardizes the well-being of suppliers, workers and consumers—who are reduced to economic objects, "things," whose value is determined by profit-maximization or economic growth.

Profits must always be related to other legitimate interests; that is, profits have a *relative* significance. Maximum profits can therefore be very *uneconomical* because they involve a distorted concept of production. In other words, a normative restructuring of the enterprise requires stewardly, economizing activity in conjunction with the realization of a number of different norms *at the same time*. Such restructuration must occur *within* the internal life of a business enterprise. Renewal does not result when the state takes over the control of the enterprise but when the enterprise is called back to its proper task delineated by the norm of stewardship. When for legitimate reasons the state must assume ownership or control of an enterprise, it does not thereby have the right to operate this enterprise as an extension of the state, but it must even then accord the enterprise room to obey the norm of economic stewardship.

A struggle is now going on between two contrasting forces—the left and the right—over the control and makeup of the business corporation. The one believes that primacy must be accorded to the individual (but many individuals are trampled on); and the other believes that primacy must be accorded to the collective (but genuine community does not result). Is this a meaningful dilemma and can this struggle be resolved? In light of these questions, the following issues are crucial: ownership, authority, production and consumption.

Ownership

The Scriptures clearly show that the modern view of ownership—namely, the notion that individuals have absolute property rights and can do with their property what they want—is erroneous. Instead, ownership must be understood in the context of the Creator's absolute claim on His creation. All ownership, therefore, must be seen in terms of stewardship, that is, a person may own a certain property (the Old Testament term is *inheritance*), but the "rights" in that property are *weighted* with the obligation to serve God and one's fellowmen. People are to give an account of the use of their possessions, for the Lord God of heaven and earth is the only absolute owner. When the people of Israel were given the promised land, they were instructed that no one's possessions might be permanently estranged from them. In case a person would encounter hard times and was forced to sell their property, the sale could only be effective until the year of redemption—the year of Jubilee which occurred every fifty years. Then it had to be returned to the original owner. The Lord instructed His people as follows: "The land shall not be sold in perpetuity, for the land is mine; for you are strangers and sojourners with me. And in all the country you possess, you shall grant a redemption of the land."[15]

This rule was designed to prevent the emergence of gross inequalities in possessions, yet the Lord's law for economic life provided for development and a dynamic unfolding of life. That is evident, for example, in the distinction the Lord made between property in the walled cities and in the open country. The latter was the source of food and income, and therefore, was essential for a family's livelihood. However, life in the walled cities already began to show a measure of differentiation; therefore, the sale of houses in the cities was allowed without the provision of redemption in the year of Jubilee.[16] Despite this "openness" in the laws for economic exchange—and *the unfolding of economic life* since the Lord gave his laws to the people of Israel *has made fantastic strides*—the underlying norm revealed in the Old Testament law against the sale of property in perpetuity still holds today: gross inequality in possessions is condemned by the Lord. He demands that justice be done also in property relations. It is up to us to obey that norm in ways that are suitable for a much more differentiated society than Old Testament Israel.

The Biblical norm for property has often been disobeyed in our society. Under the influence of major thinkers, particularly John Locke (1632-1704) and Adam Smith (1723-1790), property rights are considered to be absolute. With respect to the corporate form of ownership, all power has been vested in those who supply the capital, by virtue of their property rights. The business corporation is a cooperative arrangement whereby large amounts of capital are supplied by many investors. Such concentration of capital is not necessarily wrong; but a business enterprise cannot be defined in terms only of its source of capital since its internal structure encompasses other elements as well, especially the work force. Therefore, today extra safeguards against abuse are needed, because the more power people have—and concentration of capital involves power—the more damage can be done through abuse of such power. Corporations, under the influence of the capitalist credo, have concentrated their efforts on the narrow goal of profits and self-aggrandizement. They have been very successful and grown to a place of dominance in our society. In this process the goal of profit making has crowded out all other objectives and life has become oriented toward the purposes of business. Especially in North America, business interests have become dominant and have led to a distorted development. To overcome that distortion, the goals of business must be broadened so that genuine well-being is promoted.

A reform of the corporation must therefore begin with a new vision of ownership. Property rights must be relativized. Various forms of sharing and spreading responsibility within the corporation are to be sought. That should be done by shareholders and especially by those who work within the corporation—the employees. It is helpful here to distinguish between the corporation as a legal entity and the enterprise as a community of people. The latter cannot be owned by anyone. As Goudzwaard has pointed out:

> What is an enterprise? It is first of all a relationship in which *people* live and work together, people who, in this economically qualified co-operation, use means of production which have been financed by the providers of capital. Now we can generally say of the Christian view of ownership of property that it regards ownership of persons, living persons, as principially objectionable; slavery is a denial of the principial equality of all people before God. This, of course, is true not only of individual persons, but also of persons who constitute a societal relationship. For that reason, those who provide the money can never and may never be the owners of the enterprise, which is a societal relationship of living people. Providers of capital are merely owners of the capital goods, of the *means of production* of the enterprise. Their ownership right is a limited one which can never apply to the entire enterprise and the activities of its members. [17]

An implication of the foregoing is that the rightful claims of shareholders do not go beyond a fair return on investments and that their involvement within the enterprise is minimal.

Authority

The prevailing ideas about ownership are closely related to the issue of authority since authority within the enterprise has historically been derived from the property rights of the *investors*. The corporation has developed in keeping with an exaggerated notion of these rights and with profit as an end in itself, in accordance with the dominant conception of self-fulfilment. Consequently, authority is executed in such a manner that the freedom and responsibility of those subject to this authority are jeopardized. (We can here leave aside the fact that ownership rights are now mostly vested in institutional, large-scale investors—thus disconnecting the *direct* link between ownership and control—since this phenomenon has not affected the theory that managerial rights are derived from property rights.)

The exercise of authority within a (work) community of people must aim at the fulfilment of a *common* task of the community and must therefore contribute to the well-being of those subject to authority—so that they can better fulfill their task and office. As Bernard Zylstra has written: "Authority is office, that is, a channel for the realization of divine norms in a social relationship."[18] Those in authority may not selfishly use their authority (power) to enrich themselves at the expense of their subordinates. Whenever they do, relationships become distorted and injustice and disharmony set in. Much in human history indicates that authority often deteriorates into naked power and is used to exploit and oppress. This is all too evident in the history of the Industrial Revolution and the manner in which corporations have assumed a dominant place.

Early forms of abuse of power were obvious and resulted in oppression and degradation. Working people were helpless in the face of cruel and oppressive working conditions. Much has changed since the nineteenth century, and living and working conditions have tremendously improved—at least in the Western world. But in other important ways, the situation has not improved much. As a matter of fact, there are powerful forces at work in our society that increasingly stand in the way of genuine human fulfilment and the establishment of meaningful human relationships within the work community.

Reactions against selfish use of authority have not been lacking. One of them is the modern trade union movement. Another has been political action in the various forms of Marxism and socialism. Often the two streams interact and overlap. A few words about each are in order.

The North American trade union movement arose to protect the workers against the power of corporations. It resulted in a bitter struggle, and even today the relationship between unions and management is characterized by the adversary spirit. The unions opposed the power of the corporations in order to safeguard and defend the interests of the workers and in that they accomplished much. However, the trade union movement was, and is, infected by the same fundamental belief that so powerfully helped shape the corporations, namely, the belief that man is autonomous and able to find fulfilment in achieving mastery over nature for the sake of material abundance. The struggle between the two sides is often severe, but it centres on the division of the economic pie since unions do not find themselves in fundamental disagreement with the goals of the corporation. (The term business unionism, often used to describe North American unions, is revealing in this regard.) Consequently, problems related to abuse of power within corporations are not attacked except in a pragmatic way. Hence the underlying cause of distortions within the enterprise is not removed. This is why the problem of meaningless, oppressive and dehumanizing forms of work, which is a major problem of the corporation, is being largely ignored by the unions.[19]

In the second place, and in a more radical way, opposition against corporate power has come from the Marxists. They view modern history as a struggle between two contending classes and they anticipate the victory of the working class over their enemies. This will then, according to their belief, usher in the classless society in which the means of production will be owned by the workers via the state. The state eventually is to wither away. Man's relationship to the means of production is the key relationship. Under capitalism, the means of production are privately owned; under Marxism they are publicly owned. This element is central because the Marxists view man essentially as a producer (*homo faber*). In other words, man's relationship to his tools is determinative. Marx came to this conclusion because, as a child of the Enlightenment, he too believed in man's autonomy and freedom in terms of his mastery over nature. At this fundamental point, there is no difference between capitalism and Marxism and this explains why the latter is unable to overcome the distortions and contradictions of the former.

Much of the current talk of workers' control is inspired by the Marxist belief. But all Marxist movements are plagued by the immense propensity for disagreement and schisms. In the light of the history of the Marxist movement, it takes an extraordinarily stubborn belief to hold fast to the notion of a homogeneous working class. This so-called class is constantly torn apart by internal disagreement and rivalry. A unified class simply does not exist except in ideology, and unity is only achieved through strong-arm tactics. The belief in the existence of a single "proletarian" class is contradicted by history.

The adversary approach of labour-management relations seeks to sabotage authority within the enterprise;[20] the Marxist solution aims at the total elimination of the current authority structures within the enterprise. But in both instances the problem of authority is not resolved. That resolution can occur only within the context of a true vision of a business enterprise as a genuine work community. The Biblical vision of man as a responsible being before the face of God suggests that the reform of authority does not lie in the elimination of authority but in rechanneling it in such a way that the calling of those under authority is respected and the opportunities for fulfilling that calling are safeguarded. This implies that the concentration of authority in the top echelons of the corporation and the subsequent loss of freedom in the ranks below must make way for an "open" structure.

Employees within an enterprise should be recognized as responsible beings who must have maximum opportunities to make decisions with respect to their own immediate work situation and to the general direction of the enterprise as a whole. That calls for a restructuring of the corporation so that employees are able to share in decision making. The object must be to change the corporation from a battleground of conflicting interests—which now seeks to maintain itself by a ruthless usurpation of power in the hands of management—to a genuine work community in which the contributions of shareholders, management and workers are combined to provide goods and services that serve the meaningful unfolding of life. The foregoing requires the reorganization of work so that it can be experienced as an integrated and meaningful part of life. And that confronts us with the need to come to grips with the production process itself. In that connection, the role of modern technique is of crucial importance.

Production

The modern method of production can be understood by viewing it within the context of a generally prevailing ideology concerning man's self-realization through his mastery over nature. That perspective sets the tone and provides the driving spirit. Technology is the key ingredient in the modern production process. Not only is it the key; it has a nearly overwhelming tendency to assume a life of its own. The "one best way" of performing a task is predetermined technically and thereafter it is the *only* way.

To understand the modern method of production, we need to reflect on the essential features of "scientific management," a term associated with the pioneering work performed in this area by Frederick Winslow Taylor (1856-1915). Scientific management endeavoured to control human activity in the workplace with the aim of attaining maximum efficiency in terms of unit output. Taylor devised a system of rational (scientific) analysis of work. He accomplished this by breaking any given task down to its simplest fragment and then reconstructing the actual work process in a logical (that is, in terms of the end product) sequence. Because Taylor's emphasis was on scientific analysis, abstraction and efficiency, the resulting work process was completely fragmented as far as workers were concerned. This was not considered to be a problem in view of Taylor's original intention (maximum efficiency) and his concept of the worker (shared by management in general). Taylor, like many of his contemporaries, endorsed the concept of economic man, which entails the belief that people are motivated by economic self-interest. Consequently, if scientific managment were to succeed in raising productivity and wages, it was believed that harmony and general well-being would be realized.[21] Thus the foundation of the modern mass production system was firmly put in place and contributed mightily to the arrival of the mass production and mass consumption era.

The objective of scientific management was to raise efficiency and reduce costs. However, the real cost in terms of the human situation was extremely high. Scientific management attempted as much as possible to *eliminate* the human element because it involves unpredictability, individuality and lack of control, whereas the aim was *rationality* and *control.* This is very much evident from Taylor's own observations. He explained that what is required of the worker "is not to produce more by his own initiative but to execute punctually the orders given extending into the smallest details."[22]

Peter Drucker has described what has happened to the worker in the modern industrial system as follows:

> Denial of the existence of an individual with social status and function is really the essence of the new approach. In mass production technology the worker is only one sloppily designed machine. To bring this human machine to the full mechanical and automatic efficiency which its Maker apparently failed to achieve is the main aim of the new science of "human engineering." That means, however, that the individual must cease to exist. The new technique demands standardized, freely interchangeable, atomic labor without status, without function, without individuality.[23]

Drucker understands that the result of this attempt to fit man to the machine will lead to intolerable tensions and conflicts. He views the power of the corporations and their ability to "legitimize" their power as the key issue of modern society. Such legitimization requires what he calls the integration of the individual member of society. Drucker asserts that we have the choice "either to build a functioning industrial society or to see freedom itself disappear in anarchy and tyranny."[24]

The scientific management method attempts to push division of labour to its technical limits. The result has been fragmentation and isolation, not only with respect to the work to be done, but also among the persons who perform the fragmented jobs. It isolates workers from their work and thus downgrades the significance of real workmanship, and it also isolates workers from each other. The effect of this method of work is a loss of a sense of participation and responsibility. When one cannot see the overall context of work and the end product is far removed, it is impossible to maintain a sense of importance about one's work. The term *alienation* is a much-used word to describe this result of the fragmentation of jobs. Especially the Marxists and neo-Marxists have popularized this theme.

Another phenomenon has aggravated the problems surrounding

production. Increased complexity in production methods has raised the capital requirement of equipment. This in turn has given rise to ever larger industrial units. In the technologically advanced sectors, oligopolies dominate the scene. Their immense size further minimizes the possibilities of establishing meaningful human relations. Instead, the technique of social organization is further relied on to provide the integration among large numbers and countless separate functions. The triumph of technique is ensured, but men are reduced to expendable and interchangeable units of production and organization.

There are two more ways in which the blind pursuit of efficiency in production, aided by the scientific approach to management, has led to serious structural dislocations. The first is the damage inflicted on the natural world through the pollution of air and water, and through the destruction of the landscape. Secondly, an emphasis on economic growth and an ever rising standard of living, especially since it is accompanied by much waste and built-in obsolescence, has resulted in rapid depletion of nonrenewable resources. Thus a threefold crisis has arisen at the heart of the modern productive system, intimately affecting man in his relationship to his work, his neighbour and his environment. All three are bound together and are directly related to the worship of science and technique in man's quest for mastery over nature and for material abundance. They also underlie the structural distortions of our economy, especially high inflation and unemployment levels.[25]

Because belief in progress, coupled with the materialistic vision of man and the world, is deeply imbedded in modern culture, it will require a principled change of direction and even a change of heart for us to find our way out of the present crisis. Some are extremely pessimistic about the human prospect. They are particularly negative toward the role of technique since they view it as a necessarily enslaving and homogenizing force in modern history. Jacques Ellul has convincingly argued this point of view. But the question remains whether his evaluation and prognosis are correct.

The decisive issue is whether Western man chooses to continue worshipping science, technique and material abundance, or whether these will be viewed in terms of man's response to the Creator's mandate to develop and unfold the potentials of creation. Man's scientific and technical abilities are not something outside of God's good creation.[26] The main question therefore concerns the *direction* of technology. Will science and technique help men to "open up" and develop their lives, or will the present trend continue? Technology undoubtedly can help to lighten the burden of work, to overcome some of the limitations of time and space and to facilitate human interaction. Electricity can and does serve men to develop their talents and it can help them to relate to one another in countless ways. And one could go on and on.

The trouble starts with the belief that technique can solve all human problems, and that it is an end in itself rather than a means to an end. This is evident within the corporate structures, where rationalized efficiency is supposedly indispensable. Right at this point reform is imperative in order to make work human once more. Production must be so organized that fellowship, responsibility and concern can be expressed, even if that violates quantitative production criteria. Resources must be so used that the natural environment is not permanently destroyed. Undoubtedly, this calls for a halt to the relentless pursuit of new products and techniques for their own sake.[27] It calls for simple methods of production, for whole jobs in which workers can achieve a sense of fellowship and fulfilment, and it calls for deemphasizing high income and an ever rising number and variety of consumer goods. Obviously, this requires a fundamental reorganization and reorientation of the corporate structure, for which the participation of the *entire* work community is needed—both managers and workers. Such reforms would thoroughly alter the corporation and the work environment. Those who are quick to say that these alternatives are naive, idealistic and unrealizable should remember that the current trend cannot be maintained. Those who say that nothing can be done, that history is determined, should remember that culture is man's responsibility.

Consumption

Consumption and production are obviously two sides of the same coin. Once economic growth has become the end-all of corporate existence and the sure road to happiness, then consumption, too, tends to become an end in itself. John Kenneth Galbraith has convincingly argued that one of the ways in which "the planning system" (big, oligopolistic business) achieves security is by the management of consumer demands. He writes: "The individual serves the industrial system not by supplying it with savings and the resulting capital; he serves it by consuming its products."[28]

The message incessantly beamed at consumers in North America is: "We have the goods that can add to your happiness, self-esteem and social status; therefore buy our products." The irrelevance of the advertising message is striking; the intent is not to inform but to cajole and manipulate. Credit buying has been devised to stimulate today's spending with tomorrow's earnings. Galbraith explains that this system makes for reliable workers. "Ideally, his wants are kept slightly in excess of his income. Compelling inducements are then provided for him to go into debt. The pressure of the resulting debt adds to his reliability as a worker."[29]

The rise of the mass production corporations has been accompanied by an absence of price competition and an emphasis on product differentiation, often in minor details, such as packaging, style, brand name and marketing techniques. The new is held up as the superior simply because it is new. Billions of dollars are spent in research and development aimed at staying ahead in the race for novel products, but little or no attention is given to quality and meaning. As a matter of fact, quality is purposely deemphasized so that the products will have to be replaced sooner.[30]

The revolution of rising expectations, assiduously cultivated by the advertisers, works in the interest of consumption. The underlying theme is hedonistic and destructive, for it plays on man's greed and views the purpose of life as an incessant pursuit of pleasure. Here is where the contradiction between the rigours imposed on men and women in production on the one hand, and the consumption ethic on the other hand has contributed to the loss of coherence so evident in our time. Richard Barnet and Ronald Müller have summarized this aspect of the current emphasis on consumption as follows:

> By marketing the myth that the pleasures of consumption can be the basis of community, the global corporation helps to destroy the possibilities of real community—the reaching out of one human being to another. The decline of political community and the rise of consuming communities are related. Each TV viewer sits in front of his own box isolated from his neighbor but symbolically related through simultaneous programmed activity and shared fantasy. How much the pervasive sense of meaninglessness in modern life can be attributed to the organizational strategies and values of the huge corporation we are only beginning to understand, but for the longer run the psychological crises associated with the emerging socioeconomic system are potentially the most serious of all, for they undermine the spirit needed to reform that system.[31]

The management of consumer demands has assumed grotesque proportions and methods. The cost of advertising in the U.S. and Canada climbed to $21 billion annually by 1973.[32] But advertising is also used in Latin America and other poor countries to persuade people with a very low income that their status will improve if they spend their meagre resources for goods produced by Western technology. Advertising is popular in poor countries because it creates a make-believe sense of prosperity. Large, multinational corporations are constructing what Barnet and Müller have called a "Global Shopping Center," complete with the technology to spread the advertisers' message that happiness and consumption are interdependent.

Inequality is an obvious characteristic of current income and consumption patterns. To some extent it is present within our own country, although a large segment of the population has obtained mass consumption status. But inequality is starkly present on the international scene where the rich nations consume many times the resources used in the poor countries.

There is a huge gap between the lowest and the highest 10 per cent of income receivers. At the top of the scale there is immense wealth and much conspicuous consumption, whereas at the bottom there is poverty and deprivation. In between the two extremes, at least in the developed countries, is a large segment of income receivers who participate in the mass consumption market. But as inflation takes hold, the percentage of those who must spend all their income for basic necessities rises. Consequently, those groups who are able to muster bargaining power step up their demands for a larger share of the economic pie. This is a vicious circle with wage and salary increases chasing inflation and vice versa. Meanwhile, social and political tensions build up which, if not deflated, may well result in the destruction of society on the rock of individual and group selfishness.

The restraints advocated by the corporate elite with respect to wage demands is drowned out by the voices of their paid propagandists extolling the virtues of consumption. The two kinds of advice conflict but are addressed to the same people except that in the first instance they are producers, whereas in the second they are consumers.

While there is still much disparity in the distribution of wealth in Canada (and in other developed countries including the U.S.), the contrasts on a world scale are staggering. The poor of Latin America, Asia and Africa are falling further behind the developed countries. In his 1977 annual address to the Board of Governors of the World Bank, Robert S. McNamara, the president of the Bank, reported that the growth rate of per capita income in the poorest countries was the lowest in the world (1.1 per cent). He referred to the one billion people who make up the world's "absolute poor" as "those trapped in conditions so limited by illiteracy, malnutrition, disease, high infant mortality and low life expectancy as to be denied the very potential of the genes with which they were born. Their basic human needs are simply not met."[33]

There is good reason to assume, in view of the limits of the earth's resources, that as long as the rich countries continue to enjoy the current high standard of living, the poor countries are condemned to a perpetual position of dependency and poverty. Conversely, what is obviously and urgently needed is a structural realignment between rich and poor countries, whereby the former transfer some of their wealth to the latter. This will require a lower material standard of living in the rich countries, or at least a drastic reduction in the rate of economic growth as we have conceived it in the past, that is, based on an ever-increasing consumption pattern.

As long as economic growth of a conventional nature is the overriding goal of the developed economies, there is no prospect for an equitable distribution of the world's production, and many more of the world's poor are condemned to starvation or a brief life of hunger and despair. A drastic reappraisal of our own approach to income distribution on a national scale is required, but no less important is the need to redress the imbalance among nations. That may well be the most significant issue before us in the last quarter of the twentieth century.

God has given the world to all mankind and we are responsible for seeking a just redistribution of income, so that all men have an opportunity to develop their lives. It is ironic and tragic that at a time when technology has expanded man's abilities to exploit the earth's resources, and has facilitated consumption of an endless array of often useless and even harmful goods, large segments of the world's population are deprived of even the most basic necessities. There is absolutely no justification for this glaring injustice.

Summary

Men believed that their technical powers would enable them to master their environment, but this has not happened. On the contrary, we are beholding the strange paradox of human helplessness over against the forces he himself has set in motion—the automated process.

Space travel and moon landings have been made possible through men's scientific and technical power. But the astronaut is totally dependent on an artificially constructed system in which he functions as a minutely programmed and monitored technical operator. Nothing is left to his own choice and he must train himself to be completely at one with the machine; there is no room for variety and spontaneity. All direct, human interaction with fellowmen is suspended and contact is maintained only through a purely technical system of *indirect* communication. He is in a hostile environment that tolerates no deviations from a carefully predesigned and controlled series of manipulations. The astronaut is in that sense a perfect and advanced prototype of modern man in surroundings where technique has assumed a power of its own. He represents power in every sense that men have come to worship power, but he also bespeaks powerlessness and dependency. William Barrett has aptly described this contradiction as follows:

> Every step forward in mechanical technique is a step in the direction of abstraction. This capacity for living easily and familiarly at an extraordinary level of abstraction is the source of modern man's power. With it he has transformed the planet, annihilated space, and trebled the world's population. But it is also a power which has, like everything human, its negative side, in the desolating sense of rootlessness, vacuity, and the lack of concrete feeling that assails modern man in his moments of real anxiety.[1]

It is this paradox that lies at the centre of the problematics surrounding large-scale business corporations.

The corporation is nourished by man's desire for power and control over nature. But power is also exercised over men within the corporate structure; they are made subservient to the organization's interests. That power is increasingly realized through the process of automation understood in the broadest sense. Not only have mechanical processes been automated but society itself is being organized in the same way. This automation in turn reinforces those qualities which serve the organization but stand in the way of genuine, human interactions. Lewis Mumford, writing on the self-enforcing discipline of the automated system, asserts that its smooth operation requires "equally underdimensioned men, whose values are those needed for the operation and the continued expansion of the system itself. The minds that are so conditioned are incapable of imagining any alternatives. Having opted for automation, they are committed to flouting any subjective reaction and to wiping out human autonomy or indeed any organic process that does not accept the system's peculiar limitations."[2]

The machine that man built now threatens man himself. Conversely, a way out must be found through reestablishing man's relationship with his fellowmen and with nature. That requires a shift from ever more and ever bigger to the simple, the direct, the nonviolent, and the small-scale. That does not require the elimination of all technique, but it requires pushing technique back to a position where it extends, rather than frustrates and stifles, human capabilities. This is not so much a matter of all kinds of different and detailed reforms, but first of all a decision regarding the goal of our lives. Christians know that they need the redeeming power of their God to find their way. This conviction does not, however, relegate them to passiveness and hopelessness but spurs them on to strive for the renewal of human relations and societal structures in concrete ways.

Suggestions for Corporate Reform

With respect to the business enterprise, its internal structure and its role in society, a number of major reforms are needed. Among these the following stand out:

All persons employed within an enterprise must be considered participants entitled to such a status in law and in fact. This would, among other things, call for representation of workers on the board of directors. At all other levels provision must also be made for participation and joint decision making by those who perform the work. Because of the radicalness of this proposal and the danger of failure, it is advisable that these changes be phased in gradually over a certain period—but with a definite timetable—beginning with the largest corporations. This will provide time for adjustments and retraining on the part of unions and management. Care must be taken that the independence of day-to-day management is respected.

Production processes and work methods must be simplified and restructured so that teamwork and workmanship can be experienced by workers. All built-in obsolescence must be discontinued. Violent and harmful production techniques must be phased out.

Holding companies designed to provide a shield of secrecy and to dominate markets must be disallowed, and all oligopolistic corporations must be broken up.

The number of directorships held by any one person should be limited to a small number, say three. Crossing over of directorships between financial and nonfinancial corporations must be disallowed.

Advertising must be drastically curtailed, especially that which stimulates wasteful and damaging consumption, for example, the use of liquor, tobacco and automobiles, deodorants and nonnutritious foods.

Products from underdeveloped countries must be imported without tariff barriers—to be phased out gradually—and for a fair price. Multinational corporations should use their superior know-how and power to stimulate a balanced economic development in the poor countries, especially with an eye to the need for labour-intensive technology, a healthy agricultural base, local entrepreneurship, ownership and production.

International cooperation is needed to establish a uniform system of information gathering, taxation policies and incorporation regulations.

The much-needed resetting of production and consumption patterns will undoubtedly cause changes in employment patterns. Governments, and representatives of labour and management, and other groups as well will need to cooperate in developing other employment opportunities in keeping with genuine human needs and ecological balance.

The key elements in these suggestions are: the acceptance of the need to lower the aggregate standard of living in the rich countries; the preservation of scarce resources; a more even spread of income; the introduction of nonviolent and nonalienating methods of work; and assistance to the poor countries to achieve a balanced and wholesome economic development.

CONCLUSIONS

It would be spiritually so much more valuable, and psychologically so much easier, to adopt the principle of self-limitation—and to achieve it through prudent self-restriction.[1]

Alexander Solzhenitsyn

We must face reality. Unless we are prepared within the next eight to ten years to change our way of life, to develop new sets of values, to create a less materialistically oriented society, and to find new ways of growing as a people, other than by an ever-increasing consumption of our natural resources, we will have missed perhaps the last chance open to us. Have we the wisdom—have we the courage?[2]

Alexander B. Campbell

The expressions of the Christian paradox are so familiar that it is easy to forget their elemental power and their almost startling relevance to our age. It is nothing new to say that a society with a frantic desire for security needs to learn that the saved life is the lost one; those who have no longer any joy in work would find a deep satisfaction in the conception of the service which is perfect freedom; and the anxious self-expressionists might even be glad to hear that it is the meek who inherit and the humble who are exalted. Only through the acceptance of these noble paradoxes can, in the Christian view, the present chaos, insecurity and weakness in the social scene be turned to order, peace and strength.[3]

Vincent Massey

The issues surrounding foreign direct ownership in Canada are complex and difficult, but they are part of a much more fundamental problem. It is imperative that we gain insight into the interdependence of our society. At the same time nothing makes much sense unless we perceive clearly the outlines of the underlying beliefs that give shape to Western culture. The major premise of that culture is the belief in human autonomy, which has given rise to the radical secularization of society and man's notion of progressive self-realization through the mastery of nature leading to material abundance. This belief has confronted modern man with the hollowness of his existence so starkly evident in the prevailing moral and ethical collapse—the "transvaluation" of all values. Only if we discern the radical nature of the current malaise can we have a grasp on what is happening around us. As Daniel Bell has pointed out, the crisis of our time is first of all a crisis of belief.

> The real problem of *modernity* is the problem of belief. To use an unfashionable term, it is a spiritual crisis, since the new anchorages have proved illusory and the old ones have become submerged. It is a situation which brings us back to nihilism; lacking a past or a future, there is only a void. [4]

There are many reasons to join George Grant and Jacques Ellul in their descriptions of a decaying civilization. They are right in their analysis of current trends. However, we need not, and should not, despair of the possibility for change and renewal. There is no shortage of doomsayers—and in their defence it must be said they understand better what is happening than the superficial optimists—but it is also necessary to underscore that side of the Gospel which speaks to us of renewal and reconciliation. It should never be forgotten that the Lord of heaven and earth is able to blow the breath of life into dead bones so that they become living beings again (see Ezekiel 37).

We cannot pin our hopes on the Christian church in its present form. That church is seriously divided and marked by impotence and irrelevance because it has lost its prophetic perspective. It has become what George Grant calls "flatterer to modernity"—at least its liberal wing. The fundamentalist segment tends to abandon the world for a private religion. In both instances the renewing and redeeming power of the Gospel has been muted. Fortunately this is not the whole story; there is still faith in Canada, but the emphasis today must be on our stirring up that faith, on self-criticism and on a total reliance on the Lord's power to redeem our lives and the structures of our society again.

Os Guinness, British author and lecturer, in his *The Dust of Death* has presented us with a prophetic and highly readable account of the Christian faith and its promise for our time. After offering a lucid and fair description of the "establishment" and the counterculture, he then argues for the third way, the way of the Gospel. This book is not another of the many shallow and moralistic revivalist exhortations. It has a refreshing and stimulating ring to it because of its Biblical outlook. Guinness understands that to choose the Christian alternative is not to choose against man and this world. He asserts that the Biblical view of man calls for a defence of his humanness over against the low Eastern view of man, over against the determinist view of man which saps human significance, as well as over against the humanist view because the latter does not account for the aberrations of man. "When a man is guilty, he needs to be confronted with the guilt; when he is weak, he needs help; when he is in sorrow, he needs comfort." In this perceptive summary he catches what may be the central truth about the human condition in the world:

> The Christian community must affirm that human identity is valuable. It must affirm that human aspirations are valid and that a substantial fulfilment of them is possible. It must affirm that man's dilemmas are real and that a substantial resolution is possible. As they build homes, administer hospitals and run their businesses, Christians must struggle for human environments in cities and communities. In every area, from integrity in advertising to morality and justice in national defense, humanness in living must be demonstrated. The effects of this will be cultural, social, moral, political, educational and aesthetic; they will permeate the fabric of society at every level. If any new order is achieved, any "re-formation," then it will be important to recognize that these new forms are themselves not final and that, however closely they approximate Christian principles, they must not be made into absolutes.[5]

There is a basic similarity between the roots of the liberal as well as of the Marxist ideology. However there are important differences between the Soviet Union, China and their satellites on the one hand and Canada on the other. We have not yet arrived at a complete convergence, and before this happens we would be wise to use the relative openness of Canadian society to help redirect that society. There are many areas sealed off, but there are still others that show openness and possibilities for variety and freedom. Christians should learn to make much more effective use of opportunities that are still available. Their failure to act lies not in the first place in the opposition from without but in the Christian community's own lack of prophetic vision. It is here that renewal must begin.

Moreover, with respect to the multinationals, the fact that the inroads of foreign ownership into Canada are so extensive is the fault of the Canadian people and especially their policy makers. Therefore, we must begin with self-criticism. Charles Pachter, painter and graphic artist, in his contribution to *Getting It Back*, a publication of the Committee for An Independent Canada, rightly points out:

> We cannot go on blaming "foreigners" for our failures; we must look to ourselves for the sources of positive change. . . . By greeting exploiters with open arms, by exchanging the more difficult role of innovator for the passive role of follower, Canada took the easy way out. It is more expedient and less risky to copy than to produce something original. Burdened with an outdated Oedipus Complex towards Britain and a colonial dependence on American capital, we were loathe to endure the growing pains of awkward adolescence.[6]

To build up our sense of nationhood by being anti-American will not get us very far. An example of this kind of anti-Americanism was presented by Heather Robertson in the April 1975 issue of *Maclean's*.[7] She informs us that anti-Americanism is a Canadian tradition which built this country and keeps it together. Such a negative base is a poor foundation for any nation. What we should not forget is that there are Americans, too, who are disenchanted with the direction of their society. Some of them are

Christians, for example, Senator Mark Hatfield[8] and New York attorney William Stringfellow.[9] There are many others, including Barry Commoner, author of *The Closing Circle* and *Science and Survival*, and Ronald Müller and Richard Barnet, authors of *Global Reach*. These men have strongly opposed the trends in American life and they have called for abandoning the glorification of success in terms of materialistic goals. We would do well to seek out those Americans who are critical of the materialism of their own country and to extend them the hand of friendship.

Politically, *Canadians* will have to decide on an economic and industrial policy, including a policy with respect to foreign investment. This is no easy task, considering the critical and complex national and international economic problems, but it must be given priority in light of our need to downgrade the importance of the economic side of life so that the noneconomic sides can develop more fully. We must aim for more responsible and less wasteful ways of developing our economy. For that reason alone, there is an urgent need for more political and economic leeway to make our own decisions—not so that we can reap more economic reward ourselves, but so that we can make those decisions necessary to redirect our national priorities. While emphasizing that our first priority must be to discern the secular faith undergirding our culture and to challenge it on the basis of the Scriptural view of man and the world, we must simultaneously focus on concrete problem areas where change and renewal are needed.

To summarize the foregoing, the following are priority items within the context of a redirection of our national goals:

Plurality in education and employment. A pluralist structure of society must be undergirded by free choices in education and employment. Differently motivated communities—not in the first place ethnic communities, but rather *faith* communities—must have full and equal rights and opportunities to establish the kind of schools and labour unions that are in harmony with their own convictions.

Internal reform of corporations. The reform of corporations as advocated in the previous chapter will serve to remove, or at least lessen, friction. By spreading responsibility and providing greater opportunities for participation, also at the board of directors' level, suspicion and secrecy will be allayed and a broader range of concerns and interests will be incorporated in company policies.

Industrial policy. The emphasis must shift to the kind of industrial development in which human needs receive prior attention. That will require more emphasis on rewarding work, the conservation of non-renewable resources, simple technology and a greater emphasis on local production for local use. There must be less emphasis on the expansion of imports and exports. The federal government must assume responsibility—with full cooperation and participation from the provinces—for formulating a cohesive industrial development policy that takes special cognizance of the priorities mentioned here and of the need to combat what has been called "the law of unequal development."

In all major industrial sectors, including petroleum, automobiles, chemicals, rubber and electronics, Canadian-owned corporations —whether public, private or joint—must be established or expanded. The reason for this is not only to enhance Canadian economic independence but also to provide more room for developing alternative technologies in these areas. This is especially pressing in the case of automobiles and energy resources.

Corporate size and power. In keeping with the earlier suggestion that oligopolistic corporate structures be eliminated and holding companies restricted, mergers such as those contemplated a few years ago between the Argus and Power corporations should be prohibited.

Energy policy. The emphasis must be on conservation and on alternative, less-damaging sources of energy. The example of the former NDP government of British Columbia in deciding not to use nuclear energy should be followed by the federal and all provincial governments, in view of the extreme hazards connected with nuclear power production and waste disposal.

Energy revenues. Private oil and gas companies should be restricted to a fair return on investments. The excessive surplus profits, created by the increase in the price of oil, should be channeled into a fund—an Energy Security Fund for Canada—along the lines suggested by Premier Allan Blakeney of the Province of Saskatchewan at the April 9-10, 1975, Federal-Provincial Conference of First Ministers.[10] Premier Blakeney suggested that this fund be placed under the direction of the federal government and that it be used to make Canada self-sufficient in energy. In this connection priority should be given to finding alternative energy sources.

Inflation. The federal government must provide leadership in this area by continuing its effort to establish agreement among the various sectors of the economy about the limits of price and wage increases, especially in view of real productivity increases, our relationship to the Third World and a meaningful incomes policy. This must be done within the framework of the proposed reforms of the corporation and the collective bargaining system as a whole.

Incomes policy. An incomes policy is required that will distribute the rewards more equally and serve to oppose inflation. Speculation in land and food must be eliminated as much as possible.

Foreign direct investment. An overall industrial policy must incorporate measures to stimulate the channeling of Canadian savings into Canadian investments. Alternatives to the wholly-owned subsidiary, such as joint ventures, licensing arrangements and technology purchases, must be used more extensively. Positive steps must be undertaken to reduce the overall level of foreign ownership, while strengthening our manufacturing base. Special grants should not be paid to foreign-based multinational companies. The Canadian financial institutions must give priority to channeling finance capital into Canadian-owned businesses. The federal government must take the lead in formulating and enforcing a long-range policy regarding foreign direct investment.

A public forum. We must search for new ways to facilitate public debate and interaction. A nonpartisan orientation is needed. Therefore a body should be established to serve as a forum for public debate, and to offer advice with respect to the major socioeconomic issues now facing us. Priority attention must be given to inflation and unemployment and a long-range industrial strategy, including the establishment of investment priorities, development of energy resources and major technologies. This body must be made up of a broad range of persons with expertise who would help to bring into the open the decision making that is now often done in the privacy of corporate and government boardrooms by a small number of persons, despite the farreaching effects of these decisions.

The issue of foreign ownership in Canada must be approached in the context of a fundamental review of economic and technological expansion. We should not merely reject American domination in Canada, but we should attack head-on the larger problems of technology and industrialization. In this connection it is important to realize, as George Grant has observed, that Canadians, like the Americans, have embraced the god of progress. This aggravates the problem confronting us, for our efforts must be expended on two fronts simultaneously.

In view of the fact that there appears to be a great deal of lethargy in Canada with respect to our national existence vis-à-vis the U.S., one may understandably be doubtful of the possibilities for arousing interest in the even more fundamental issues raised here. How will we ever succeed in persuading our fellow Canadians that we should be prepared to repudiate the gods of our age? Yet, it is somewhat encouraging that among those who are concerned about Canada's national integrity there is an awareness of the need to come to grips with technology and the assumptions underlying Western culture in general. It is also encouraging that there is a growing sense of urgency among deeply concerned men and women of other countries.

The Christian community is obligated to involve itself in the problems surrounding Canada's nationhood because the Christian faith opens up real perspectives for individuals, families, communities and nations. We need to become thoroughly acquainted with the issues, including the forces and ideas that have given shape to our nation and to the world. We have to interact with others who are concerned about the same issues, albeit from a different perspective than our own. In some instances we will be able to agree; in others we will have to take an alternative position. What must come through persistently in our participation is the conviction that our nation needs the healing power of our God who long ago told His people:

> Therefore, you shall keep the commandments of the Lord your God, to walk in His ways and to fear Him. For the Lord your God is bringing you into a good land, a land of brooks of water, of fountains and springs, flowing forth in valleys and hills; a land of wheat and barley, of vines and fig trees and pomegranates, a land of olive oil and honey; a land where you shall eat food without scarcity, in which you shall not lack anything; a land whose stones are iron, and out of whose hills you can dig copper. [11]

One more thing remains to be said, especially in view of our inclination to rely on blueprints, models and systems. There is something *mysterious*, something intangible about the core of human existence. Exactly what happiness really is can never be fully defined because of the mystery at the centre of our being. The delineation of "the good life" escapes us. The good life is a gift that occurs when the Lord blesses His creatures. These words of Christ reveal how that blessedness can be experienced:

> For this reason I say to you, do not be anxious for your life, as to what you shall eat, or what you shall drink; nor for your body, as to what you shall put on. Is not life more than food, and the body than clothing? . . . And why are you anxious about clothing? Observe how the lilies of the field grow; they do not toil nor do they spin. . . . Do not be anxious then, saying, "What shall we eat?" or "What shall we drink?" or "With what shall we clothe ourselves?". . . But seek first His kingdom, and His righteousness; and all these things shall be added to you. [12]

Notes

A Personal Preface

1 Walter L. Gordon, **A Choice for Canada** (Toronto: McClelland and Stewart Limited, 1966), p.x.
2 John Kenneth Galbraith, **Economics & The Public Purpose** (Boston: Houghton Mifflin Company, 1973), pp. 171-72.
3 George Grant, "To Be a Citizen in North America," in William Kilbourn, ed., **Canada: A Guide to the Peaceable Kingdom** (Toronto: The Macmillan Company of Canada Limited, 1970), p. 221.
4 See Maurice Strong, "Canada in a Planetary Society," Address to the Men's Canadian Club of Ottawa, February 12, 1974.
5 Hugh G.J. Aitken, **American Capital and Canadian Resources** (Cambridge: Harvard University Press, 1961), p. 85.
6 James Laxer, **Canada's Energy Crisis** (Toronto: James Lewis and Samuel, Publishers, 1974), p. 129.
7 For an articulation of this view of life and religion, see H.E. Runner, **The Relation of the Bible to Learning** (Toronto: Wedge Publishing Foundation, 1970), 167 pp.; **Scriptural Religion and Political Task** (Toronto: Wedge Publishing Foundation, 1974), 123 pp. See also this statement by the same author: "The most fundamental battle of our time is not to be thought of in the first place as one for the preservation of a familiar and so-called orthodox church organization, or of an abstract system of theological propositions. The struggle of our time goes much deeper: it is a struggle for the religious direction of human society in its totality. . . . A church organization, or a world of Christian theological activity, standing alone within a culture all the other activities of which are directed by an anti-Christian spirit must remain impotent and has become irrelevant, and it will in the long run fade away. Even to preserve the organized church therefore we must fight for an integral Christian society." H. Evan Runner, **Can Canada Tolerate the C.L.A.C.?: The Achilles Heel of a Humanistic Society** (Toronto: Christian Labour Association of Canada, 1967), pp. 14-15.
8 Peter L. Berger, **Facing up to Modernity: Excursions in Society, Politics, and Religion** (New York: Basic Books, Inc., 1977), p. 206.
9 See, e.g., Paul's words about the wisdom of God versus the foolishness of the world in I Corinthians 1.
10 See in this connection Willem A. Visser 't Hooft, **The Background of the Social Gospel in America** (St. Louis, Missouri: The Bethany Press, 1928). This is an outstanding study of the social gospel in which especially its notion of divine immanence is criticized.
11 J.S. Woodsworth, **The First Story of the Labor Church and Some Things For Which It Stands** An Address in the Strand Theatre, Winnipeg, April 5th, 1920 (Labor Church, Winnipeg), p. 13.
12 Salem G. Bland, **The New Christianity** (1920; reprint ed., Toronto: University of Toronto Press, 1973), p. 72.
13 **Ibid.**, p. 79.
14 See the translated lectures by G. Groen van Prinsterer, **Unbelief and Revolution: Lectures VIII and IX** (Amsterdam: The Groen van Prinsterer Fund, 1975), 87 pp. and **Unbelief and Revolution: Lecture XI** (Amsterdam: The Groen van Prinsterer Fund, 1973), 68 pp.

15 In 1898 Kuyper presented the Stone Lectures at Princeton University. See Abraham Kuyper, **Lectures on Calvinism** (Grand Rapids: Wm. B. Eerdmans Publishing Company, 1953), 199 pp. See also Abraham Kuyper, **Christianity and the Class Struggle** (Grand Rapids: Piet Hein Publisher, 1950), 64 pp.
16 Dooyeweerd's major work has been translated in English. See Herman Dooyeweerd, **A New Critique of Theoretical Thought,** 4 vols. (Amsterdam: H.J. Paris; Philadelphia: Presbyterian and Reformed Publishing Company, 1953-1958); Herman Dooyeweerd, **In the Twilight of Western Thought** (Philadelphia: Presbyterian and Reformed Publishing Company, 1960), 195 pp. See also L. Kalsbeek, **Contours of a Christian Philosophy: An Introduction to Herman Dooyeweerd's Thought** (Toronto: Wedge Publishing Foundation, 1975); Arthur Holmes, "Christian Philosophy," **Encyclopaedia Britannica** (1974 edition), vol. 4, pp. 555-56; James William Skillen, "The Development of Calvinistic Political Theory in the Netherlands, with Special Reference to the Thought of Herman Dooyeweerd" (Ph.D. dissertation, Duke University, 1973), 459 pp.

Chapter 1

1 Harry G. Johnson, "Economic Benefits of the Multinational Enterprise," in H.R. Hahlo, J. Graham Smith, Richard W. Wright, eds., **Nationalism and the Multinational Enterprise: Legal, Economic and Managerial Aspects** (Dobbs Ferry, New York: Oceana Publications, Inc., 1973), p. 167.
2 Carl A. Gerstacker, quoted in S. Prakash Sethi and Richard H. Holton, eds., **Management of the Multinationals: Policies, Operations, and Research** (New York: The Free Press, 1974), p. 78.
3 Johnson, "Economic Benefits," pp. 166-67.
4 Frank Tannenbaum, "The Survival of the Fittest," in Courtney C. Brown, ed., **World Business: Promise and Problems** (New York/London: Macmillan, 1970), p. 165.
5 **Ibid.,** p. 166.
6 George Ball, "The Promise of the Multinational Corporation," **Fortune,** June 1967, p. 80.
7 Arnold Toynbee, "Are Businessmen Creating a New Pax Romana?" **Forbes,** April 15, 1974, p. 68.
8 Mira Wilkins, **The Emergence of Multinational Enterprise: American Business Abroad from the Colonial Era to 1914** (Cambridge: Harvard University Press, 1970), p. 17.
9 **Ibid.,** p. 28.
10 **Ibid.,** pp. 47-69.
11 The following warning, given in 1902, indicates that the current concern over American prominence is not new: "We are becoming the hewers of wood and drawers of water, while the most skilled, the most profitable, and the easiest trades are becoming American. . . . The purchase outright of British manufacturers by Americans is a blow to our prestige. But in many instances the American purchasers settle in our midst, and become English in their turn. England has in the past showed great powers of absorbing other peoples; in the future she will show the same. To build high barriers against America would be folly. If we wish to hold what America is taking from us we must do so by proving ourselves as good men as the Americans, as good in business energy, in education, in technical training, in working capacity, and in inventive skills." F.A. McKenzie, **The American Invaders** (London: Grant Richards, 1902), pp. 120-21; quoted in Jack N. Behrman, **National Interests and the Multinational**

Enterprise: Tensions Among the North Atlantic Countries (Englewood Cliffs, New Jersey: Prentice-Hall, Inc., 1970), p. 153.

12 Wilkins, **Emergence of Multinational Enterprise,** p. 83.

13 **Ibid.,** p. 201.

14 Christopher Tugendhat, **The Multinationals** (London: Eyre & Spottiswoode, 1971), p. 12.

15 **Ibid.,** p. 20.

16 **Ibid.,** pp. 22-23.

17 **Ibid.,** p. 24.

18 **Multinational Corporations in World Development** (New York: United Nations, 1973), p. 139.

19 **Ibid.,** p. 7.

20 See Tugendhat, **Multinationals,** p. 32.

21 See Thomas Aitken, **The Multinational Man: The Role of Managers Abroad** (London: George Allen and Unwin Ltd., 1973), chapter 2, "The Small Multinationals," pp. 22-35.

22 James K. Sweeney, "A Small Company Enters the European Market," **Harvard Business Review,** September-October 1970, p. 128.

23 This is the meaning assigned to the term multinational in **Multinational Corporations in World Development,** p. 5.

24 **U.S. Multinationals: The Dimming of America,** A Report prepared for the AFL-CIO Maritime Trades Department, Executive Board meeting February 15, 16, 1973, p. 22.

25 **The Multinational Corporation: Studies on U.S. Foreign Investment,** vol. I, (U.S. Department of Commerce, 1972), section one, p. 7.

26 Raymond Vernon, **Sovereignty at Bay: The Multinational Spread of U.S. Enterprises** (New York/London: Basic Books, Inc., 1971), pp. 14-15.

27 See Louis Turner, **Invisible Empires: Multinational Companies and the Modern World** (New York: Harcourt Brace Jovanovich, Inc., 1970), pp. 177-80.

28 Vernon, **Sovereignty at Bay,** p. 134.

29 See Tugendhat, **Multinationals,** p. 25.

30 **The Multinational Corporation: Studies on U.S. Foreign Investment,** vol. I, section one, p. 35.

31 **Ibid.,** section one, p. 38.

32 See Vernon, **Sovereignty at Bay,** pp. 85, 90.

33 **Ibid.,** p. 90.

34 These figures are from **Gaps in Technology, Analytical Report** (Paris: Organization for Economic Co-operation and Development, 1970), quoted in **Multinational Corporations in World Development,** p. 49.

35 See Vernon, **Sovereignty at Bay,** p. 92.

36 Turner, **Invisible Empires,** p. 9.

37 See Tugendhat, **Multinationals,** p. 132.

38 **Ibid.,** p. 134. For further details on this problem, see pp. 134-37. These multinationals included Canadian ones: see Behrman, **National Interests and the Multinational Enterprise,** pp. 80-81. See also Turner, **Invisible Empires,** pp. 81-85.

39 Charles Levinson, **International Trade Unionism** (London: George Allen and Unwin Ltd., 1972), pp. 72-73.

40 Charles Levinson, **Capital, Inflation and the Multinationals** (London: George Allen and Unwin Ltd., 1971), pp. 70-71.

41 "How the Multinationals Play the Money Game," **Fortune,** August 1973, p. 138.

42 **Fortune,** August 1973, p. 62.
43 See **Fortune,** August 1973, p. 62. For a brief discussion on proposals for tax reforms in the U.S. which would result in much higher tax rates paid by the U.S. parent companies on the profits earned abroad, see "The Push to Make Them Pay More Taxes," **Fortune,** August 1973, p. 57.
44 Richard Barnet, Ronald Müller, **Global Reach: The Power of the Multinational Corporations** (New York: Simon and Schuster, 1974), p. 278.
45 Quoted in Tugendhat, **Multinationals,** p. 143.
46 Levinson, **International Trade Unionism,** p. 72.
47 Turner, **Invisible Empires,** p. 78.
48 For a detailed description of this incredible, large-scale swindle, see Robert A. Hutchison, "The Looting of I.O.S.," **Fortune,** March 1973, pp. 126ff.
49 See Richard J. Barber, **The American Corporation: Its Power, Its Money, Its Politics** (New York: E.P. Dutton & Co., Inc., 1970), pp. 61-62; also Walter Stewart, "Beneath the Sheltering Palms," **Maclean's,** November 17, 1975, pp. 30ff.
50 Turner, **Invisible Empires,** p. 79.
51 For details on the Eurocurrency market I have drawn on Frederick Heldring, "Multinational Banking Strives for Identity," in Brown, ed., **World Business,** pp. 214-21; and Tugendhat, **Multinationals,** pp. 156-63.
52 Quoted in Tugendhat, **Multinationals,** p. 160.
53 Jane Sneddon Little, **Euro-Dollars: The Money-Market Gypsies** (New York: Harper and Row Publishers, 1975), p. 1.
54 Levinson, **Capital, Inflation and the Multinationals,** p. 147. Other details in this paragraph are derived from pp. 144-51. See also Barnet and Müller, "A Reporter At Large: Global Reach II," in **The New Yorker,** December 9, 1974, pp. 102-107, for a brief description of the enormous assets controlled by the large American banks. They report that the top fifty banks in the U.S. had 39 per cent of all commercial bank assets in 1960; ten years later that had increased to 85 per cent of all assets in commercial banking. In 1971 U.S. banks had $557 billion in corporate securities in their portfolios; they controlled an additional $336 billion in trust funds. The Rockefeller-Morgan group, with the six largest banks (Chase Manhattan, First National City Bank, Manufacturers Hanover Trust, Chemical Bank of New York, Morgan Guaranty Trust, and Bankers Trust) is singled out as the core of the U.S. banking industry.
55 **The Financial Post 300,** Summer 1977, pp. 20, 45.
56 Quoted in Peter C. Newman, "The Bankers, Part Two," **Maclean's,** March 1972, p. 29.
57 **Ibid.,** p. 29.
58 Cf. this comment: "Thus, nine-tenths of American investment in Europe is financed from European sources. In other words, *we pay them to buy us*." J.J. Servan-Schreiber, **The American Challenge,** trans. Ronald Steel (New York: Avon Books, 1969), p. 43.
59 For a brief discussion of these and other beneficial effects of foreign direct investment, see Behrman, **National Interests and the Multinational Enterprise,** pp. 21-26.
60 Vernon, **Sovereignty at Bay,** p. 166.
61 Sanford Rose, "Multinational Corporations in a Tough New World," **Fortune,** August 1973, p. 55.
62 **The Multinational Corporation: Studies on U.S. Foreign Investment,** vol. I, section one, p. 65.
63 **Ibid.,** section three, p. 11.
64 Quoted by S. Prakash Sethi and Adam F. Cuhney, "The Domestic Inter-

national Sales Corporation (DISC): Problems and Prospects," in Sethi and Holton, eds., **Management of the Multinationals,** p. 102.

65 Behrman, **National Interests and the Multinational Enterprise,** p. 98.

Chapter 2

1 Samuel Pisar, "The Transideological Corporation: New Hope for the Third World," **Economic Impact,** no. 5, p. 43.

2 In this section I have relied extensively on these sources: Charles Levinson, **International Trade Unionism** (London: George Allen and Unwin Ltd., 1972), chapter 5, and **Capital, Inflation and the Multinationals** (London: George Allen and Unwin Ltd., 1971), chapter 4; Herbert E. Meyer, "A Plant that Could Change the Soviet Industry," **Fortune**, November 1974, pp. 150ff; Hedrick Smith, "The Russians Mean Business About Business," **The Atlantic Monthly**, December 1974, pp. 41-48; and Pisar, "The Transideological Corporation: New Hope for the Third World," pp. 43-47.

3 "The U.S. Trade Lag With Eastern Europe," **Business Week**, February 23, 1976, p. 44.

4 See "Yugoslavia: A Door Slightly Ajar for U.S. Investment," **Business Week,** February 6, 1978, pp. 54-55.

5 Smith, "The Russians Mean Business About Business," p. 44.

6 Herbert E. Meyer, "Why the Outlook Is So Bearish for U.S.-Soviet Trade," **Fortune**, Jan. 16, 1978, pp. 102-104.

7 Levinson, **Capital, Inflation and the Multinationals,** p. 118.

8 Pisar, "The Transideological Corporation: New Hope for the Third World," p. 47.

9 Lenin wrote in Pravda of April 28, 1918: "The task that the Soviet government must set the people in all its scope is—learn to work. The Taylor system, the last word of capitalism in this respect, like all capitalist progress, is a combination of the refined brutality of bourgeois exploitation and a number of the greatest scientific achievements in the field of analyzing mechanical motions during work, the elimination of superfluous and awkward motions, the elaboration of correct methods of work, the introduction of the best system of accounting and control, etc. The Soviet Republic must at all cost adopt all that is valuable in the achievements of science and technology in this field. The possibility of building socialism depends exactly upon our success in combining the Soviet power and the Soviet organisation of administration with the up-to-date achievements of capitalism. We must organize in Russia the study and teaching of the Taylor system and systematically try it out and adapt it to our own ends." James E. Connor, **Lenin on Politics and Revolution** (New York: Pegasus, 1968), p. 260.

10 Smith, "The Russians Mean Business About Business," p. 48. At the time of this writing, Russia has renounced the 1972 trade agreement with the U.S., which removed the discriminatory tariffs against Russia, because it objected to the attached condition that the emigration of Jews from Russia be liberalized.

11 Quoted in Robert Scheer, "The Doctrine of Multinational Sell," **Esquire,** April 1975, p. 160.

12 **Ibid.,** p. 164.

13 Richard Barnet and Ronald Müller, **Global Reach: The Power of the Multinational Corporations,** (New York: Simon and Schuster, 1974), p. 190.

14 **Multinational Corporations in World Development** (New York: United Nations, 1973), p. 175.

15 **Ibid.**, pp. 20-21.
16 **Ibid.**, p. 193.
17 Louis Turner, **Multinational Companies and the Third World** (New York: Hill and Wang, Inc., 1973), p. 56.
18 **The Economist**, May 28, 1977, p. 85.
19 Barnet and Müller, **Global Reach**, p. 153.
20 **The Multinational Corporation: Studies on U.S. Foreign Investment**, vol. I, (U.S. Department of Commerce, 1972), section three, p. 5.
21 Many of the figures and other details in this section have been derived from Barnet and Müller, **Global Reach**.
22 Turner, **Multinational Companies and the Third World**, p. 58.
23 Barnet and Müller, "A Reporter At Large: Global Reach I," **The New Yorker**, December 2, 1974, p. 99.
24 Turner, **Multinational Companies and the Third World**, p. 49.
25 Barnet and Müller, "A Reporter At Large: Global Reach I," p. 69.
26 **Multinational Corporations in World Development**, p. 195.
27 Turner, **Multinational Companies and the Third World**, p. 53.
28 For a well-documented critique of this issue from a Marxist perspective, see Pierre Jalée, **The Pillage of the Third World**, trans. Mary Klopper (New York/London: Monthly Review Press, 1968).
29 **The Economist**, May 28, 1977, p. 86.
30 Albert Stridsberg, "New Marketing, Ad Methods May Save Underdeveloped Nations," **Advertising Age**, Sept. 22, 1969, p. 64.
31 See Barnet and Müller, **Global Reach**, p. 183.
32 Building "runaway plants" and employing cheap labour in Taiwan, Singapore, Brazil and other low-wage countries, for the manufacture of mass consumption goods, provides some much-needed jobs. The wages, though low compared to Western standards, are of obvious benefit to the local workers, but this form of using the low-wage manpower in the Third World amounts to exploitation. These workers are extremely vulnerable to layoffs and economic slumps, in the absence of unemployment, sickness and other benefits. Moreover, this type of employment is not integrated into the country's development and functions as an "enclave" that often obstructs a balanced development in the long run.
33 Barnet and Müller, **Global Reach**, p. 166.
34 For a refreshing discussion on the challenge of the Third World, see E.F. Schumacher, **Small Is Beautiful: A Study of Economics As If People Mattered** (London: Blond and Briggs Ltd., 1973), especially pp. 152-206.
35 Turner, **Multinational Companies and the Third World**, pp. 163-65.

Chapter 3

1 William C. Hood, "The Canadian Economy: An Overview," in Richard H. Leach, ed., **Contemporary Canada** (Toronto: U. of T. Press, 1968), pp. 60-61.
2 **Foreign Direct Investment in Canada** (Ottawa: Information Canada, 1972), p. 26.
3 Kari Levitt, **Silent Surrender: The Multinational Corporation in Canada** (Toronto: Macmillan, 1970), p. 142.
4 Melville H. Watkins, "A Staple Theory of Economic Growth," **Canadian Journal of Economics and Political Science**, vol. 29, no. 2, May 1963, p. 157.
5 D.W. Carr, **Recovering Canada's Nationhood** (Ottawa: Canada Publishing Company, 1971), p. 20.
6 "Innis was a liberal nationalist for whom Canada, having sprung from

liberalism, must develop its own national version. He recognized liberal (American) imperialism, but he did not abandon his faith in Canadian liberalism. The resulting tension made him personally highly productive but socially increasingly irrelevant. His contemporaries, unable to accept his analysis of liberal imperialism, became continentalists." Melville H. Watkins, "Economics in Canada," in Ian Lumsden, ed., **Close the 49th Parallel etc.: The Americanization of Canada** (Toronto: U. of T. Press, 1970, 1973), p. 205.

7 R.T. Naylor, "The Rise and Fall of the Third Commercial Empire of the St. Lawrence," in Gary Teeple, ed., **Capitalism and the National Question in Canada** (Toronto: U. of T. Press, 1972), p. 2.

8 Jim Laxer, "Introduction to the Political Economy of Canada," in Robert Laxer, ed., **(Canada) Ltd.: The Political Economy of Dependency** (Toronto: McClelland and Stewart Ltd., 1973), pp. 28-29.

9 Hugh G.J. Aitken, **American Capital and Canadian Resources** (Cambridge: Harvard University Press, 1961), p. 131.

10 V.C. Fowke, "The National Policy—Old and New," in W.T. Easterbrook and M.H. Watkins, eds., **Approaches to Canadian Economic History** (Toronto: McClelland and Stewart Ltd., 1967), p. 240.

Another Canadian economist provides the following summary of the National Policy: "At the heart of the National Policy was the determination to strengthen Canada's east-west axis by the construction of a transcontinental railroad. This would offset the increasing north-south pull of American markets and at the same time make possible agricultural expansion into the western prairies beyond the intervening barrier of the pre-Cambrian Shield. Central Canada—now the provinces of Ontario and Quebec—would become the manufacturing and financial centre of the new dominion, and by the transcontinental railroad manufactured goods could be sent west to the prairie market and agricultural produce east to the St. Lawrence provinces and Europe. To this grand design all other aspects of the National Policy were to contribute. The protective tariff would check the importation of American manufactures and funnel freight of Canadian origin along the east-west artery." H.G.J. Aitken, "Defensive Expansion: The State and Economic Growth in Canada," in Easterbrook and Watkins, eds., **Approaches to Canadian Economic History**, pp. 204-205.

11 Craig Brown, "The Nationalism of the National Policy," in Peter Russell, ed., **Nationalism in Canada** (Toronto: McGraw-Hill, 1966), p. 162.

12 Jim Laxer, "Introduction to the Political Economy of Canada," p. 31. See also Michael Bliss, "Canadianizing American Business," in Lumsden, ed., **Close the 49th Parallel etc.**, p. 32.

13 See Naylor's summary: "As we have seen, the Macdonald tariff produced industry in Canada but no Canadian industry, because it was not intended to produce Canadian firms. It was a mercantile rather than an industrial protective tariff, designed explicitly to augment the quantity of productive factors available to the economy by attracting foreign capital. To the merchant capitalist ruling class, the nationality of the industrial sector was irrelevant: what counted was its size and its location in central Canada. The federal government did not play the role of entrepreneur, as is often suggested, but that of financial intermediary and provider of social overhead capital." Naylor, "The Rise and Fall of the Third Commercial Empire," p. 25.

14 Bliss, "Canadianizing American Business," p. 32.

15 For the distinction between foreign direct and portfolio investment, see Levitt, **Silent Surrender**, pp. 58-59.

16 **Ibid.**, pp. 64-68.

17 **Ibid.**, pp. 60-70. See also Carr, **Recovering Canada's Nationhood**, pp. 45-53, 183-84.

18 U.S. Department of Commerce, **Survey of Current Business**, October 1977, p. 23.

19 See Carr, **Recovering Canada's Nationhood**, pp. 185-87.

20 **Foreign Direct Investment in Canada**, p. 26.

21 Walter L. Gordon, "Last Chance for Canada," **Maclean's**, September 1972, p. 72.

22 Aitken, **American Capital and Canadian Resources**, p. 112.

23 Pierre L. Bourgault, **Innovation and the Structure of Canadian Industry**, Background Study for the Science Council of Canada (Ottawa: Information Canada, 1972), p. 51.

24 **Ibid.**, p. 83.

25 Mel Watkins, "Resources and Underdevelopment," in Laxer, ed., **(Canada) Ltd.**, p. 111.

26 See, for example, the case of Canadair in Montreal which was owned by General Dynamics in the U.S. until 1976. The parent company had allowed Canadair to languish by keeping its projects and investment money at home. After the Canadian government bought this company, it began to thrive; as explained by one observer: "Autonomy from the U.S. unleashed management ambitions and a new atmosphere was felt throughout the company." Dean Walker, "Launching a stunning comeback," **Executive**, November 1977, p. 67.

27 See **Foreign Ownership and the Structure of Canadian Industry: Report of the Task Force on the Structure of Canadian Industry** (Ottawa: Information Canada, 1968), pp. 154-59.

28 See Abraham Rotstein and Gary Lax, eds., **Getting It Back: A Program for Canadian Independence** (Toronto/Vancouver: Clarke, Irwin & Company Limited, 1974), p. 9.

29 **Ibid.**, p. 10.

30 See **Foreign Direct Investment in Canada**, pp. 137-46. See also Rotstein and Lax, eds., **Getting It Back**, pp. 49-66.

31 Levitt, **Silent Surrender**, p. 77.

32 Robert L. Perry, **Galt U.S.A.: The 'American Presence' in a Canadian City** (Toronto: Maclean-Hunter Ltd., 1971), p. 63.

33 Arthur J. Cordell, **The Multinational Firm, Foreign Direct Investment, and Canadian Science Policy**, Background Study for the Science Council of Canada, no. 22, 1971, p. 62.

34 **Ibid.**, p. 64.

35 **Ibid.**, p. 65.

36 Bourgault, **Innovation and Structure**, p. 124.

37 See Richard Liskeard, "Computers: Caught in the Continental Web," in Mark Starowicz and Rae Murphy, eds., **Corporate Canada: 14 Probes Into the Workings of a Branchplant Economy** (Toronto: James Lewis and Samuel, Publishers, 1972), pp. 100-107.

38 **Towards a National Science Policy for Canada**, Science Council of Canada Report No. 4 (Ottawa: Queen's Printer, 1968), p. 42.

39 Liskeard, "Computers: Caught in the Continental Web," p. 103.

40 **A Trans-Canada Computer Communications Network**, Science Council of Canada, Report No. 13 (Ottawa: Information Canada, 1971), p. 26.

41 The crucial distinction between debt and equity capital, described previously, should be kept in mind in this section.

42 Cy Gonick, "Foreign Ownership and Political Decay," in Lumsden, ed., **Close the 49th Parallel etc.**, pp. 64-65.
43 **CALURA, Report for 1971** (Ottawa: Statistics Canada), p. 18.
44 Levitt, **Silent Surrender,** pp. 137, 138.
45 **Foreign Direct Investment in Canada,** p. 90.
46 Levitt, **Silent Surrender,** p. 140.
47 Quoted in Mel Hurtig, **A Submission to the Select Committee on Foreign Investment of the Government of Alberta** (Edmonton, 1972), p. 29. (Mimeographed.)
48 Describing his difficulties in borrowing money at this time, McClelland blames Canadian investors for shortsightedness and greed. For the difficulties experienced by him and other Canadian businessmen in borrowing capital from Canadian investors and investment institutions, see Perry, **Galt U.S.A.,** especially pp. 82-91.
49 Hurtig, **A Submission to the Select Committee,** p. 23.
50 **Ibid.,** pp. 22, 30. For a critical description of the various aid programs and special arrangements sponsored by the federal and provincial governments, see David Lewis, **Louder Voices: The Corporate Welfare Bums** (Toronto: James Lewis and Samuel, Publishers, 1972), pp. 62-96.
51 Carr, **Recovering Canada's Nationhood** pp. 156-57.
52 A.E. Safarian, "Some Myths About Foreign Business Investment in Canada," **Journal of Canadian Studies,** August 1971, p. 17.
53 Mel Watkins, "A New National Policy," in Trevor Lloyd and Jack McLeod, eds., **Agenda 1970: Proposals for a Creative Politics** (Toronto: U. of T. Press, 1968), p. 173.
54 See Levitt, **Silent Surrender**, pp. 49-57, 142-53; Carr, **Recovering Canada's Nationhood,** pp. 35-44.
55 Aitken, **American Capital,** p. 178.
56 Levitt, **Silent Surrender,** p. 55. For a detailed description of the current English Canada-Quebec controversy and the problems of the Canadian economy viewed from a socialist perspective, see James and Robert Laxer, **The Liberal Idea of Canada: Pierre Trudeau and the Question of Canada's Survival** (Toronto: James Lorimer & Company Publishers, 1977), 234 pp.
57 **Foreign Ownership and the Structure of Canadian Industry,** p. 49.
58 **Foreign-Owned Subsidiaries in Canada** (Ottawa: Information Canada, 1974). This is how an American author describes the way multinational corporations affect the U.S. balance of payments: "The impact of multinational companies on the U.S. balance of payments is an important but very elusive issue. Multinational companies exert all sorts of unmeasurable influences on the balance. . . . When the companies send capital overseas, they obviously hurt the balance of payments. They import goods from their foreign affiliates, which also hurts. But they sell a lot to their foreign affiliates, which helps. And each year the affiliates send home dividends, royalties, and management fees—which help a lot." Sanford Rose, "Multinational Corporations in a Tough New World: A Big Boost for the B.O.P.," **Fortune,** August 1973, p. 64.
59 **Foreign Direct Investment in Canada,** p. 289.
60 Levitt, **Silent Surrender,** p. 15.
61 See Wayne Cheveldayoff, "Canada Faces Prospect of Crisis in Payments," **The Globe and Mail,** August 19, 1976, p. B-1.
62 Levitt, **Silent Surrender,** p. XIII.
63 **Foreign Direct Investment in Canada,** p. 271.
64 **Ibid.,** p. 292.

65 **Ibid.**, pp. 296-97.
66 For details see Paul Audley, "Book Publishing in Canada," in Rotstein and Lax, eds., **Getting It Back,** pp. 201-21.
67 See John Warnock, "All the News it Pays to Print," in Ian Lumsden, ed., **Close the 49th Parallel etc.**, pp. 117-34.
68 See Denis Smith, **Gentle Patriot: A Political Biography of Walter Gordon** (Edmonton: Hurtig Publishers, 1973), p. 228.
69 **Ibid.,** p. 231.
70 See Hurtig, **A Submission to the Select Committee,** p. 19.
71 See James Steele and Robin Mathews, "The Universities: Takeover of the Mind," in Lumsden, ed., **Close the 49th Parallel etc.**

Chapter 4

1 Peter F. Drucker, **Management: Tasks, Responsibilities, Practices** (New York: Harper and Row, 1973), p. 753.
2 Richard J. Barnet and Ronald E. Müller, **Global Reach: The Power of the Multinational Corporations** (New York: Simon and Schuster, 1974), p. 373.
3 J.J. Servan-Schreiber, **The American Challenge,** trans. Ronald Steel (New York: Avon Books, 1969), p. 43.
4 **Ibid.,** p. 42.
5 **Ibid.,** pp. 115-16.
6 See **Summary of the Hearings Before the Group of Eminent Persons to Study the Impact of Multinational Corporations on Development and on International Relations** (New York: United Nations, 1974).
7 **The Impact of Multinational Corporations on Development and on International Relations** (New York: United Nations, 1974), p. 129.
8 **Ibid.,** p. 54.
9 **Summary of the Hearings Before the Group,** p. 216.
10 **Ibid.,** p. 218.
11 "An American Proposal," **Fortune,** May 1942, p. 63.
12 **Summary of the Hearings Before the Group,** p. 237.
13 **Ibid.,** p. 254.
14 Richard Armstrong, "Suddenly it's Mañana in Latin America," **Fortune,** August 1974, p. 143.
15 See Raymond Vernon, **Storm over the Multinationals: the Real Issues** (Cambridge: Harvard University Press, 1977), p. 197.
16 "Northrop's Punishment for Campaign Giving," **Business Week,** February 24, 1975, pp. 60ff. See also "Northrop: Fame in Aircraft, Shame in Politics," **The New York Times,** May 18, 1975, sec. 3, pp. 1, 12.
17 See Michael C. Jensen, "How 3M Got Tangled Up in Politics," **The New York Times**, March 9, 1975, sec. 3, pp. 2f.
18 For a description of the action against IBM, see William D. Smith, "Curtain Time for the I.B.M. Case," **The New York Times,** May 18, 1975, sec. 3, pp. 1, 2; see also Edward Cowan, "Wanted: A Lawyer to Take on A.T. & T.," **The New York Times**, Sunday, March 12, 1978, sec. 3, pp. 2f.
19 Marylin Bender, "Management Braces for Annual Meetings," **The New York Times,** March 23, 1975, sec. 3, pp. 1f.
20 Neil H. Jacoby, **Corporate Power and Social Responsibility: A Blueprint for the Future** (New York: Macmillan, 1973), p. 177.
21 Robert F. Buckhorn, **Nader the People's Lawyer** (Englewood Cliffs, New Jersey: Prenctice-Hall, Inc., 1972), p. 38.

22 Ralph Nader and Mark J. Green, eds., **Corporate Power in America** (New York: Grossman, 1973), pp. vii-viii.
23 Cf. Andrew Hacker, "Citizen Counteraction?" in Nader and Green, eds., **Corporate Power in America,** p. 173.
24 **Ibid.,** p. 176.
25 **Ibid.,** pp. 176, 177.
26 Drucker, **Management,** p. 761.
27 **Ibid.,** p. 758.
28 In this context Drucker's remarks about the Canadian situation are of interest: "The key case is, of course, Canada. That Canadian industry is so heavily owned by foreign, and especially by U.S., companies is the result of **Canadian** decisions and actions, and especially of the deliberate policy of the Liberal governments of Canada in the thirty years after the Great Depression of the thirties, to channel Canadian capital into 'infrastructure' investments such as public works and leave industrial investment to the foreigner. The result, in economic terms, has been a brilliant success. . . . Politically the result has, however, been undesirable. A major economic power, which is what Canada has become, cannot be 'owned' abroad." **Ibid.,** pp. 758-59.
29 See Raymond Vernon, **Sovereignty at Bay: The Multinational Spread of U.S. Enterprises** (New York/London: Basic Books, 1971), p. 270.
30 Jack N. Behrman, **National Interests and the Multinational Enterprise: Tensions Among the North Atlantic Countries** (Englewood Cliffs, N.J.: Prentice-Hall, Inc., 1970), p. 171.
31 Barnet and Müller, **Global Reach,** p. 364.
32 **Ibid.,** p. 373.
33 **Ibid.,** p. 210.
34 John K. Galbraith, **The New Industrial State** (Boston: Houghton Mifflin, 1967), p. 164.
35 John K. Galbraith, **Economics and the Public Purpose** (Boston: Houghton Mifflin, 1973), pp. 170, 172.
36 Galbraith, **The New Industrial State,** p. 370.
37 Galbraith, **Economics and the Public Purpose,** p. 242.
38 **Ibid.,** p. 242.
39 **U.S. Multinationals: The Dimming of America,** A Report prepared for the AFL-CIO Maritime Trades Department, Executive Board meeting February 15, 16, 1973, p. 1.
40 **Ibid.,** p. 4.
41 **Ibid.,** p. 49.
42 **Ibid.,** p. 60.
43 **Ibid.,** p. 57.
44 See Irwin Ross, "Labor's Big Push for Protectionism," **Fortune,** March 1973, pp. 92ff.
45 Barnet and Müller, **Global Reach,** p. 216.
46 Cf. this comment on the AFL-CIO's push in late 1977 for protectionist measures similar to those envisaged in the earlier Burke-Hartke bill (which would undoubtedly work against the interests of those countries in which American subsidiaries are located): "If a trade bill in this form were to be revived in Congress, it could mean the end of the multilateral trade talks in Geneva. . . . And if a restrictive AFL-CIO trade bill got Congressional approval, it could produce a 1930s style trade war with the industrial nations vying with each other to raise tariffs and keep out imports." Peter Cook, "AFL chief pushes for more restrictive U.S. trade law," **Financial Times of Canada,** Nov. 14-20, 1977, p. 16.

47 **The Multinational Corporation: Studies on U.S. Foreign Investment**, vol. I, (U.S. Department of Commerce, 1972), section two, p. 31.
48 **Ibid.**, section two, p. 15. The Harvard Business School study found that the Canadian investment yielded immediate positive results to the U.S. in terms of employment and the balance of payments. The net employment gain to the U.S. economy was thirty-five man-years of employment on the basis of machinery exports to the Canadian subsidiary. The balance-of-payments gain was an inflow to the U.S. beginning at $1.9 million in the first year. (This is because the investment was made with a Canadian bank loan, so no outflow from the U.S. occurred.) During the next six years (transitional period) the yearly inflow was also $1.9 million. After that the yearly inflow to the U.S. parent was $2.8 million.
49 **U.S. Multinationals: The Dimming of America**, p. 84.

Chapter 5

1 Eric Kierans, "Towards a New National Policy," in Abraham Rotstein and Gary Lax, eds., **Independence: The Canadian Challenge** (Toronto: Web Offset Publications Ltd., 1972) pp. 111-12.
2 Alan Heisey, **The Great Canadian Stampede: The Rush to Economic Nationalism—Right or Wrong** (Toronto: Griffin House, 1973), p. v.
3 Abraham Rotstein, **The Precarious Homestead: Essays on Economics, Technology and Nationalism** (Toronto: New Press, 1973), p. 77.
4 For a summary of the Report of the Royal Commission on Canada's Economic Prospects, see Albert A. Shea, **Canada 1980** (Toronto: McClelland and Stewart Ltd., 1960). For a helpful look at the political background of this Report, see Denis Smith, **Gentle Patriot: A Political Biography of Walter Gordon** (Edmonton: Hurtig Publishers, 1973), chapter 2, pp. 31-50.
5 Smith, **Gentle Patriot**, p. 32.
6 **Ibid.**, p. 44.
7 **Foreign Ownership and the Structure of Canadian Industry** (Ottawa: Information Canada, 1968).
8 **Ibid.**, p. 392.
9 **Ibid.**, p. 394
10 Abraham Rotstein, **The Precarious Homestead**, p. 53.
11 **Foreign Direct Investment in Canada** (Ottawa: Information Canada, 1972), p. 429.
12 Editorial committee of *The Canadian Forum,* **A Citizen's Guide to the Gray Report** (Toronto: New Press, 1971), p. 6.
13 For a brief review of these and other measures aimed at safeguarding certain sectors of the Canadian economy from foreign domination, see **Foreign Ownership and the Structure of Canadian Industry,** pp. 383-94. See also **Foreign Direct Investment,** pp. 319-37.
14 For the complete text of the letter containing these guidelines, see **Foreign-Owned Subsidiaries in Canada 1964-1967** (Ottawa: Queen's Printer, 1970), pp. 67-70.
15 A.W. Cockerill, "Canada: Economic Colony," **The Guardian,** December 4, 1971.
16 See H. Anthony Hampson, "The CDC: Friend or Foe?" Speech delivered by H. Anthony Hampson, President and Chief Executive Officer of the Canada Development Corporation, to the International Conference sponsored by the Chemical Institute of Canada and the Commercial Development Association Inc., Montreal, December 4, 1974. (Mimeographed.) Hampson states: "We are

not asked to preempt takeovers, to act as a buyer of last resort, to be a 'buy-back' agency, or to assume some special responsibility for employment and regional development, even though we believe we can make a useful contribution on the last two fronts—as you can also—through creating successful and growing enterprises, the only lasting way to achieve rising employment and standards of living." See also Daniel Stoffman, "Canada Development Corp. Still Won't Sell You a Share," **The Toronto Star,** April 17, 1975, p. C-3.

17 Roger Croft, "Foreign Takeovers: Is Anyone On Guard?" **The Toronto Star,** March 13, 1976, p. B-1.

18 Kari Levitt, **Silent Surrender: The Multinational Corporation in Canada** (Toronto: Macmillan of Canada, 1970), p. 146.

19 Jim Laxer, "Canadian Manufacturing and U.S. Trade Policy," in Robert M. Laxer, ed., **(Canada) Ltd.: The Political Economy of Dependency** (McClelland and Stewart, 1973), p. 135.

20 Hugh G.J. Aitken, **American Capital and Canadian Resources** (Toronto: House of Anansi Press Ltd., 1967), p. 136.

21 Quoted in D.W. Carr, **Recovering Canada's Nationhood** (Ottawa: Canada Publishing Company, 1971), p. 62.

22 Smith, **Gentle Patriot,** p. 311.

23 See John Fayerweather, **Foreign Investment in Canada: Prospects for National Policy** (Toronto: Oxford University Press, 1974), p. 20.

24 **Ibid.,** p. 166.

25 Harry G. Johnson, **The Canadian Quandary: Economic Problems and Policies** (Toronto: McGraw-Hill Company of Canada Limited, 1963), p. 23.

26 **Ibid.,** p. 127.

27 **Ibid.,** p. 17.

28 **Ibid.,** p. 12.

29 Walter L. Gordon, **A Choice for Canada: Independence or Colonial Status** (Toronto/Montreal: McClelland and Stewart Ltd., 1966), pp. 123-24.

30 Walter L. Gordon, "Last Chance for Canada," **Maclean's,** September 1972, p. 72.

31 See Walter L. Gordon, **Storm Signals: New Economic Policies for Canada** (Toronto: McClelland and Stewart Limited, 1975), pp. 105-14.

32 Quoted in Dave Godfrey and Mel Watkins, eds., **Gordon to Watkins to You: A Documentary: The Battle for Control of Our Economy** (Toronto: New Press, 1970), pp. 50-51.

33 Eric Kierans, "The Cosmocorporation: An Unsympathetic View," in H.R. Hahlo, J. Graham Smith, Richard W. Wright, eds., **Nationalism and the Multinational Enterprise: Legal, Economic and Managerial Aspects** (Dobbs Ferry, New York: Oceana Publications Inc., 1973), p. 171.

34 **Ibid.,** p. 179.

35 **Ibid.,** p. 180.

36 Kierans, "Towards a New National Policy," p. 116.

37 Rotstein and Lax, eds., **Independence: The Canadian Challenge,** p. xi.

38 Abraham Rotstein and Gary Lax, eds., **Getting It Back: A Program for Canadian Independence** (Toronto/Vancouver: Clarke, Irwin & Company Limited, 1974).

39 **Ibid.,** p. xii

40 **Ibid.,** pp. xiv-xv.

41 Philip Sykes, **Sellout: The Giveaway of Canada's Energy Resources** (Edmonton: Hurtig Publishers, 1973).

42 See Ian A. McDougall, et al., "Economic Development with Environmental Security," a brief to the Canadian Council of Resource and Environment

Ministers, 1972; for an excellent critique of Canada's resource policies written from a Christian perspective, see John Olthuis, "Canada's Energy Policy," **C.J.L. Working Paper** (Toronto: C.J.L. Foundation, 1974).
43 Sykes, p. 12.
44 Rotstein, **The Precarious Homestead,** p. 12.
45 **Ibid.,** p. 94.
46 **Ibid.,** p. 98.
47 **Ibid.,** p. 66.
48 See Godfrey and Watkins, eds., **Gordon to Watkins to You,** pp. 103-109.
49 Rotstein, **The Precarious Homestead,** p. 72.
50 **Ibid.,** p. 213.
51 **Ibid.,** p. 23.
52 **Ibid.,** p. 331.
53 Godfrey and Watkins, eds., **Gordon to Watkins to You,** p. 105.
54 **Ibid.,** p. 107.
55 See Virginia Hunter, "Why I Left the Waffle," **The Canadian Forum,** March 1975, pp. 17-20.
56 John Hutcheson, "Class and Income Distribution in Canada," in Laxer, ed., **(Canada) Ltd.,** p. 82.
57 John Smart, "Populist and Socialist Movements in Canadian History," in Laxer, ed., **(Canada) Ltd.,** p. 215.
58 Hutcheson, "Class and Income Distribution in Canada," p. 174.
59 Mel Watkins, "Contradictions and Alternatives in Canada's Future," in Laxer, ed., **(Canada) Ltd.,** p. 268.
60 Quoted in Godfrey and Watkins, eds., **Gordon to Watkins to You,** p. 136.
61 Charles Taylor, "The Agony of Economic Man," in Laurier LaPierre et al, eds., **Essays on the Left** (Toronto/Montreal: McClelland and Stewart Ltd., 1971), p. 226.

Chapter 6

1 George Grant, **Lament for a Nation: The Defeat of Canadian Nationalism** (Toronto: McClelland and Stewart Limited, 1965), p. 90.
2 Robert S. McNamara, "McNamara on the 'Gap' " in J.J. Servan-Schreiber, **The American Challenge,** trans. Ronald Steel (New York: Avon Books, 1969), p. 93.
3 Barry Commoner, **The Closing Circle: Nature, Man and Technology** (New York: Alfred A. Knopf, 1971), p. 26.
4 Walter L. Gordon, **A Choice for Canada: Independence or Colonial Status** (Toronto/Montreal: McClelland and Stewart Ltd., 1966), p. xiv.
5 D.W. Carr, **Recovering Canada's Nationhood** (Ottawa: Canada Publishing Company, 1971), p. 148.
6 George Grant, **Technology and Empire: Perspectives on North America** (Toronto: House of Anansi, 1969), p. 70.
7 Grant, **Lament for a Nation,** p. 86.
8 **Ibid.,** p. 53.
9 Grant, **Technology and Empire,** p. 113.
10 **Ibid.,** p. 114.
11 Grant, **Lament for a Nation,** p. 46.
12 **Ibid.,** p. 47.
13 **Ibid.,** p. 54.
14 Grant, **Technology and Empire,** p. 137.
15 **Ibid.,** p. 64.

16 **Ibid.**, p. 44.
17 Jacques Ellul, **The Technological Society**, trans. John Wilkinson (New York: Vintage Books, 1964), p. xxv.
18 **Ibid.**, pp. xxxii-xxxiii.
19 **Ibid.**, p. 6.
20 **Ibid.**, p. 221.
21 **Ibid.**, p. 356. One of the major experiments carried on by the "human relations" school was conducted at the Hawthorne Works of Western Electric Co. in the late 1920s. This experiment clearly showed that the intention was indeed to adapt men to the machine. Elton Mayo, the Harvard professor in charge of this "experiment," wrote that "these various studies—biochemical, medical, industrial, anthropological—show signs of developing a coherent unity of relation which, if it continues to advance, will greatly increase our understanding and control of the human problems of an industrial civilization." Elton Mayo, **The Human Problems of an Industrial Civilization** (New York: The Viking Press, 1933), p. 161.
22 Ellul, **The Technological Society**, p. 436. See in this connection E.O. Wilson's comments on human behaviour: "[T]here is every justification from both genetic theory and experiments on animal species to suppose that rapid behavioral evolution is at least a possibility in man. By rapid I mean significant alteration in, say, emotional and intellectual traits within no more than ten generations—or about 300 years." Quoted in Robert L. Heilbroner, **An Inquiry into the Human Prospect** (New York: W.W. Norton and Company, Inc., 1974; Toronto: George J. McLeod Limited, 1974), p. 120.
23 Robert L. Heilbroner, **The Economic Problem** (Englewood Cliffs, New Jersey: Prentice-Hall, Inc., 1968), p. 633.
24 Robert L. Heilbroner, **An Inquiry into the Human Prospect** (New York: W.W. Norton and Company, Inc., 1974; Toronto: George J. McLeod Limited, 1974), p. 22.
25 **Ibid.**, p. 57.
26 **Ibid.**, p. 77.
27 **Ibid.**, p. 94.
28 **Ibid.**, pp. 135-36.
29 **Ibid.**, p. 137.
30 **Ibid.**, pp. 143-44.
31 Donella H. Meadows, Dennis L. Meadows, Jørgen Randers, William W. Behrens III, **The Limits to Growth: A Report for the Club of Rome's Project on the Predicament of Mankind** (Washington, D.C.: New American Library—a Signet Book, 1972), p. 197.
32 E.J. Mishan, **The Costs of Economic Growth** (London: Staples Press, 1967).
33 **Ibid.**, p. 7.
34 **Ibid.**, p. 15.
35 **Ibid.**, p. 144.
36 **Ibid.**, p. 146.
37 **Ibid.**, p. 173.
38 **Ibid.**, p. 174.
39 E.F. Schumacher, **Small is Beautiful: A Study of Economics As If People Mattered** (London: Blond & Briggs Ltd., 1973).
40 **Ibid.**, p. 137.
41 **Ibid.**, pp. 275-76.
42 Raymond Aron, **The Industrial Society: Three Essays on Ideology and Development** (New York: Simon and Schuster, a Clarion Book, 1968), p. 14.
43 **Ibid.**, p. 15.

44 Bob Goudzwaard, "The Dynamic of the Word of God in Economics" (2), **The Guide,** May 1974, p. 9.
45 See in this connection E. Schuurman, **Techniek en Toekomst** (Assen: Van Gorcum and Comp. N.V., 1972). This book contains an excellent English summary, pp. 399-425.

Chapter 7

1 Donald Creighton, **Canada's First Century 1867-1967** (Toronto: Macmillan of Canada, 1970), p. 355.
2 Vincent Massey, **Speaking of Canada: Addresses by the Right Hon. Vincent Massey** (Toronto: The Macmillan Company of Canada Ltd., 1959), p. 208.
3 Bruce Hutchison, "Where Do We Go From Here?" **Maclean's,** July 1971, pp. 46-47.
4 Bruce Hutchison, "The Storming of the World," **Maclean's,** September 1972, pp. 27ff.
5 Donald Creighton, **Dominion of the North: A History of Canada** (Toronto: The Macmillan Co. of Canada Ltd., 1944, 1957), p. 575.
6 **Ibid.,** pp. 576, 579.
7 Creighton, **Canada's First Century,** p. 354.
8 **Ibid.,** p. 356.
9 See Donald Creighton, "We've Been Fat Too Long and Now it's Too Late," **Maclean's,** April 1975, pp. 26-28.
10 **Ibid.,** p. 28. Another distinguished Canadian must not be omitted from this discussion. He is the late Vincent Massey (1887-1967) who served as the Canadian Governor-General from 1952-1959. He demonstrated keen insight into the nature of the crisis besetting our society. A devout Christian, he was aware that this crisis was at bottom religious and could only be overcome by a return to Biblical faith. See his collection of speeches, in Massey, **Speaking of Canada,** especially, "The Good Canadian," pp. 36-41 and "Christian Social Order in a Changing World," pp. 203-209.
11 See John Porter, **The Vertical Mosaic: An Analysis of Social Class and Power in Canada** (Toronto: University of Toronto Press, 1965).
12 James L. Heap, ed., **Everybody's Canada: The Vertical Mosaic Reviewed and Re-examined** (Toronto: Burns and MacEachern Ltd., 1974), p. viii.
13 Porter, **The Vertical Mosaic,** p. 557.
14 **Ibid.,** p. 108.
15 **Ibid.,** p. 558.
16 Wallace Clement, **The Canadian Corporate Elite: An Analysis of Economic Power** (Toronto: McClelland and Stewart Ltd., 1975).
17 **Ibid.,** pp. xxv-xxvi.
18 **Ibid.,** p. 5.
19 **Ibid.,** p. 150.
20 **Ibid.,** p. 355.
21 Peter C. Newman, **The Canadian Establishment,** volume 1 (Toronto: McClelland and Stewart Limited, 1975), 480 pp.
22 **Ibid.,** chapter 5, pp. 143-73.
23 Cf. **Canada Yearbook 1973** (Ottawa: Information Canada, 1973), pp. 373-75.
24 **A Science Policy for Canada: Report of the Senate Special Committee on Science Policy, Vol. 2** (Ottawa: Information Canada, 1972), p. 365.
25 **A Science Policy for Canada: Report of the Senate Special Committee on Science Policy, Vol. 1** (Ottawa: Information Canada, 1970), p. 271.

26 See **Ibid.**, pp. 282-83.
27 **Economic Targets and Social Indicators: Eleventh Annual Review,** Economic Council of Canada (Ottawa: Information Canada, 1974), p. 7.
28 **Ibid.**, pp. 9-10.
29 **Ibid.**, p. 8
30 Quoted in Andrew H. Wilson, **Science, Technology, and Innovation: Special Study No. 8,** Economic Council of Canada (Ottawa: Information Canada, 1968), pp. 108-109.
31 To my knowledge, very little attention has been paid to this phenomenon. Charles Lynch, veteran political columnist, alerted his readers to the collectivistic overtone of the **Eleventh Annual Review** of the ECC. He wrote: "Here we are just 10 years away from George Orwell's 1984, and the Economic Council is striving mightily to fulfill his dire prophecy that, by that time, we shall all be programmed into a master computer, run by Big Brother." See Charles Lynch, "Who Needs Economic Council as Big Brother?" **The Vancouver Sun,** November 28, 1974.

Lynch laments the fact that under the Council's program individual rights and responsibilities will be hollowed out into four outputs, and aspirations will be quantified. But his critique lacks depth and is a one-shot attempt. (How else can you write for a newspaper audience?) The next day Lynch will move on to a different subject, and the juggernaut grinds on. There is reason to believe that this type of reporting plays somewhat of a similar role to the one played by the Russian magazine **Krokodil** (see p. 133). It creates the illusion of a vigorous and critical press, but nothing changes. I do not write this to blame Lynch in the first place, but first of all his readers who prefer to be left undisturbed.

32 Wilson, **Special Study No. 8,** pp. 103-104. A different and much more appealing advice comes from Barry Commoner with respect to this same issue. He points out that the isolation of science from the practical problems, resulting in the destruction of our environment through the introduction of new industrial and agricultural production technologies, limits public knowledge about the real causes. He insists that public knowledge is essential to the solution of the environmental problems because these solutions depend not only on scientific data but on public judgement. The environmental crisis represents hidden costs which must be made explicit and balanced against the benefits of technology in open public debate.

Commoner continues: "But this debate will not come easily. For the public has little access to the necessary scientific data. Much of the needed information has been, and remains, wrapped in government and industrial secrecy. Unearthing the needed information and disseminating it to the public is, I believe, the unique responsibility of the scientific community. For to exercise its right of conscience, the public must have the relevant scientific facts in understandable terms. As the custodians of this knowledge, we in the scientific community owe it to our fellow citizens to help inform them about the crisis in the environment." Barry Commoner, **The Closing Circle: Nature, Man and Technology** (New York: Alfred A. Knopf, 1971), p. 198.

33 Walter Stewart, **Shrug: Trudeau in Power** (Toronto: New Press, 1971.
34 **Ibid.**, p. 152.
35 **Ibid.**, p. 188.
36 **Ibid.**, p. 182.
37 Pierre Elliott Trudeau, **Federalism and the French Canadians** (Toronto: Macmillan of Canada, 1968), p. 203.
38 Stewart, **Shrug: Trudeau in Power,** p. 2.

39 **Ibid.**, chapter: "The Press: The Flattering Friends," pp. 203ff.
40 Donald Smiley, "The Managed Mosaic," in Viv Nelles and Abraham Rotstein, **Nationalism or Local Control** (Toronto: New Press, 1973), p. 74.
41 **Ibid.**, p. 74.
42 **Ibid.**, pp. 74-75.
43 Erich Fromm, **The Revolution of Hope: Toward a Humanized Technology** (New York: Harper and Row, Publishers, Inc., 1968), p. 1.
44 George Grant, **Lament for a Nation: The Defeat of Canadian Nationalism** (Toronto: McClelland & Stewart Ltd., 1965), p. 76.
45 **Canadian Industrial Relations: The Report of the Task Force on Labour Relations** (Ottawa: Privy Council Office, 1968), p. 119.
46 Cf. this observation: "Unions, like management, have failed in this new and more challenging area, although they have responded comparatively well to worker concerns about their terms and conditions of employment and their subordinate status in relation to their employers. To some extent this failure is due to the fact that unions and collective bargaining were not designed to handle problems growing out of the nature of work itself." **Canadian Industrial Relations**, p. 98.
47 I cannot help but observe here that this type of report does not seem to serve an important function despite the talents and expense devoted to its preparation. When a report such as this is issued, it results in a few items in the newspaper; each side in the labour-management contest selects what it approves for use in the continuing propaganda battle; no new and innovative alternatives are pursued, but the patchwork of labour legislation is simply updated a bit. Furthermore, this type of inquiry gives the appearance of real action being taken and real participation occurring. In reality it provides the government with some more time to shelve the problem.
48 **Information**, 15/77, Labour Canada, July 21, 1977.
49 In a **Globe and Mail** article, Joe Morris, President of the Canadian Labour Congress, accused the federal government of wanting to centralize power via the anti-inflation control program, and he warned that the Congress has "no other option but to resist with all the strength at its command, even to the point where it must eventually defy the Government." Joe Morris, "Trudeau's True Purpose Is to Centralize Power," **The Globe and Mail**, January 10, 1975, p. 7.
50 See Canadian Labour Congress, "Labour's Manifesto for Canada," adopted at convention held in Quebec City, May 17-21, 1976, 14 pp.; and "Discussion Paper for the Meeting with the Prime Minister and Members of the Cabinet," July 12, 1976, 8 pp. (Mimeographed.)
51 For a more detailed description of reforming the enterprise and labour-management relations, see the submissions of the Christian Labour Association of Canada: 1) "A Re-Evaluation of Collective Bargaining," presented to the Conference on Labour Legislation, Victoria, B.C., April 13-15, 1973; 2) "A proposal to Re-Structure Collective Bargaining in the Province of British Columbia," June 7, 1973; 3) "Submission to the Royal Commission Inquiry in Certain Sectors of the Building Industry," Commissioner His Honour Harry Waisberg, March 1974. (Mimeographs.)
52 In connection with the increasing unrest in Canadian industry, an article by Paul Johnson on the British trade unions is particularly relevant. Johnson, who is a socialist, in a remarkably hard-hitting article, accuses the British unions of incompetence and greed, and he holds them responsible for the current social-economic crisis in Britain. See Paul Johnson, "A Brotherhood of National Misery," **New Statesman**, May 16, 1975, pp. 652-56.

53 See Arnold Toynbee, "Continual Recession is Foreseen," **The Toronto Star,** April 20, 1974, p. A-12.
54 For an excellent description of the spirit of modernity and its presence in the political left as well as the right, see Bernard Zylstra, "Modernity and the American Empire," **International Reformed Bulletin,** No. 68, 1977, pp. 3-19.
55 Trudeau, **Federalism and the French Canadians,** p. 196.
56 J.A. Corry and J.E. Hodgetts, **Democratic Government and Politics** (Toronto: University of Toronto Press, 1946, 1964), p. 230.
57 See Nelles and Rotstein, eds., **Nationalism or Local Control,** p. 6.
58 **Ibid.,** p. 6.
59 Quoted in Ross Terrill, "China Moves Away From Mao and to Modernization," **The Toronto Star,** December 16, 1977.

Chapter 8

1 William Barrett, **Irrational Man: A Study in Existential Philosophy** (New York: Doubleday and Co. Inc., 1958, 1962), p. 274.
2 Bernard Zylstra, "The Bible, Justice and the State," **International Reformed Bulletin,** no. 55, 1973, pp. 15, 8, 9.
3 Kenneth D. McRea, ed., **Consociational Democracy: Political Accommodation in Segmented Societies** (Toronto: McClelland and Stewart Ltd., 1974), pp. 300-301.
4 Gad Horowitz, "Creative Politics, Mosaics and Identity," in Heaps, ed., **Everybody's Canada,** p. 27.
5 Charles Taylor, **The Pattern of Politics** (Toronto: McClelland and Stewart Limited, 1970, 1975), pp. 124-25.
6 Hoogendoorn vs. Greening Metal Products and Screening Equipment et al, Ontario Court of Appeal, 1967, CCH-C.L.L.R., par. 14,017, pp. 11, 179.
7 Cf. H. Evan Runner, **Can Canada Tolerate the CLAC?: The Achilles Heel of a Humanistic Society** (Toronto: Christian Labour Association of Canada, 1967), p. 22ff.
8 Crane Brinton, **The Shaping of Modern Thought** (Englewood Cliffs, New Jersey: Prentice-Hall, Inc., 1950), pp. 82-83. See also this succinct description about the period 1789-1848 by another eminent historian: "For in a sense there was only one *Weltanschauung* of major significance, and a number of other views which, whatever their merits, were at bottom chiefly negative critiques of it: the triumphant, rationalist, humanist 'Enlightenment' of the eighteenth century. Its champions believed firmly (and correctly) that human history was an ascent, rather than a decline or an undulating movement about a level trend. They could observe that man's scientific knowledge and technical control over nature increased daily. They believed that human society and individual man could be perfected by the same application of reason, and were destined to be so perfected by history. On these points bourgeois liberals and revolutionary proletarian socialists were at one." E.J. Hobsbawm, **The Age of Revolution: 1789-1848** (New York: The New American Library, a Mentor Book, 1962), p. 278.
9 Cf. this analysis: " . . . what I find striking today is the radical disjunction between the social structure (techno-economic order) and the culture. The former is ruled by an economic principle defined in terms of efficiency and functional rationality, the organization of production through the ordering of things, including men as things. The latter is prodigal, promiscuous, dominated by an anti-rational, anti-intellectual temper in which the self is taken as the

touchstone of cultural judgments, and the effect on the self is the measure of the aesthetic worth of experience." Daniel Bell, **The Cultural Contradictions of Capitalism** (New York: Basic Books, Inc., 1976), p. 37.

10 For an excellent discussion of this Biblical principle, see H. Van Riessen, **The Society of the Future** (Philadelphia: The Presbyterian and Reformed Publishing Co., 1952), especially chapter III, "Structural Principles of Society," pp. 68-86. See also H. Evan Runner, "Sphere Sovereignty," **Christian Perspectives** (Hamilton: Guardian Publishing Company Ltd., 1961), pp. 53-87.

11 Van Riessen, **Society of the Future,** pp. 71-72.

12 Cf. this author's claim: "The superiority of private capitalism over collectivism is essentially the superiority of God's revelation over man's human reason and faulty logic. . . . We should be enthusiastic about private capitalism as a system designed to guard something priceless—our freedom to choose. . . . The United States is a free country because every citizen is free to fashion his life according to his own plans. . . . The philosophy of free enterprise is based on the belief that an economic system that makes it possible for each to pursue his own best interests will achieve the greatest welfare for all. The foundations of free enterprise are also the foundations of democracy." John R. Richardson, **Christian Economics: Studies in the Christian Message to the Market Place** (Houston, Texas: St. Thomas Press, 1966), pp. 32-33.

13 Cf. this statement of the Special Senate Committee on Poverty: "The welfare system, at all levels, costs Canadians more than six billion dollars a year, yet it has not significantly alleviated poverty let alone eliminated it. The problems grow; costs go up and up and will, in time, suffocate the taxpayer. The welfare system is increasingly unable to deal with the needs of its clients. It has failed to achieve its humanitarian goals. It deprives its recipients of dignity and provides no incentive or rewards to escape from poverty. It has become punitive and demeaning. It is a mess—a social wasteland and an economic morass." **Highlights from the Report of the Special Senate Committee on Poverty** (Ottawa: Information Canada, 1971, 1972), p. 10.

A 1978 study concluded that the relative position of the poor in Canada had declined further during the 1970s. See W. Irwin Gillespie, **In Search of Robin Hood: The Effect of Federal Budgetary Policies During the 1970s on the Distribution of Income in Canada** (Montreal: C.D. Howe Research Institute, 1978), 61 pp.

14 Bob Goudzwaard, "Economic Stewardship Versus Capitalist Religion" (Toronto: Institute for Christian Studies, 1972), p. 55. (Mimeographed.)

15 Leviticus 25:23, 24 (NAS).

16 Leviticus 25:29-31 (NAS).

17 Bob Goudzwaard, **The Christian and the Modern Business Enterprise** (Toronto: Christian Labour Association of Canada, 1967), p. 12.

18 Zylstra, "The Bible, Justice and the State," p. 11.

19 Cf. this observation: "In union ranks, there are many leaders who prefer to operate in an atmosphere of discontent and opposition. Without discontent, members may cease to believe that unions are necessary. Without an opponent, union officials may lack a symbol to use in whipping up militancy and determination among the rank and file. To these leaders, the newer concepts of work may be distasteful because they blur the lines between workers and management and weaken the adversary spirit." John T. Dunlop and Derek C. Bok, **Labor and the American Community** (New York: Simon and Schuster, 1970), p. 360.

20 Here it is in order to point to the split-personality character of North American business unionism. Unions, on the one hand, assume an opposition stance; on the other hand, they conclude agreements with management which then must be enforced.

21 See Taylor's confident prediction regarding the beneficial effect of his system: "Scientific management, on the contrary, has for its very foundation the firm conviction that the true interests of the two are one and the same; that prosperity for the employer cannot exist through a long term of years unless it is accompanied by prosperity for the employee, and vice versa; and that it is possible to give the workman what he most wants—high wages—and the employer what he wants—a low labor cost—for his manufactures." F.W. Taylor, **The Principles of Scientific Management** (1911; reprint ed., New York: W.W. Norton & Company, 1967), p. 10.

22 Quoted in Georges Friedman, **Industrial Society: The Emergence of the Human Problems of Automation** (Toronto: Collier-Macmillan Canada Ltd., Free Press Paperback Edition, 1964), p. 365.

A chilling example of this perspective and the attempt to eliminate the human element is provided by Alfred Krupp of the famous Krupp family, the German steel makers. He obviously had absorbed Taylor's lessons well. He stated: "What I shall attempt to bring about [in the Krupp works] is, that nothing shall be dependent on the life or existence of any particular person; that nothing of importance shall happen or be caused to happen without the foreknowledge and approval of the management; that the past and the determinable future of the establishment can be learned in the files of management without asking a question of any mortal." Quoted in Loren Baritz, **The Servants of Power: A History of the Use of Social Science in American Industry** (New York: John Wiley and Sons, 1960), pp. 5-6.

23 Peter F. Drucker, **The Future of Industrial Man** (New York: The John Day Company, 1942), p. 110.

24 **Ibid.,** p. 129.

25 Barry Commoner has perceptively described the interdependence of energy, technology and employment. The corporation's drive for profit demands more capital-intensive equipment, which is not labour intensive while it invariably increases the consumption of scarce energy resources. This results in capital shortage and unemployment simultaneously. Barry Commoner, "A Reporter At Large: Energy III," **The New Yorker,** February 16, 1976, pp. 64ff.; see especially p. 84.

26 As E. Schuurman, Dutch professor of philosophy, writes: "The meaning of technology is not exhausted in human existence: it transcends man. In technology man unfolds the nature that is created by God. Accordingly, technology at bottom is service of God, and therein service of fellow man and development of culture." E. Schuurman, **Techniek en Toekomst [Technology and the Future]** (Assen, the Netherlands: Van Gorcum en Co. N.V., 1972), p. 420.

27 In this connection, we can think of many examples. To mention only one: the current drift into the so-called cashless society should be fundamentally re-examined since it reinforces those trends that further enhance the power of the machine and the automated process. But the federal government blithely supports this new development. See, for example, **Towards an Electronic Payment System** (Ottawa: Information Canada, 1975).

28 John Kenneth Galbraith, **The New Industrial State** (Boston: Houghton Mifflin Company, 1973), pp. 37-38.

29 **Ibid.**, p. 273.
30 See Vance Packard, **The Waste Makers** (New York: Pocket Book, Inc., David McKay edition, 1960).
31 Richard J. Barnet and Ronald E. Müller, **Global Reach: The Power of the Multinational Corporations** (New York: Simon and Schuster, 1974), p. 365.
32 Wilson Bryan Key, **Subliminal Seduction: Ad Media's Manipulation of a Not So Innocent America** (Englewood Cliffs, New Jersey: Prentice-Hall, Inc., 1973), p. 8.
33 Robert S. McNamara, Address to the Board of Governors, International Bank for Reconstruction and Development, Sept. 26, 1977, p. 11.

Summary

1 William Barrett, **Irrational Man: A Study in Existential Philosophy** (New York: Doubleday and Co. Inc., 1958, 1962), p. 31.
2 Lewis Mumford, **The Myth of the Machine: The Pentagon of Power** (New York: Harcourt Brace Jovanovich, 1964), pp. 183-84.

Conclusions

1 Alexander Solzhenitsyn, ed., **From Under The Rubble** (Boston/Toronto: Little, Brown and Company, 1975), pp. 137-38.
2 Premier Alexander B. Campbell of Prince Edward Island, at Federal-Provincial Conference, April 9, 1975.
3 Vincent Massey, **Speaking of Canada: Addresses by the Right Hon. Vincent Massey** (Toronto: The Macmillan Company of Canada Ltd., 1959), p. 207.
4 Daniel Bell, **The Cultural Contradictions of Capitalism** (New York: Basic Books, Inc., 1976), pp. 28-29.
5 Os Guinness, **The Dust of Death: A Critique of the Establishment and the Counter Culture—and a Proposal for a Third Way** (Downers Grove, Illinois: Inter-Varsity Press, 1973), pp. 378-79.
6 Abraham Rotstein and Gary Lax, eds., **Getting It Back: A Program for Canadian Independence** (Toronto/Vancouver: Clarke, Irwin & Company Limited, 1974), p. 287.
7 See Heather Robertson, "Confessions of a Canadian Chauvinist Pig," **Maclean's,** April 1975, p. 96.
8 See Mark Hatfield, "A Time to Share," **The Guide,** December 1974, pp. 6ff.
9 See William Stringfellow, "The Case Against Christendom and the Case Against Pierre Berton," in William Kilbourn, ed., **The Restless Church: A Response to the Comfortable Pew** (Toronto/Montreal: McClelland and Stewart Ltd., 1966), pp. 11-32.
10 See Document No. F.P.-4171, Federal-Provincial Conference of First Ministers, April 9-10, 1975, Ottawa.
11 Deuteronomy 8:6-9 (NAS).
12 Matthew 6:25, 28, 31, 33.

Bibliography

BOOKS

Adler-Karlsson, Gunnar. **Reclaiming the Canadian Economy: A Swedish Approach through Functional Socialism**. Toronto: House of Anansi Press Ltd., 1967, 96 pp.

Aitken, Hugh G.J. **American Capital and Canadian Resources.** Cambridge: Harvard University Press, 1961, 212 pp.

Aitken, Thomas. **The Multinational Man: The Role of the Manager Abroad.** London: George Allen and Unwin Ltd., 1973, 176 pp.

Barber, Richard J. **The American Corporation: Its Power, Its Money, Its Politics**. New York: Dutton and Co. Inc., 1970, 309 pp.

Baritz, Loren. **The Servants of Power: A History of the Use of Social Science in American Industry**. New York: John Wiley and Sons, 1960, 273 pp.

Barnet, Richard J., and Müller, Ronald E. **Global Reach: The Power of the Multinational Corporations.** New York: Simon and Schuster, 1974, 508 pp.

Barrett, William. **Irrational Man: A Study in Existential Philosophy.** New York: Doubleday Anchor Books, 1962, 314 pp.

Behrman, Jack N. **National Interests and the Multinational Enterprise: Tensions Among the North Atlantic Countries.** Englewood Cliffs, New Jersey: Prentice-Hall, Inc., 1970, 194 pp.

Bell, Daniel. **The Cultural Contradictions of Capitalism**. New York: Basic Books, Inc., 1976, 301 pp.

Berger, Peter L. **Facing up to Modernity: Excursions in Society, Politics, and Religion**. New York: Basic Books, Inc., 1977, 233 pp.

Berle, Adolph A., and Means, Gardiner C. **The Modern Corporation and Private Property**. New York: Harcourt, Brace and World, Inc., 1967, 380 pp.

Bland, Salem G. **The New Christianity.** 1920; reprint ed., Toronto: University of Toronto Press, 1973, 89 pp.

Brinton, Crane. **The Shaping of Modern Thought.** Englewood Cliffs, New Jersey: Prentice-Hall, Inc., 1950, 249 pp.

Brown, Courtney C., ed. **World Business: Promise and Problems.** New York /London: The Macmillan Company, 1970, 338 pp.

Buckhorn, Robert F. **Nader the People's Lawyer.** Englewood Cliffs, New Jersey: Prentice-Hall, Inc., 1972, 310 pp.

Carr, D.W. **Recovering Canada's Nationhood.** Ottawa: Canada Publishing Company, 1971, 213 pp.

Clement, Wallace. **The Canadian Corporate Elite: An Analysis of Economic Power.** Toronto: McClelland and Stewart Ltd., 1975, 479 pp.

Commager, Henry. **The American Mind.** New Haven: Yale University Press, 1950, 476 pp.

Commoner, Barry. **The Closing Circle: Nature, Man and Technology.** New York: Alfred A. Knopf, 1971, 326 pp.

______. **The Poverty of Power: Energy and the Economic Crisis.** New York: Alfred A. Knopf, 1976, 314 pp.

______. **Science and Survival.** New York: The Viking Press, 1966, 150 pp.

Connor, James E. **Lenin on Politics and Revolution.** New York: Pegasus, 1968, 377 pp.

Corry, J. A., and Hodgetts, J.E. **Democratic Government and Politics.** Toronto: University of Toronto Press, 1946, 1964, 691 pp.

Creighton, Donald. **Canada's First Century 1867-1967.** Toronto: Macmillan of Canada Ltd., 1970, 372 pp.

______. **Dominion of the North: A History of Canada.** Toronto: The Macmillan Company of Canada Ltd., 1944, 1957, 619 pp.

Dooyeweerd, Herman. **A New Critique of Theoretical Thought.** 4 vols. Amsterdam: H.J. Paris; Philadelphia: Presbyterian and Reformed Publishing Company, 1953-1958.

______. **In The Twilight of Western Thought.** Philadelphia, Pennsylvania: The Presbyterian and Reformed Publishing Company, 1960, 195 pp.

Drucker, Peter F. **Concept of the Corporation.** New York: John Day Company, 1946; reprint ed., Boston: Beacon Press, 1960, 301 pp.

______. **Management: Tasks, Responsibilities, Practices.** New York: Harper and Row, 1973, 839 pp.

______. **The Future of Industrial Man**. New York: John Day Company, 1942, 298 pp.

______. **The New Society: The Anatomy of Industrial Order.** New York: Harper and Row, 1962; Harper Torch Books, 1973, 362 pp.

Dunlop, John T., and Bok, Derek C. **Labor and the American Community.** New York: Simon and Schuster, 1970, 542 pp.

Ellul, Jacques. **Hope in Time of Abandonment.** Translated by C. Edward Hopkin. New York: The Seabury Press, 1973, 306 pp.

______. **The Technological Society**. Translated by John Wilkinson. New York: Vintage Books, 1964, 449 pp.

Fayerweather, John. **Foreign Investment in Canada: Prospects for National Policy.** Toronto: Oxford University Press, 1974, 194 pp.

Fleisher, Frederic. **The New Sweden: The Challenge of a Disciplined Democracy.** New York: David McKay Company, Inc., 1967, 365 pp.

Fromm, Erich. **The Revolution of Hope: Toward a Humanized Technology.** New York: Harper and Row, Publishers, Inc., 1968, 162 pp.

Galbraith, John K. **Economics and the Public Purpose**. Boston: Houghton Mifflin, 1973, 334 pp.

______. **The New Industrial State.** Boston: Houghton Mifflin, 1967, 427 pp.

Godfrey, Dave, and Watkins, Mel, eds. **Gordon to Watkins to You: A Documentary: The Battle for Control of Our Economy.** Toronto: New Press, 1970, 258 pp.

Gordon, Walter L. **A Choice for Canada.** Toronto: McClelland and Stewart Limited, 1966, 125 pp.

______. **Storm Signals: New Economic Policies for Canada.** Toronto: McClelland and Stewart Limited, 1975, 140 pp.

______. **Troubled Canada: The Need for New Domestic Policies.** Toronto: McClelland and Stewart Limited, 1961, 134 pp.

Goudzwaard, Bob. **Aid for the Overdeveloped West.** Toronto: Wedge Publishing Foundation, 1975, 89 pp.

Goyder, George. **The Responsible Company.** Oxford: Basil Blackwell, 1961, 192 pp.

Grant, George P. **Lament for a Nation: The Defeat of Canadian Nationalism.** Toronto: McClelland and Stewart Limited, 1965, 97 pp.

______. **Philosophy in the Mass Age.** Vancouver/Toronto/Montreal: The Copp Clark Publishing Co. Ltd., 1959, 117 pp.

______. **Technology and Empire: Perspectives on North America.** Toronto: House of Anansi, 1969, 143 pp.

Guinness, Os. **The Dust of Death: A Critique of the Establishment and the**

Counter Culture—and a Proposal for a Third Way. Downers Grove, Illinois: Inter-Varsity Press, 1973, 419 pp.

Hahlo, H.R.; Smith, Graham J.; and Wright, Richard W., eds., **Nationalism and the Multinational Enterprise.** Leiden: A.W. Sijthoff, 1973; Dobbs Ferry, New York: Oceana Publications, Inc., 1973.

Hart, Hendrik. **The Challenge Of Our Age.** Hamilton: Guardian Publishing Company, 1968, 148 pp.

Heap, James L., ed. **Everybody's Canada: The Vertical Mosaic Reviewed and Re-examined.** Toronto: Burns and MacEachern Ltd., 1974, 178 pp.

Heilbroner, Robert L. **An Inquiry into the Human Prospect.** New York: W.W. Norton and Company, Inc.; Toronto: George J. McLeod Limited, 1974, 150 pp.

Heilbroner, Robert L., and others. **In the Name of Profit: Profiles in Corporate Irresponsibility.** New York: Doubleday & Company, 1972, 273 pp.

Heisey, Alan. **The Great Canadian Stampede: The Rush to Economic Nationalism Right or Wrong.** Toronto: Griffin House, 1973, 148 pp.

Hobsbawm, E. J. **The Age of Revolution: 1789-1848.** New York: The New American Library, A Mentor Book, 1962, 416 pp.

Hunnius, Gerry; Garson, David G.; and Case, John, eds. **Workers Control: A Reader on Labor and Social Change.** New York/Toronto: Vintage Books, Random House, 1973, 493 pp.

Huntford, Roland. **The New Totalitarians.** New York: Stein and Day Publishers, 1971, 354 pp.

Hutcheson, John. **Dominance and Dependency: Liberalism and National Policies in the North Atlantic Triangle.** Toronto: McClelland and Stewart Limited, 1978, 182 pp.

Jacoby, Neil H. **Corporate Power and Social Responsibility: a Blueprint for the Future.** New York: The Macmillan Company, 1973, 282 pp.

Jalée, Pierre. **Pillage of the Third World.** Translated by Mary Klopper. New York/London: Monthly Review Press, 1968.

Johnson, Harry G. **The Canadian Quandary: Economic Problems and Policies.** Toronto/Montreal: McGraw-Hill Company of Canada Limited, 1963, 352 pp.

Kalsbeek, L. **Contours of a Christian Philosophy: An introduction to Herman Dooyeweerd's Thought.** Toronto: Wedge Publishing Foundation, 1975, 360 pp.

Kerr, Clark; Dunlop, John T.; Harbison, Frederick; and Myers, Charles A. **Industrialism and Industrial Man.** New York: Oxford University Press, 1960, 239 pp.

Key, Wilson Bryan. **Subliminal Seduction: Ad Media's Manipulation of a Not So Innocent America.** Englewood Cliffs, New Jersey: Prentice-Hall, Inc., 1973, 206 pp.

Kierans, Eric W. **Challenge of Confidence: Kierans on Canada.** Toronto/Montreal: McClelland and Stewart Limited. 1967, 125 pp.

Kilbourn, William, ed. **Canada: A Guide to the Peaceable Kingdom.** Toronto: Macmillan of Canada, 1970, 345 pp.

______. **The Restless Church: A Response to the Comfortable Pew.** Toronto/Montreal: McClelland and Stewart Ltd., 1966, 196 pp.

Kindleberger, Charles P., ed. **The International Corporation.** Cambridge /London: The M.I.T. Press, 1970, 415 pp.

Kuyper, Abraham. **Christianity and the Class Struggle.** Grand Rapids: Piet Hein, 1950, 64 pp.

______. **Lectures on Calvinism.** Grand Rapids: Wm. B. Eerdmans Publishing Company, 1953, 199 pp.

Laxer, James. **Canada's Energy Crisis.** Toronto: James Lewis & Samuel, Publishers, 1974, 135 pp.

______. **The Energy Poker Game: The Politics of the Continental Resources Deal.** Toronto/Chicago: New Press, 1970, 72 pp.

Laxer, Robert M., ed. **[Canada] Ltd.: The Political Economy of Dependency.** Toronto: McClelland and Stewart Limited, 1973, 268 pp.

Laxer, James and Robert. **The Liberal Idea of Canada: Pierre Trudeau and the Question of Survival for Canada.** Toronto: James Lorimer & Company, Publishers, 1977, 234 pp.

Leach, Richard H., ed. **Contemporary Canada.** Toronto: Duke University Commonwealth-Studies Center, 1968, 318 pp.

Levin, Malcolm, and Sylvester, Christine, eds. **Foreign Ownership.** Don Mills, Ontario: PaperJacks, A Division of General Publishing Co. Limited, 1972, 107 pp.

Levinson, Charles. **Capital, Inflation and the Multinationals.** London: George Allen and Unwin Ltd., 1971, 229 pp.

______, ed. **Industry's Democratic Revolution.** London: George Allen and Unwin Ltd., 1974, 350 pp.

______. **International Trade Unionism.** London: George Allen and Unwin Ltd., 1972.

Levitt, Kari. **Silent Surrender: The Multinational Corporation in Canada.** Toronto: Macmillan Company of Canada Limited, 1970, 184 pp.

Lewis, David. **Louder Voices: The Corporate Welfare Bums.** Toronto: James and Lewis, 1972, 118 pp.

Lumsden, Ian, ed. **Close the 49th Parallel etc.: The Americanization of Canada.** Toronto: University of Toronto Press, 1970, 334 pp.

Massey, Vincent. **Speaking of Canada: Addresses by the Right Honourable Vincent Massey.** Toronto: The Macmillan Company of Canada Ltd., 1959, 244 pp.

Mathias, Philip. **Forced Growth.** Toronto: James Lewis & Samuel, Publishers, 1971, 179 pp.

McCullum, Hugh and Karmel, and Olthuis, John. **Moratorium: Justice, Energy, the North, and the Native People.** Toronto: Anglican Book Centre, 1977, 208 pp.

McNaught, Kenneth. **A Prophet in Politics: A Biography of J.S. Woodsworth.** Toronto: University of Toronto Press, 1973, 339 pp.

McRea, Kenneth D., ed. **Consociational Democracy: Political Accommodation in Segmented Societies.** Toronto: McClelland and Stewart Ltd., 1974, 311 pp.

Meadows, Donella H.; Meadows, Dennis L.; Randers, Jørgen; Behrens III, William W. **The Limits to Growth: A Report for the Club of Rome's Project on the Predicament of Mankind.** Washington, D.C.: New American Library—a Signet Book, 1972.

Mishan, E. J. **Technology and Growth: The Price We Pay.** New York/Washington: Praeger Publishers, 1969, 1970, 193 pp.

Moorcraft, Colin. **Must the Seas Die?** Boston: Gambit, 1973, 223 pp.

Mumford, Lewis. **The Myth of the Machine: The Pentagon of Power.** New York: Harcourt Brace Jovanovich, 1964, 496 pp.

Nader, Ralph, and Green, Mark J., eds. **Corporate Power in America.** New York: Grossman Publishers, 1973, 309 pp.

Nelles, Viv, and Rotstein, Abraham, eds. **Nationalism or Local Control.** Toronto: New Press, 1973, 97 pp.

Newman, Peter C. **The Canadian Establishment.** Toronto: McClelland and Stewart Limited, 1975, 480 pp.

Packard, Vance. **The Waste Makers.** New York: Pocket Books Inc., David McKay edition, 1960, 306 pp.

Park, Libbie, and Park, Frank. **Anatomy of Big Business.** Toronto: James Lewis and Samuel, Publishers, 1962, 1973, 271 pp.

Perry, Robert L. **Galt U.S.A.: The 'American Presence' in a Canadian City.** Toronto: MacLean-Hunter Limited, 1971, 123 pp.

Pope, W.H. **The Elephant and the Mouse: A Handbook on Regaining Control of Canada's Economy.** Toronto/Montreal: McClelland and Stewart Limited, 1971, 158 pp.

Porter, John. **The Vertical Mosaic: An Analysis of Social Class and Power in Canada.** Toronto: University of Toronto Press, 1965, 626 pp.

Quinn, T.K. **Giant Business: Threat to Democracy.** New York: Exposition Press, 1953, 321 pp.

Radwanski, George. **Trudeau.** Toronto: Macmillan Company of Canada Limited, 1978, 372 pp.

Raynauld, Andre. **The Canadian Economic System.** Toronto: The Macmillan Company of Canada Limited, 1967, 420 pp.

Rotstein, Abraham, ed. **An Industrial Strategy for Canada.**Toronto: New Press, 1972, 130 pp.

______. **The Precarious Homestead.** Toronto: New Press, 1973, 331 pp.

Rotstein, Abraham, and Lax, Gary, eds. **Getting It Back: A Program For Canadian Independence.** Toronto/Vancouver: Clarke, Irwin & Company Limited, 1974, 293 pp.

______. **Independence: The Canadian Challenge.** Toronto: Web Offset Publications Limited, 1972, 272 pp.

Runner, H. Evan. **Scriptural Religion and Political Task.** Toronto: Wedge Publishing Foundation, 1974, 123 pp.

______. **The Relation of the Bible to Learning.** Toronto: Wedge Publishing Foundation, 1970, 167 pp.

Russell, Peter, ed. **Nationalism in Canada.** Toronto: McGraw-Hill Company of Canada Limited, 1966, 377 pp.

Safarian, A.E. **Foreign Ownership of Canadian Industry.** Toronto: University of Toronto Press, 1973, 312 pp.

Scheer, Robert. **America After Nixon: The Age of the Multinationals.** New York/Toronto: McGraw-Hill Book Company, 1974, 326 pp.

Schmidt, Larry, ed. **George Grant in Process: Essays and Conversations.** Toronto: House of Anansi Press Limited, 1978, 223 pp.

Schumacher, E.F. **Small is Beautiful: A Study of Economics as if People Mattered.** London: Blond and Briggs Ltd., 1973, 288 pp.

Servan-Schreiber, J.J. **The American Challenge.** Translated by Ronald Steel. New York: Avon Books, 1969, 255 pp.

Sethi, Prakash S., and Holton, Richard H., eds. **Management of the Multinationals: Policies, Operations, and Research.** New York: The Free Press, 1974. London: The Macmillan Co., 1974, 431 pp.

Shea, Albert A. **Canada 1980.** Toronto: McClelland and Stewart Limited, 1960, 105 pp.

Sider, Ronald J. **Rich Christians in an Age of Hunger: A Biblical Study.** Downers Grove, Ill.: Intervarsity Press, 1977, 254 pp.

Smith, Denis. **Gentle Patriot: A Political Biography of Walter Gordon.** Edmonton: Hurtig Publishers, 1973, 364 pp.

Solzhenitsyn, Alexander, ed. **From Under The Rubble**. Boston/Toronto: Little, Brown and Company, 1975, 308 pp.

Sorokin, P.A. **The Crisis of Our Age: The Social and Cultural Outlook.** New York: E.P. Dutton & Co., Inc., 1941, 338 pp.

Starowicz, Mark, and Murphy, Rae, eds. **Corporate Canada: 14 Probes into the Workings of a Branch-Plant Economy.** Toronto: James Lewis & Samuel, Publishers, 1972, 156 pp.

Stewart, Walter. **Shrug: Trudeau in Power.** Toronto: New Press, 1971, 240 pp.

Sturmthal, Adolf. **Workers Councils: A Study of Workplace Organization on Both Sides of the Iron Curtain.** Cambridge: Harvard University Press, 1964, 217 pp.

Sykes, Philip. **Sellout: the Giveaway of Canada's Energy Resources.** Edmonton: Hurtig Publishers, 1973, 235 pp.

Taylor, Charles. **The Pattern of Politics.** Toronto: McClelland and Stewart Ltd., 1970, 1975, 160 pp.

Taylor, F.W. **The Principles of Scientific Management.** 1911; reprint ed., New York: W.W. Norton & Company, 1967, 144 pp.

Teeple, Gary, ed. **Capitalism and the National Question in Canada.** Toronto: University of Toronto Press, 1972, 247 pp.

Trudeau, Pierre Elliott. **Federalism and the French Canadians.** Toronto: Macmillan of Canada, 1968, 212 pp.

Tugendhat, Christopher. **The Multinationals.** London: Eyre & Spottiswoode (Publishers) Ltd., 1971, 221 pp.

Turner, Louis. **Invisible Empires: Multinational Companies and the Modern World.** New York: Harcourt Brace Jovanovich, Inc., 1970, 228 pp.

______. **Multinational Companies and the Third World.** New York: Hill and Wang, Inc., 1973.

Van Prinsterer, Groen G. **Unbelief and Revolution.** Lecture XI. Amsterdam: The Groen Van Prinsterer Fund, 1973, 68 pp.

______. **Unbelief and Revolution.** Lectures VIII & IX. Amsterdam: The Groen Van Prinsterer Fund, 1975, 87 pp.

Van Riessen, H. **The Society of the Future.** Philadelphia: The Presbyterian and Reformed Publishing Co., 1952, 320 pp.

Vernon, Raymond. **Sovereignty at Bay: The Multinational Spread of U.S. Enterprises.** New York/London: Basic Books, Inc., 1971, 326 pp.

Westell, Anthony. **The New Society.** Toronto: McClelland and Stewart Limited, 1977, 237 pp.

Wilkins, Mira. **The Emergence of Multinational Enterprise: American Business Abroad from the Colonial Era to 1914.** Cambridge Harvard University Press, 1970, 310 pp.

______. **The Maturing of Multinational Enterprise: American Business Abroad from 1914 to 1970.** Cambridge: Harvard University Press, 1974, 590 pp. 590 pp.

ARTICLES

Armstrong, Richard. "Suddenly it's Mañana in Latin America." **Fortune,** August 1974, p. 143.

Ball, George. "The Promise of the Multinational Corporation." **Fortune,** June 1967, p. 80.

Barnet, Richard J., and Müller, Ronald E. "A Reporter At Large: Global Reach I." **The New Yorker,** December 2, 1974, pp. 53ff.

______. "A Reporter At Large: Global Reach II." **The New Yorker,** December 9, 1974, pp. 100ff.

Bender, Marylin. "Management Braces for Annual Meetings." **The New York Times,** March 23, 1975, sec. 3, pp. 1ff.

"The Canadian Paradox: Rich and Dependent." Toronto: Inter-Church Committee for World Development Education, September 1974, 13 pp. (Mimeographed.)

Cheveldayoff, Wayne. "Canada Faces Prospect of Crisis in Payments." **The Globe and Mail,** August 19, 1976, p. B1.

Cook, Peter. "AFL Chief Pushes for More Restrictive Trade Law." **Financial Times of Canada,** Nov. 14-20, 1977, p. 16.

Cowan, Edward. "Wanted: A Lawyer to Take On A.T.&T." **The New York Times,** Sunday, March 12, 1978, sec. 3, pp. 2ff.

Creighton, Donald. "We've Been Fat Too Long and Now it's Too Late." **Maclean's,** April 1975, pp. 26-28.

Croft, Roger. "Foreign Takeovers: Is Anyone on Guard?" **The Toronto Star,** March 13, 1976.

Frank, Richard A. "The Law at Sea." **The New York Times Magazine,** May 18, 1975, p. 14.

Gordon, Walter. "If There's a Will, Gordon says this is the Way." **The Financial Post,** October 5, 1974, p. 7.

______. "Last Chance for Canada." **Maclean's,** September 1972, pp. 68-72.

Goudzwaard, Bob. "The Dynamic of the Word of God in Economics." Two installments. **The Guide:** April 1974, pp. 10 ff.; May 1974, pp. 8 ff.

______. "Economic Life: A Confession." Two installments, **The Guide:** May 1978, pp. 6 ff.; June 1978, pp. 8 ff.

Hampson, H. Anthony. "The CDC: Friend or Foe?" Speech presented to the International Conference sponsored by the Chemical Institute of Canada and the Commerical Development Association Inc., Montreal, December 4, 1974. (Mimeographed.)

Hatfield, Mark. "A Time to Share." **The Guide,** December 1974, pp. 6ff.

"How the Multinationals Play the Money Game," **Fortune,** August 1973, pp. 59ff.

Hunter, Virginia. "Why I Left the Waffle." **The Canadian Forum,** May 1975, pp. 17-20.

Hurtig, Mel. "We're Reaching A Point of No Return in Foreign Ownership." **The Financial Post,** October 5, 1974, p. C-4.

Hutchison, Bruce. "Where Do We Go From Here?" **Maclean's,** July 1971, pp. 23ff.

______. "The Storming of the World." **Maclean's,** September 1972, pp. 27ff.

______. "Canada's Time Of Troubles." **Foreign Affairs,** October 1977, pp. 175-89.

Hutchison, Robert A. "The Looting of I.O.S." **Fortune,** March 1973, pp. 12ff.

Jensen, Michael C. "How 3M Got Tangled Up in Politics." **The New York Times,** March 9, 1975, sec. 3, pp. 2ff.

Johnson, Paul. "A Brotherhood of National Misery." **New Statesman,** May 16, 1975, pp. 652-56.

Kierans, Eric. "Foreign Guidelines and Canada's Economic Future." In **The Nation Keepers: Canadian Business Perspectives,** pp. 205-215. Edited by Isaiah A. Litvak. Toronto: McGraw-Hill, 1967.

______. "The Day the Cabinet was Misled." **The Canadian Forum,** March 1974, pp. 4-8.

______. "Beware of Slogans Like National Integrity." **The Vancouver Province,** September 22, 1972, p. 4.

Lynch, Charles. "Who Needs Economic Council as Big Brother?" **The Vancouver Sun,** November 28, 1974.

Macdonald, H. Ian. "Productivity: the Key to a New Economic Policy." **Cost and Management,** March-April 1978, pp. 4-12.

Merklein, H.A. "Mid-East Petrodollars: Enough to buy Corporate America?" **World Oil,** November 1974, p. 95.

Meyer, Herbert E. "A Plant that Could Change the Soviet Industry." **Fortune,** November 1974, pp. 150ff.

______. "Why the Outlook is so Bearish for U.S.-Soviet Trade." **Fortune,** Jan. 16, 1978, pp. 102-104.

Newman, Peter C. "The Bankers." **Maclean's,** Part One, February 1972, pp. 21ff. and Part Two, March 1972, pp. 29ff.

"Northrop: Fame in Aircraft, Shame in Politics." **The New York Times,** May 18, 1975, sec. 3, pp. 1, 12.

"Northrop's Punishment for Campaign Giving." **Business Week,** February 24, 1975, pp. 60ff.

Nycander, Svante. "Working Environment in Sweden: Industrial Relations and Workers' Participation." **Current Sweden** 41 (September 1974).

Olthuis, John. "Can Less Be More?" **C.J.L. Foundation Newsletter,** February 1974, pp. 1ff.

______. "Toward a Just Energy Policy for Canada." **C.J.L. Foundation Newsletter,** August 1974, December 1974, February 1975 and May 1975.

Ophuls, William. "The Scarcity Society." **Harper's,** April 1974, pp. 47-52.

Pisar, Samuel. "The Transideological Corporation: New Hope for the Third World." **Economic Impact,** no. 5, pp. 43-47.

Robertson, Heather. "Confessions of a Canadian Chauvinist Pig." **Maclean's,** April 1975, p. 96.

Rose, Sanford. "Multinational Corporations in a Tough New World." **Fortune,** August 1973, pp. 52ff.

______. "Why the Multinational Tide is Ebbing." **Fortune,** August, 1977, pp. 111-20.

Rosenbluth, Gideon. "Concentration of Ownership and Control in the Canadian Economy." In **Economics: Canada,** pp. 67-75. Edited by M.H. Watkins and D.F. Forster. Toronto: McGraw-Hill Company of Canada Limited, 1963.

Ross, Irwin. "Labour's Big Push for Protectionism." **Fortune,** March 1973, pp. 92ff.

Rotstein, Abraham. "It's Too Expensive to Buy Back Canada. It's Probably Not a Good Idea to Steal it Back. So Why Not Figure Out How We Can Control It." **Saturday Night,** October 1970, pp. 26-30.

______. "Canada: The New Nationalism." **Foreign Affairs,** October 1976, pp. 97-118.

Safarian, A.E. "Foreign Ownership and Control of Canadian Industry." In **The Prospect of Change**, pp. 220-44. Edited by Abraham Rotstein. Toronto: McGraw-Hill Company of Canada Limited, 1965.

______. "Some Myths About Foreign Business Investment in Canada." **Journal of Canadian Studies,** August 1971, pp. 3-21.

Scheer, Robert. "The Doctrine of Multinational Sell." **Esquire,** April 1975, p. 160.

Schrotenboer, Paul. "Development: Its Disappointment and Challenge."

International Reformed Bulletin, no. 65, first and second quarter 1977, pp. 36-48.

Sinclair, George. "Canada's Real Problem is Not Foreign Ownership." **The Financial Post,** September 1973.

Smith, Hedrick. "The Russians Mean Business About Business." **The Atlantic Monthly,** December 1974, pp. 41-48.

Smith, William D. "Curtain Time for the IBM Case." **The New York Times,** May 18, 1975, sec. 3, pp. 1, 2.

"Stateless Money: A New Force on World Economies," **Business Week,** August 21, 1978, pp. 76ff.

Stewart, Walter. "All Canada Wants for Christmas Is Itself." **Maclean's,** December 1971, pp. 23ff.

______. "Baby It Was Cold Inside: Eric Kierans Reveals How Trudeau Froze Him Out." **Maclean's,** July 1971, pp. 32ff.

______. "Beneath the Sheltering Palms." **Maclean's,** November 17, 1975.

Stoffman, Daniel. "Canada Development Corp. Still Won't Sell You a Share." **The Toronto Star,** April 17, 1975, p. C-3.

Stridsberg, Albert. "New Marketing, Ad Methods May Save Underdeveloped Nations." **Advertising Age,** September 22, 1969, p. 64.

Strong, Maurice. "Canada in a Planetary Society." Address by Maurice Strong to the Men's Canadian Club of Ottawa, February 1974, 5 pp. (Mimeographed.)

Teasdale, Philip. "New Foreign Control Wave Washes Over Fira's Dike." **The Financial Post,** February 25, 1978, pp. 1ff.

Toynbee, Arnold. "Are Businessmen Creating a New Pax Romana?" **Forbes,** April 15, 1974.

______. "Continual Recession is Foreseen." **The Toronto Star,** April 20, 1974, p. A-12.

"The U.S. Trade Lag With Eastern Europe." **Business Week,** February 23, 1976, p. 44.

Viner, Jacob. "American Capital and the Canadian Economy." In **Economics: Canada,** pp. 188-94. Edited by M.H. Watkins and D.F. Forster. Toronto: McGraw-Hill Company of Canada Limited, 1963.

Watkins, Mel. "A New National Policy." In **Agenda 1970: Proposals For a Creative Politics,** pp. 159-76. Edited by Trevor Lloyd and Jack McLeod. Toronto: University of Toronto Press, 1968.

Yanchula, Joseph. "The Politics of Petroleum: An Inside Look at Alberta Oil." **The Canadian Forum,** November-December 1974, pp. 5-8.

"Yugoslavia: A Door Slightly Ajar for U.S. Investment." **Business Week,** February 6, 1978, pp. 54-55.

Zylstra, Bernard. "A Neoconservative Critique of Modernity: Daniel Bell's Appraisal." **Christian Scholar's Review,** vol. 7, no. 4, 1978, pp. 337-55.

______. "Do Christians Have a Political Future?" Two installments, **Vanguard:** "The Scope of Politics." March-April 1972, pp. 13ff.; "Developing a Policy for Christian Political Action." August-September 1972, pp. 12ff.

______. "Karl Marx: Radical Humanist." **Vanguard,** December 1973, pp. 9ff.

______. "Modernity And The American Empire." **International Reformed Bulletin,** no. 68, 1977, pp. 3-19.

______. "The Bible, Justice And The State." **International Reformed Bulletin,** no. 55, 1973, pp. 2-18.

GOVERNMENT PUBLICATIONS

Bourgault, Pierre L. **Innovation and the Structure of Canadian Industry.** Science Council of Canada, Special Study No. 23. Ottawa: Information Canada, 1972, 135 pp.

Canadian Industrial Relations: The Report of the Task Force on Labour Relations. Ottawa: Privy Council Office, 1968, 250 pp.

Cordell, Arthur J. **The Multinational Firm, Foreign Direct Investment, and Canadian Science Policy.** Science Council of Canada, Special Study No. 22. Ottawa: Information Canada, 1971, 95 pp.

Corporations and Labour Unions Returns Act, Report for 1974 Part I: Corporations. Ottawa: Statistics Canada, 1977, 270 pp.

Economic Council of Canada. **Economic Targets and Social Indicators: Eleventh Annual Review.** Ottawa: Information Canada, 1974, 264 pp.

Eleventh Report of the Standing Committee on External Affairs and National Defense Respecting Canada—United States Relations. Ottawa: Information Canada, 1970, 169 pp.

Foreign Direct Investment in Canada. Ottawa: Information Canada, 1972, 523 pp.

Foreign Ownership and the Structure of Canadian Industry: Report of the Task Force on the Structure of Canadian Industry. Ottawa: Information Canada, 1968, 427 pp.

Foreign-Owned Subsidiaries in Canada 1964-1967. A Report on operations and financing by the larger subsidiary companies. Ottawa: Queen's Printer, 1970, 148 pp.

Foreign-Owned Subsidiaries in Canada 1964-1971. A Report on operations and financing by the larger subsidiary companies. Ottawa: Information Canada, 1974, 92 pp.

Highlights from the Report of the Special Senate Committee on Poverty in Canada. Ottawa: Information Canada, 1971, 1972, 23 pp.

The Impact of Multinational Corporations on Development and on International Relations. New York: United Nations, 1974, 162 pp.

Multinational Corporations in World Development. Department of Economic and Social Affairs. New York: United Nations, 1973, 195 pp.

Science Council of Canada. Report No. 21. **Strategies of Development for the Canadian Computer Industry.** Ottawa: Information Canada, 1973, 80 pp.

______. Report No. 13. **A Trans-Canada Computer Communications Network: Phase I of a Major Program on Computers.** Ottawa: Information Canada, 1971, 41 pp.

A Science Policy for Canada: Report of the Senate Special Committee on Science Policy, Volume 1, **A Critical Review: Past and Present.** Ottawa: Queen's Printer, 1970, 327 pp.

A Science Policy for Canada: Report of the Senate Special Committee on Science Policy, Volume 2, **Targets and Strategies for the Seventies.** Ottawa: Information Canada, 1972, 281 pp.

Summary of the Hearings Before the Group of Eminent Persons to Study the Impact of Multinational Corporations on Development and on International Relations. New York: United Nations, 1974, 455 pp.

U.S. Department of Commerce. **The Multinational Corporation: Studies on U.S. Foreign Investment,** Volume 1. U.S. Department of Commerce, March 1972, 74 pp.

Wilson, Andrew H. **Science, Technology, and Innovation.** Economic Council of Canada, Special Study No. 8. Ottawa: Information Canada, 1968.

MISCELLANEOUS DOCUMENTS

Gillespie, W. Irwin. **In Search of Robin Hood: The Effect of Federal Budgetary Policies During the 70s on the Distribution of Income in Canada.** Montreal: C.D. Howe Research Institute, 1978, 61 pp.

Goudzwaard, Bob. **Economic Stewardship Versus Capitalist Religion.** Toronto: Institute for Christian Studies, 1972, 92 pp. (Mimeographed.)

"A presentation by the Christian Labour Association of Canada and the C.J.L. Foundation to the Royal Commission on Corporate Concentration." Toronto: Christian Labour Association of Canada, May 1976, 7 pp.

"A proposal to Restructure Collective Bargaining in the Province of British Columbia." Toronto: Christian Labour Association of Canada, June 27, 1973, 14 pp. (Mimeographed.)

"A Re-evaluation of Collective Bargaining presented by Christian Labour Association of Canada." Conference on Labour Legislation held by B.C. Department of Labour, Victoria, April 13-15, 1973, 29 pp. (Mimeographed.)

"Response to a Better Work Environment for Canadians." Addressed to The Honourable John Munro, Minister of Labour, Canada. Toronto: Christian Labour Association of Canada, May 1977, 7 pp.

Runner, H. Evan. **Can Canada Tolerate the CLAC?: The Achilles' Heel of a Humanistic Society.** Toronto: Christian Labour Association of Canada, 1967, 31 pp.

Skillen, James William. "The Development of Calvinistic Political Theory in the Netherlands, with Special Reference to the Thought of Herman Dooyeweerd." Unpublished Ph.D. dissertation, Duke University, 1973, 459 pp.

Submissions of the Christian Labour Association of Canada to the Royal Commission Inquiry on Certain Sectors of the Building Industry. Toronto: Christian Labour Association of Canada, March 1974, 54 pp. (Mimeographed.)

U.S. Multinationals: The Dimming of America. The report prepared for the AFL-CIO Maritime Trades Department Executive Board meeting, February 15-16, 1973, 96 pp. (Mimeographed.)

Index